Minor League Baseball
Community Building Through Hometown Sports

THE HAWORTH PRESS
Contemporary Sports Issues
Frank Hoffmann, PhD, MLS
Martin Manning
Senior Editors

Minor League Baseball: Community Building Through Hometown Sports by Rebecca S. Kraus

Baseball and American Culture: Across the Diamond edited by Edward J. Rielly

Minor League Baseball
Community Building Through Hometown Sports

Rebecca S. Kraus, PhD

The Haworth Press®
New York • London • Oxford

© 2003 by The Haworth Press, Inc. All rights reserved. No part of this work may be reproduced or utilized in any form or by any means, electronic or mechanical, including photocopying, microfilm, and recording, or by any information storage and retrieval system, without permission in writing from the publisher. Printed in the United States of America.

The Haworth Press, Inc., 10 Alice Street, Binghamton, NY 13904-1580.

Cover design by Lora Wiggins.

Library of Congress Cataloging-in-Publication Data

Kraus, Rebecca S.
   Minor league baseball : community building through hometown sports / Rebecca S. Kraus.
     p. cm.
   Includes bibliographical references (p.) and index.
   ISBN 0-7890-1755-5 (hardcover : alk. paper)—ISBN 0-7890-1756-3 (paperback : alk. paper)
    1. Minor league baseball—United States. 2. Minor league baseball—United States—Sociological aspects. I. Title.
GV863.A1 K72 2003
796.357'64'0973—dc21

                                                            2002015022

For Mom and Dad
who encouraged my love of the game

ABOUT THE AUTHOR

Rebecca Susan Kraus received her PhD in sociology from The Catholic University of America in Washington, DC. Her research interests have focused on community sociology, sport sociology, and social movements. A member of the Washington-Baltimore chapter of the Society of American Baseball Research (SABR), Dr. Kraus assisted the Maryland-National Capital Parks and Planning Commission in developing an exhibit on the Negro Leagues and sandlot baseball in Prince George County and is the historian for the YWCA of the National Capital Area. Her work has appeared in publications such as the *Sociology of Education* and the *Journal of Sport Sociology*.

NOTES FOR PROFESSIONAL LIBRARIANS AND LIBRARY USERS

This is an original book title published by The Haworth Press, Inc. Unless otherwise noted in specific chapters with attribution, materials in this book have not been previously published elsewhere in any format or language.

CONSERVATION AND PRESERVATION NOTES

All books published by The Haworth Press, Inc. and its imprints are printed on certified pH neutral, acid free book grade paper. This paper meets the minimum requirements of American National Standard for Information Sciences-Permanence of Paper for Printed Material, ANSI Z39.48-1984.

CONTENTS

Acknowledgments	xi
Chapter 1. Introduction	1
Safe at Home	1
Minor League Baseball Through Time	3
Minor League Basics	4
Minor League Reviews	8
Play Ball!	9
Chapter 2. Baseball Coast to Coast	11
National Association of Professional Baseball Leagues (NAPBL)	11
Independent Leagues	43
Conclusion	53
Chapter 3. The Lure of Minor League Baseball	57
The Nation Awakens	57
Academics Take Notice	58
Sociology and Minor League Communities	72
Chapter 4. The Evolution of Minor League Baseball	87
Historical Overview	87
Minor League Baseball As a Different Kind of Business	95
Franchise Relocation and Name Changes	98
Corporate Sponsorship	111
Conclusion	111
Chapter 5. A Tale of Two Minor League Cities	113
Baseball As a Maryland Tradition	114
Hagerstown, Maryland	116
Bowie, Maryland	122

Chapter 6. The Impact of Minor League Baseball   **127**

   Theory Revisited   127
   Minor League History   129
   Hagerstown and Bowie: Theory in Action   130
   Conclusion   131

Epilogue: A Shelter in the Storm   **133**

Appendix A: Minor League Attendance and Number of Teams, by Year and Era, 1947 to 1990   **137**

Appendix B: Development of the Data Set   **141**

   Hypotheses   141
   Construction of the Data Set   142
   Data Used   144
   Statistical Methods and Models   155

Notes   **167**

Index   **187**

Acknowledgments

This book could not have been completed without the support and encouragement of my friends, family, and colleagues. Walter and Elizabeth Kraus, a.k.a. Mom and Dad, are responsible for everything I have accomplished, and are the first people who told me that I could actually do this. And, of course, without my older siblings—Mark, Terry, and Kathy—arguing with me, competing with me, harassing me, and supporting me, I still might not know my ABCs.

As always, my friends played important roles in this project. Kelly and David were always there to remind me that I could, and indeed had to, finish this book. Thank you, Mr. Chambers, for your most excellent editing, and thank you, Cousin John, for your photographs and assistance. I also want to recognize my friends, Sharon, Kim, Denise, and Margaret, who have always been there for me, even when I should have been working on my book instead.

I would like to thank Dr. John McCarthy for agreeing that baseball is worthy of sociological study, and for his encouragement throughout my graduate school experience at The Catholic University of America. I would also like to thank Dr. Zampelli, Dr. D'Antonio, Dr. Lee, and Dr. Hanson for their helpful advice and critical review of my work.

Every good baseball researcher needs the support of the Society of American Baseball Research (SABR) and its network of baseball enthusiasts and professionals. In particular, I am proud to belong to and know the members of the Washington-Baltimore chapter of SABR. Another extremely important resource has been almost all of the publications of Baseball America, Inc. Their annual directories and *The Encyclopedia of Minor League Baseball* are invaluable resources for any research on Minor League Baseball. I am also very appreciative of the Internet Web site of Minor League Baseball, <www.milb.com>, and all of its links to Minor League Baseball teams across the country.

I am extremely grateful for the chance to prepare a book on my first love—Minor League Baseball. I want to express my appreciation to The Haworth Press for providing me with this opportunity, to Martin Manning and Frank Hoffmann, senior editors; Dawn Krisko and Peg Marr, senior production editors and Binghamton Mets fans; and the rest of the Haworth family for supporting this project.

Chapter 1

Introduction

SAFE AT HOME

Tucked away safely in my suburban home on a warm summer night, I hear the rumbling begin. It is slow and distant at first, then it grows, becoming increasingly powerful. At the shopping center across the street, people stop to watch the bursts of light in the sky. It's another Saturday night postgame fireworks show. I smile, comforted by the fact that I live in a minor league town. Life is good.

A seasoned journalist and published author once gave me the following advice: "Don't write about Minor League Baseball." Short and to the point, the reasoning behind his words of wisdom was that not everyone cares as much about Minor League Baseball as I do. As a resident of a minor league town and an avid baseball fan, I still find it hard to believe that other people don't follow the fortunes of their team, or even know where the closest Major League Baseball team has minor league connections. Meanwhile, as a self-described baseball sociologist, I have noticed a trend toward the commercialization and marketing of Minor League Baseball since the 1990s. Surely, there has to be some effects from these recent changes in Minor League Baseball.

With the rise in popularity of Minor League Baseball in the 1990s, it became fashionable to attend games in towns such as Asheville, North Carolina; Salem, Oregon; and Frederick, Maryland. These towns were little known on the national scene, yet seemingly overnight became popular, at least among the baseball set. Box scores are often readily available in local newspapers, and are tracked with interest by residents and Major League Baseball fans alike. Tourism companies now offer convenient packages to tour both major and minor league stadiums and attend games in cities across the country. Other companies have published vacation guides to minor league cities (e.g., Fodor's).

Indeed, I have taken personal tours of major and minor league stadiums across the country. One summer I trekked from San Francisco to Seattle, seeing six games in eight days. While en route to a family reunion several summers later, I stopped at as many minor league stadiums as I could between Washington, DC, and Asheville, North Carolina. I was two days late for the weeklong reunion. Some call it an obsession; I call it my passion, and an intellectual pursuit.

Over the years, baseball scholars and others have witnessed the transformation of Minor League Baseball from a mere tool of Major League Baseball to a thriving industry with a life of its own. Minor League Baseball has become more than a pastime. It is a bona fide economic and community development tool. Many communities—and baseball fans—fervently believe, "If you build it, they will come."

And people do come. Not just to watch, but to eat, shop, and even put down roots. When Minor League Baseball came to central Maryland, I hopped on the bandwagon along with many others, and took it one step further: I moved in. You see, I chose my home for the primary reason that it is located in a minor league town. Having studied the sociological phenomena of the minor leagues—and being a huge baseball fan—I wanted to live in a minor league town and experience the special relationship between town and team. Visions of the movie *Bull Durham* (1988) danced in my head as the thought of living in a minor league town completely enthralled me. I imagined lazy summer nights at Prince George's Stadium and peaceful, moonlit walks back to my house. Of course, it's not quite like that. A major highway and a lack of sidewalks separate me from the ballpark. Nonetheless, although Bowie, Maryland, is large compared to many minor league towns, it provides a unique opportunity to enjoy the impact of Minor League Baseball on the community.

In fact, the first thing I show people when I give them a tour of Bowie is Prince George's Stadium. My friends, knowing how obsessed I am with baseball, smile appreciatively as I point to the clump of trees beyond the orange façade of Home Depot, toward the ballpark that is not visible from the highway. I ignore their patronizing nods and babble on about Double A baseball, the Eastern League, and the location of Oriole affiliates past and present. I explain to them the history of the farm system and how Minor League Baseball came to be in its present form. When my less-obsessive friends nod politely and ask if it's time to go home yet, I show them the new housing and retail development that has occurred subsequent to the team moving to town in 1993, and I in 1995.

This book represents my enthusiasm for the great game of baseball, my passion for the minors, and my love of minor league towns. Much has been written about the dichotomy between Major and Minor League Baseball. Minor League Baseball has been called the purist form of baseball, where the players play hard, work hard, and don't act like a bunch of overpaid teenagers. But there is so much more to the minor leagues.

MINOR LEAGUE BASEBALL THROUGH TIME

Minor League Baseball celebrated its 100th season in 2001. Although the minors have been in existence since the 1800s, prior to 1999 the present configuration operated under the name National Association of Professional Baseball Leagues (NAPBL). The NAPBL established its relationship with Major League Baseball in 1901, and in 1963 reorganized to the present format of leagues and levels of play (see Chapter 3 for a detailed history).

Truly the national pastime at one point, minor league ball was played in cities as small as Brewster, Texas (population 6,434 in 1960), and as large as Los Angeles, California. Minor League Baseball once inhabited close to 500 cities in the United States. But as the nation progressed, the minor leagues soon had to contend with competitors for entertainment time and money, such as television and interstate travel, made easier by improved air and rail options as well as the interstate highway system. It also saw many of its more profitable cities be overtaken by Major League Baseball as it expanded, adding more major league teams across the country, particularly in places such as Los Angeles and Seattle.

By the 1970s, interest in the minors had waned due to scant investment in the teams by owners and major league affiliates. Teams were operated solely as major league training grounds, with little attention paid to attracting fans or turning a profit.[1] During this time, fewer Major League Baseball teams owned minor league teams than had in the 1950s and 1960s, and many of the remaining owners operated minor league teams merely as hobbies. Attendance dropped off considerably as the number of leagues and teams diminished. By 1975, only 106 teams were fielded. According to one sports historian, throughout this time Minor League Baseball was "as fashionable as the Edsel."[2] The lowest point came in the late 1970s when the Reading Phillies were sold for just $1.[3]

However, in the 1980s, a minor league renaissance began that continues to this day. Investors and communities began to realize the financial and communal benefits that could be reaped from obtaining a Minor League Baseball team. Thus, business-minded owners began to buy out the "mom and pop" operations that until the 1980s had been the norm in Minor League Baseball. Marketing professionals were hired to sell the minor league product to the fans, and state and local governments began to partner with team owners to turn Minor League Baseball into a profitable enterprise for investors and municipalities alike.[4] This business model for operating minor league franchises has continued into the twenty-first century. Cities now compete with one another to lure teams away and win the honor of bringing a team into the city limits to earn its place in minor league history.

What city wouldn't want to play host to an organization that brings us "Morganna, the Kissing Bandit," the nightly "Dirtiest Car in the Parking Lot" award, and "the toilet toss" contest (in which a fan attempts to toss plungers into a toilet that has been brought onto the field in order to win prizes)? Minor League Baseball goes beyond mere sport. It's a source of local pride and family entertainment. But most of all, it's a part of the fabric of the nation that is shared by many communities in the United States, as well as Canada and Mexico.

MINOR LEAGUE BASICS

The minor leagues serve as a training ground for players with aspirations of playing in the major leagues. Although Minor League Baseball teams are professional teams, the skill level of the players improves as players move up through a major league team's farm system. Today, Minor League Baseball is comprised of many leagues at varying levels of play (see Figure 1.1).

Major League Baseball teams assign players to minor league teams that are affiliated with the big league club. For example, my team—the Baltimore Orioles—had the following farm system in 2002:

- AAA affiliate: Rochester Red Wings, International League
- AA affiliate: Bowie Baysox, Eastern League
- A (advanced) affiliate: Frederick Keys, Carolina League
- A affiliate: Delmarva Shorebirds, South Atlantic League
- Short Season A affiliate: Aberdeen IronBirds, New York-Penn League
- Rookie (advanced) affiliate: Bluefield Orioles, Appalachian League
- Rookie affiliate: Sarasota Orioles, Gulf Coast League

Major League Baseball also operates or is associated with several fall and winter leagues in places such as Florida, Arizona, Venezuela, and Puerto Rico. There are other leagues as well, leagues that are not affiliated with Minor League Baseball or Major League Baseball. These independent leagues hearken back to a time when few teams had ties to major league teams and operated independent of major league rules. Since 1993, there have been several successful independent leagues (see Figure 1.2).

The independent leagues do not carry a particular classification, but leagues associated with Major League Baseball are classified into

---

Class AAA:
International League
Mexican League
Pacific Coast League

Class AA:
Eastern League
Southern League
Texas League

Class A Advanced:
California League
Carolina League
Florida State League

Class A:
Midwest League
South Atlantic League

Short Season Class A:
New York-Penn League
Northwest League

Advanced Rookie:
Appalachian League
Pioneer League

Rookie:
Arizona League
Gulf Coast League

FIGURE 1.1. Minor League Divisions, 2002

> Northern League (active since 1993)
> Frontier League (active since 1993)
> Central League (active since 1994)
> Western League (active since 1995)
> Atlantic League (active since 1998)

FIGURE 1.2. Independent Leagues, 2002

different levels. Typically, a player moves up through the leagues from the lowest level, the Rookie level, to Triple A (or AAA), which is the highest level of play (see Table 1.1). Theoretically, the next stop for a player that has proven himself at the AAA level is the big leagues. Over the years, the classifications have changed.

The leagues were restructured in 1963 by the NAPBL in conjunction with Major League Baseball. Prior to that, Class A was the highest league, followed by levels B through E. Class A was the highest classification from 1902 to 1911. In 1912, Class AA was established. That year, the American Association, the Eastern League, and the Pacific Coast League moved up from Class A to Class AA. In addition, from 1936 to 1945, there was a Class A1, which was in between A and AA. Class AAA was established in 1946. Leagues that had been Class AA in 1945, the highest league until that point, were reclassified as Class AAA.[5]

Below Class A were Classes B through D, with Class D being the lowest classification from 1902 through 1962. In 1937, Class E was added, which was restricted to players with no experience in higher leagues. However, only one league was ever classified as Class E—the Twin Ports League in 1943. In the restructuring of the leagues in 1963, all Class B, C, and D leagues were reclassified as Class A and leagues that had been in Class A and AA were moved into the new Class AA.[6]

The minors differ from the major leagues in many ways. For example, because the players are affiliated with the major league club, they can be moved up and down the leagues with little notice. Therefore, a minor league owner cannot depend on player recognition or team quality to sell tickets. Further, in the minors, not only are the stadiums smaller, so are the salaries. All minor leaguers start at a salary of $850 per month for the first year of their contract. After that, salaries vary

TABLE 1.1. Minor League Classifications, 2002

Classification	Definition	Years in Use
AAA	The highest level in the minor leagues	1946 to present
AA	An intermediate level	1912 to present
A	Entry level	1902 to present
Rookie	Primarily for first-year players	1963 to present
Independent	Leagues not affiliated with the National Association of Professional Baseball Leagues or Major League Baseball	

Source: Lloyd Johnson and Miles Wolff, eds., *The Encyclopedia of Minor League Baseball,* Second Edition (Durham, NC: Baseball America, Inc., 1997), p. 11.

according to the contract negotiated between the player and the major league team with which he signed and by league to which the player is assigned. The minimum salary for players assigned to short-season Class A teams is $850 per month. Full season Class A players can expect no less than $1,050 per month. Double A players receive a minimum of $1,500 per month, while AAA players receive at least $1,500 per month.[7] According to Judith Blahnik and Phillip S. Schulz in their guide to the minor leagues, *Mud Hens and Mavericks,*

> Life in the minors is no bed of roses. Players come to town on one day's notice from spring training with a couple suitcases in hand. The hometown booster club is critical to a player's well-being. Boosters will take players into their homes if need be, and if a player is in financial trouble, they'll try to help out.... Most kids are grateful to be taken in by the locals, even if it means getting unsolicited advice. And boosters do love to give advice, be they owners of the local hardware store or farmers from out over the hill. They know a lot about the game, and the players do well to listen. When "their boys" move on to the Show, they're so proud they could bust.[8]

Indeed, it is that special, personal connection between the town and its team that is part of the lure of Minor League Baseball. Although a major league team can represent us and bring us together, it is Minor League Baseball that is played in our own backyard, by folks such as us, who are just trying to make it in this world.

MINOR LEAGUE REVIEWS

Since the early 1990s, several authors have given the minors rave reviews:

> The appeal is obvious. Minor league ball, played largely in small and mid-sized cities and towns, retains a purity of spirit which the majors no longer possess. There are no mega-salaries, no enormous stadia. It is baseball in its simplest form—just balls, bats, gloves and lifelong dreams.[9]
>
> Bruce Adelson, Rod Beaton
Bill Koenig, and Lisa Winston
The Minor League Baseball Book

> Having spent most of my time in the United States in major league cities, I had never even been to a minor league game, but I knew the marriage was perfect: America and the minor leagues, each a metaphor for each other. It was a road that led through what for me would be virgin territory, and back into the mist of my fondest childhood memory: a love affair with a team that no longer existed, the Milwaukee Braves.[10]
>
> David Lamb
Stolen Season: A Journey Through
America and Baseball's Minor Leagues

> ... if baseball is America, then Minor League baseball is grass-roots America in its purest form. The diamond is, after all, American youth's genuine field of dreams, and those dreams that begin on the sandlots and schoolyards of this great land take real shape and gain honest purpose and unequivocal focus on the fields of the minor leagues.[11]
>
> Mike Blake
The Minor Leagues:
A Celebration of the Little Show

Minor-league parks are as comfortable as a favorite chair. Beer costs a buck. Seats are close to the field. . . . Entire neighborhoods sit together. People know the team's owner by his first name. Everybody knows the words to the national anthem.[12]

> Bruce Chadwick
> *Baseball's Hometown Teams:*
> *The Story of the Minor Leagues*

The Minor Leagues play a secondary role in professional baseball that unfortunately hides the richness of their game. Such teams as the Albuquerque Dukes, the Toledo Mud Hens, and the Pawtucket Red Sox entertain their fans and communities, but their more significant purpose is usually thought to be a training ground for future major leaguers.[13]

> Neil J. Sullivan
> *The Minors: The Struggles and the Triumph*
> *of Baseball's Poor Relation from 1876 to the Present*

There is a homey yet exuberant atmosphere of celebration in most minor league stands—a touch of Americana, straight out of the late 1940s.[14]

> Judith Blahnik and Phillip S. Schulz
> *Mud Hens and Mavericks*

The relationship between the minor leagues and their communities will undoubtedly reveal something more about the minors as their story unfolds. Minor league baseball will continue to entertain its fans, unite the community, and carry on the traditions of the national pastime.[15]

> Rebecca Kraus
> "Sport and the Community:
> The Case of Minor League Baseball, 1950s-1990s"

PLAY BALL!

This book is more than an academic inquiry into the hold Minor League Baseball has on the American people. It is also a journey to the places near and far that have welcomed the national pastime into their communities, and the story of how town and team become one, for better or worse. It shows how the past, present, and future of both a minor league team and its community are often intertwined.

So, now that a brief introduction to Minor League Baseball has been given, read on. Then, grab your glove and get out to a stadium near you to check out all the excitement. Until then, if you happen to be driving through Bowie, Maryland, around 9:30 on a Thursday or Saturday summer night, don't be alarmed by the booming noises and flashes of light in the sky over Routes 301 and 50. It's just life in a twenty-first century Minor League Baseball town.

Chapter 2

Baseball Coast to Coast

One of the many great things about Minor League Baseball is that it is often not too far away. It is played in approximately 200 towns across the United States. I am fortunate to have a minor league team play only five minutes from my home. I can also drive to four other ballparks in under two hours; and approximately three or four others are about two to three hours away.

Also, it's pretty easy to find a minor league game when I'm on the road. On a recent trip to Los Angeles, I had my choice of several minor league games to attend within ninety minutes of the city. I opted to see the Rancho Cucamonga Quakes, the Class A affiliate of the Anaheim Angels (who I'd seen just days before at their new home, Edison International Field). But you don't need to visit a major league city to find a minor league team nearby. Minor League Baseball truly reaches across America from the heartland to thriving metropolitan cities. Of course, there hasn't always been a team near my home, and the Quakes have been in Rancho Cucamonga, California only since 1993.

The leagues have experienced shifts in team membership as well as name changes, classification changes, mergers, and alliances. The following overview provides an introduction to the organization of the minor leagues as well as a glimpse at the many places where Minor League Baseball has been played throughout the years.

NATIONAL ASSOCIATION OF PROFESSIONAL BASEBALL LEAGUES (NAPBL)

On September 5, 1901, a group of men met at the Leland Hotel in Chicago, Illinois to discuss the future of the national pastime. There had been much turmoil in baseball, particularly in the minor leagues.

Teams had come and gone; leagues had folded and disappeared overnight. Owners were competitive to the point of stealing players from one another. As the nation's love of baseball increased and the number of teams quickly grew, the industry had grown increasingly unstable.[1]

At the meeting, an agreement between the major and minor leagues was reached. There would be roster and salary limits, an organized system for drafting players, and penalties for breaking the rules. In addition, the minor leagues were classified by their varying levels of play. The NAPBL was formed to represent the minors in this new arrangement.[2]

The minor leagues operated under this arrangement for several decades. However, the number of teams began to decrease in the 1950s and 1960s. After reaching a high of approximately 409 teams in 1949, only 135 remained by 1960. Major League Baseball and the NAPBL searched for ways to save Minor League Baseball. In 1956, Baseball Commissioner Ford Frick created a "Save the Minors" committee. The next year, a stabilization fund of 500,000 dollars (the Professional Baseball Fund) was established to help minor league teams. The fund was replaced three years later with the Player Development and Promotion program. Under this program, major league clubs paid minor league teams if they completed the season. Payments ranged from 22,500 dollars for class A teams, to 3,000 dollars for Class D teams.[3]

Despite these efforts, the minor leagues continued to decline. Finally, in 1962, an agreement was reached with Major League Baseball concerning the relationship between the majors and the minors. Major league teams essentially adopted minor league teams at each classification level, guaranteeing the survival of twenty AAA and AA teams and sixty lower-level teams. The Player Development Plan was approved by Major League Baseball on May 18, 1962. After that point, the majors would pay much of the minor league players' salaries and would also provide equipment and other resources for their minor league affiliates.[4]

Under this plan, the relationship between the NAPBL and the major leagues is governed by the Professional Baseball Agreement (PBA). The PBA, which is renegotiated periodically, specifies the responsibilities of the leagues and clubs. The PBA requires that a player development contract (PDC) be signed between each major league team and its minor league affiliates. The PDC specifies the expenses for which each entity is responsible.[5] Generally, the PDC specifies that all players, instructors, trainers, coaches, and managers are employees of the major league club. The PDC covers all aspects of the relationship, down to the number of games played and the maximum number of double-headers allowed during a season.[6]

As a result of the new agreement, the leagues were restructured and reclassified as part of a stabilization program. Teams that had previously been Class A and Class AA were combined into Class A. Former Class B, C, and D teams were reclassified as Class A. Two Class AAA leagues remained—the International League and the Pacific Coast League.[7]

Today, the minor leagues retain the organizational plan instituted in 1963. In 2002, there were three Class AAA leagues, three Class AA leagues, five Class A leagues (two of which are advanced A), two short-season A leagues, and four rookie leagues (two of which are advanced). In addition, six independent leagues were in operation. (See Figures 1.1 and 1.2 for a list of league names.) The following is a discussion of each league.

Class AAA Leagues

International League (IL)

Future stars of the Cleveland Indians, New York Yankees, Atlanta Braves, and eleven other Major League Baseball teams take their final steps toward the big time in the International League (IL). The IL is an intriguing blend of old and new, with several teams boasting brand new ballparks, and major league affiliations reaching back to the 1960s. The Baltimore Orioles have been affiliated with the IL's Rochester Red Wings since 1961, and the New York Mets have partnered the Norfolk Tides since 1969. Newly-built stadiums include Louisville Slugger Field, home of the Louisville Bats since 2000, and the Toledo Mud Hens' Fifth Third Field, which opened in 2002. The remaining teams play in stadiums built within the last twenty years. However, one classic park remains. Located in Rhode Island, the

Pawtucket Red Sox continue to play in McCoy Field which was built in 1946.[8]

According to minor league researcher Bill O'Neal, the International League (IL) has "achieve[d] the longest continual history of any minor league."[9] The league has been active since 1884, and was one of the original leagues in the NAPBL.[10] The IL was created by a merger of three different leagues: the New York State League, the Ontario League, and the Eastern League. The IL first organized as the Eastern League at a league meeting in Philadelphia in 1884. The original teams were located in Richmond, Virginia; Baltimore, Maryland; Wilmington, Delaware; Allentown, Harrisburg, and Reading, Pennsylvania; and Newark and Trenton, New Jersey.[11] The New York State League and the Ontario League combined to form the International League in 1886. One year later, the Eastern League joined them.[12]

In 1891, the league was reorganized as the Eastern Circuit, and in 1892, changed its name to the Eastern League. Between 1902 and 1911, it was a Class A league. In 1912, after experiencing many compositional changes—as teams moved in and out of the league to and from other competing leagues—it was renamed the International League, and moved into Class AA.[13]

However, by 1918, competition from movies and automobile travel, as well as World War I, had put the future of the IL in question. Wartime restrictions, players being called into the armed forces, declining attendance, and financial difficulties caused the league to decide to disband prior to the 1918 season.[14] Nonetheless, eight team owners decided to reorganize as the New International League.[15] The New International League was the only one out of nine leagues to complete its full schedule that year.[16] In 1920, the league name reverted to the International League.[17]

The IL dealt with wartime personnel shortages and travel restrictions again during World War II.[18] However, at the close of the war, the IL was prepared to enjoy the postwar Minor League Baseball boom, and was able to remain strong during the retraction of the industry from the 1950s through the 1970s.[19] It was so strong, in fact, that the IL was able to absorb some of the teams whose leagues disbanded. For example, when the American Association disbanded after the 1962 season, the International League expanded to include the

Little Rock and Indianapolis teams. Other American Association teams transferred to the Pacific Coast League.[20]

By 1969, the American Association was back in business, fielding six teams.[21] In 1987, the International League and the American Association announced a plan for interleague play beginning in the 1988 season. Known as the AAA Alliance, the agreement provided for forty-two interleague games to be played during the season, allowing fans to see the players from eight additional teams. It was hoped that this plan would increase attendance. Also created was the Alliance Classic, a post-season series which matched the champion teams of the IL and the American Association against each other, as well as the AAA All-Star Game, a midseason game featuring the best players of the IL, PCL, and the American Association.[22] However, after the 1997 season, the American Association disbanded. Three of its teams (Buffalo, Indianapolis, and Louisville) became part of the International League, and the other five (Iowa, Nashville, New Orleans, Oklahoma, and Omaha) were absorbed by the Pacific Coast League.[23]

Over the years, teams in the International League were located from Canada to Cuba, as well as throughout the midwestern and eastern United States. IL teams have been in several cities, including Montreal, Toronto, Ottawa, and Hamilton, Canada; Pawtucket, Rhode Island; Albany, Buffalo, and Syracuse, New York; Jersey City and Newark, New Jersey; Baltimore, Maryland; Richmond, Virginia; Little Rock, Arkansas; Charleston, West Virginia; Columbus, Ohio; Memphis, Tennessee; Atlanta, Georgia; Jacksonville, Florida; Havana, Cuba; and San Juan, Puerto Rico—just to name a few! Today, the International League operates in fourteen cities in the United States and Canada (see Table 2.1).

Pacific Coast League (PCL)

The Pacific Coast League (PCL) is a metaphor for the expansiveness of the western-most part of North America and the unique characteristics of PCL towns and cities, such as Tacoma, Washington, and Salt Lake City, Utah. An example of this is the hulking 24,500-seat PGE Park in Portland, Oregon, which has been home to the Portland Beavers since 2001, and many other Portland baseball teams since it was constructed in 1926. In comparison, from the stands at Tucson Electric Park, built in 1998, one can view the purple mountains of the

TABLE 2.1. International League Teams, 2002

Team	Location of Home Stadium	Major League Affiliate	Years in League
Buffalo Bisons	Buffalo, NY	Cleveland Indians	1886-1890, 1912-1970, 1998-present
Charlotte Knights	Fort Mill, SC	Chicago White Sox	1993-present
Columbus Clippers	Columbus, OH	New York Yankees	1955-1970, 1977-present
Durham Bulls	Durham, NC	Tampa Bay Devil Rays	1998-present
Indianapolis Indians	Indianapolis, IN	Milwaukee Brewers	1963, 1998-present
Louisville Bats	Louisville, KY	Cincinnati Reds	1998-present
Norfolk Tides	Norfolk, VA	New York Mets	1969-present
Ottawa Lynx	Ottawa, Ontario	Montreal Expos	1993-present
Pawtucket Red Sox	Pawtucket, RI	Boston Red Sox	1973-present
Richmond Braves	Richmond, VA	Atlanta Braves	1884, 1915-1917, 1954-1964, 1966-present
Rochester Red Wings	Rochester, NY	Baltimore Orioles	1885-1889, 1891-1892, 1895-present
Scranton/Wilkes-Barre Red Barons	Scranton, PA	Philadelphia Phillies	1989-present
Syracuse SkyChiefs	Syracuse, NY	Toronto Blue Jays	1885-1889, 1891-1892, 1894-1901, 1918, 1920-1927, 1934-1955, 1961-present
Toledo Mud Hens	Toledo, OH	Detroit Tigers	1889, 1965-present

Source: Compiled from *Baseball America 2002 Directory*, Nineteenth Edition (Durham, NC: Baseball America, Inc., 2002); International League Web Site, <http://www.ilbaseball.com>.

Tucson skyline as the sun sets over the Arizona Diamondbacks' Triple A affiliate, the Tucson Sidewinders.

For many years, many towns along the Pacific Coast of the United States enjoyed Minor League Baseball, without the presence—or interference—of Major League Baseball. The Pacific Coast League (PCL), established in 1903, eventually earned the nickname of the "Third Minor League."[24] In fact, the PCL was even given special status as an open-level or Class Four-A league in 1952. This classification was a step above Class AAA and was established in anticipation of the PCL becoming a part of the major leagues.[25] As early as 1945, the PCL launched a plan to achieve major league status. At the winter baseball meetings in December of that year, the PCL president requested the American and National Leagues to designate the PCL as a third major league. Major League owners, unable or unwilling to view the PCL clubs as equal to their own, denied the request. Further, of the eight cities in the PCL, they viewed only Los Angeles and San Francisco as viable markets. Nonetheless, in 1946 the major league owners did agree to pay indemnities to the local team if any of their teams relocated to a PCL city, therefore insulating the PCL from any potential invasion by the majors. The PCL continued to press for a change in its level of play until the eventual migration of Major League Baseball in 1958 took away its strongest markets.[26]

Throughout its history, the PCL has enjoyed success, in part due to its relative independence and lack of competition from other leagues. Although many leagues disbanded during the Great Depression, the PCL remained strong, drawing 1,673,123 fans in 1931.[27] Despite some declines in attendance and reductions in number of games played and roster size, the PCL remained healthy into the 1940s. According to Bill O'Neal, the league "was so stable that the 1940s would be the only decade in PCL history in which there were no franchise movements."[28]

In 1958, the PCL was threatened by the expansion of the major leagues into traditional PCL towns, that, incidentally, crushed any hope that the PCL would become a major league.[29] Then, in the 1960s and 1970s, further major league expansion chased minor league teams from Anaheim, San Diego, and Seattle. Nonetheless, the PCL survived. According to Bruce Chadwick:

> The Pacific Coast League has always been different from other leagues. For one thing, it has had glitz and glamour like no other

league has ever enjoyed. After all, with a team called the Hollywood Stars, owned by real Hollywood stars, how could it not be bathed in glamour?[30]

He continues:

> Distance has also set the PCL apart from other leagues. Until the late 1950s, most PCL franchises were more than 1,500 miles from the nearest major-league city, Saint Louis. The PCL played its games in splendid isolation, a very big fish in its own very big pond. The league had West Coast psychology on its side. Separated by days of travel until the advent of the jet airplane in the 1960s, the West Coast developed its own culture and its own lifestyle, and the PCL was its own, very precious, league.[31]

Over the years, the PCL included such teams as the Hollywood Stars, the Seattle Rainiers, the Hawaii Islanders, the Los Angeles Angels, the Salt Lake City Bees, and the Vancouver Mounties.[32] Today, the PCL operates in sixteen cities, from Edmonton in Alberta, Canada, to Nashville, Tennessee (see Table 2.2).

Mexican League

Mexico has a long history of baseball and several baseball leagues have operated in the country. In the 1950s, several Mexican cities, such as Tijuana, Nogales, and Chihuahua fielded teams that competed in the Arizona-Texas League, which was later known as the Arizona-Mexico League. In the 1960s, leagues such as the Mexican Center League, the Mexican Northern League, and the Mexican Southeast League were classified as A, B, or C like their U.S. counterparts.[33]

However, the Mexican League, or La Liga Mexicana de Béisbol, has had the longest relationship with organized baseball in the United States. This league has fielded teams since 1925 and became associated with the National Association of Professional Baseball Leagues in January 1955. Designated as a Double A league, the 1955 league fielded teams in México, D. F., Nuevo Laredo, Veracruz, Monterrey, and Yucatán. The league was upgraded to AAA level in 1967.[34]

Although the Mexican League is recognized by Minor League Baseball, its teams do not have the same relationship to Major League Baseball as other minor league teams.[35] Although teams such as the

TABLE 2.2. Pacific Coast League Teams, 2002

Team	Location of Home Stadium	Major League Affiliate	Years in League
Calgary Cannons	Calgary, Alberta	Florida Marlins	1985-present
Colorado Springs Sky Sox	Colorado Springs, CO	Colorado Rockies	1988-present
Edmonton Trappers	Edmonton, Alberta	Minnesota Twins	1981-present
Fresno Grizzlies	Fresno, CA	San Francisco Giants	1998-present
Iowa Cubs	Des Moines, IA	Chicago Cubs	1969-present
Las Vegas 51s	Las Vegas, NV	Los Angeles Dodgers	1983-present
Memphis Redbirds	Memphis, TN	St. Louis Cardinals	1998-present
Nashville Sounds	Nashville, TN	Pittsburgh Pirates	1998-present
New Orleans Zephyrs	Metairie, LA	Houston Astros	1998-present
Oklahoma RedHawks	Oklahoma City, OK	Texas Rangers	1963-1968, 1998-present
Omaha Royals	Omaha, NE	Kansas City Royals	1998-present
Portland Beavers	Portland, OR	San Diego Padres	1903-1917, 1919-1972, 1978-1993, 2001-present
Sacramento River Cats	West Sacramento, CA	Oakland Athletics	1903, 1909-1911, 1918-1960, 1974-1976
Salt Lake Stingers	Salt Lake City, UT	Anaheim Angels	1915-1925, 1958-1965, 1970-1984, 1994-present
Tacoma Rainiers	Tacoma, WA	Seattle Mariners	1904-1905, 1960-present
Tucson Sidewinders	Tucson, AZ	Arizona Diamondbacks	1969-present

Source: Compiled from *Baseball America 2002 Directory*, Nineteenth Edition (Durham, NC: Baseball America, Inc., 2002); Pacific Coast League Web Site, <http://www.pclbaseball.com>.

San Diego Padres and the Arizona Diamondbacks maintain loose affiliations with Mexican League teams and cities, often playing Spring Training games across the border in their stadiums, the teams do not have player development agreements with Major League Baseball teams. Therefore, players in the Mexican League do not move up to the U.S. major leagues with much frequency.

In 2002, the Mexican League hosted teams in the Mexican states of Campeche, Coahuila, Nuevo León, Oaxaca, Puebla, Quintana Roo, Tabasco, Tamaulipas, Veracruz, and Yucatán, as well as in México, D. F. (see Table 2.3).

TABLE 2.3. Mexican League Teams, 2002

Team	English Translation of Team Name	Location of Home Stadium
Acereros del Norte	Monclova Steelers	Monclova, Coahuila
Algodoneros de Unión Laguna	Union Laguna Cotton Pickers	Terreón, Coahuila
Broncos de Reynosa	Reynosa Broncos	Reynosa, Tamaulipas
Cafeteros de Córdoba	Cordoba Coffee Growers	Córdoba, Veracruz
Diablos Rojos del México	Mexico City Red Devils	México, D. F.
Guerreros de Oaxaca	Oaxaca Warriors	Oaxaca, Oaxaca
Leones de Yucatán	Yucatan Lions	Mérida, Yucatán
Longosteros de Cancún	Cancun Lobstermen	Cancún, Quintana Roo
Olmecas de Tabasco	Tabasco Cattlemen	Villahermosa, Tabasco
Pericos de Puebla	Puebla Parrots	Puebla, Puebla
Piratas de Campeche	Campeche Pirates	Campeche, Campeche
Rojos del Aguila de Veracruz	Veracruz Eagles	Boca del Río, Veracruz
Saraperos de Saltillo	Saltillo Sarape Makers	Saltillo, Coahuila
Sultanes de Monterrey	Monterrey Sultans	Monterrey, Nuevo León
Tecolotes de Los Dos Laredos	Two Laredos Owls	Nuevo Laredo, Tamaulipas
Tigres del México	Mexico City Tigers	México, D. F.

Source: Liga Mexicana de Béisbol, Web Site, accessed at <www.lmb.com.mx>; Minor League Baseball, Web Site, accessed at <www.milb.com>.

Class AA Leagues

Eastern League (EL)

The proximity of large cities and towns to one another on the east coast of North America makes the Eastern League a good proposition for many major league teams and their fans. With minor league affiliates nearby, Major League Baseball teams can easily shift players between the big league team and their double A affiliates.[35] The Baltimore Orioles rely on the Bowie Baysox, about twenty-five miles away, for quick player call-ups and short rehabilitation stints. Similarly, the Philadelphia Phillies and the Cleveland Indians have their Eastern League affiliates close by with the Reading Phillies and the Akron Aeros. Even the New York Mets' players do not have to go far to travel between Queens and Binghamton, New York. Although the rule of proximity does not apply in all cases, such as with the Florida Marlins and their Portland (Maine) Seadogs, it may provide a stronger fan base for the major and minor league teams that do operate near one another.[36]

The Eastern League (EL) was formed in March 1923, at the Arlington Hotel in Binghamton, New York. Its first game was played between the Williamsport Billies and the Wilkes-Barre Barons on May 9, 1923. The original league, known as the New York-Pennsylvania League, was comprised of six teams located in those two states. In 1938, after teams had moved to New Jersey and Connecticut, the league became known as the Eastern League. Since its inception in 1923, the Eastern League has fielded teams in fifty-one different cities, located in twelve states and two Canadian provinces.[37] For the 2002 season, the Eastern League sported teams in Ohio, Pennsylvania, New York, Maryland, Connecticut, Maine, and New Jersey (see Table 2.4).

Southern League

Historically, the Southern League and its predecessors provided baseball to the grand cities of the southern United States long before Major League Baseball had a presence (when the Milwaukee Braves moved to Atlanta in 1966). In the 1930s and 1940s, cities such as Savannah, Georgia; Jacksonville, Florida; and Charleston, South Carolina,

TABLE 2.4. Eastern League Teams, 2002

Team	Location of Home Stadium	Major League Affiliate	Years in League
Akron Aeros	Akron, OH	Cleveland Indians	1989-present
Altoona Curve	Altoona, PA	Pittsburgh Pirates	1999-present
Binghamton Mets	Binghamton, NY	New York Mets	1923-1937, 1940-1963, 1966-1968, 1992-present
Bowie Baysox	Bowie, MD	Baltimore Orioles	1993-present
Erie SeaWolves	Erie, PA	Detroit Tigers	1999-present
Harrisburg Senators	Harrisburg, PA	Montreal Expos	1924-1935, 1987-present
New Britain Rock Cats	New Britain, CT	Minnesota Twins	1983-present
New Haven Ravens	West Haven, CT	St. Louis Cardinals	1916-1932, 1994-present
Norwich Navigators	Norwich, CT	New York Yankees	1995-present
Portland Sea Dogs	Portland, ME	Florida Marlins	1994-present
Reading Phillies	Reading, PA	Philadelphia Phillies	1933-1935, 1952-1961, 1963-1965, 1967-present
Trenton Thunder	Trenton, NJ	Boston Red Sox	1994-present

Source: Compiled from *Baseball America 2002 Directory*, Nineteenth Edition (Durham, NC: Baseball America, Inc., 2002); *Baseball America 2001 Directory*, Eighteenth Edition (Durham, NC: Baseball America, Inc., 2001); Eastern League Web Site, <http://www.easternleague.com>.

hosted Minor League Baseball. By the 1950s, the league had expanded to Charlotte, North Carolina, and Montgomery, Alabama. In the 1960s and 1970s, the league stretched out to include cites such as Evansville, Indiana, and Lynchburg, Virginia.[38]

Although the Southern League has been a member of the NAPBL since 1964, the league can trace its history back to the Southern League of Professional Baseball Clubs that was formed in 1885.[39] The league played intermittently, from 1885 to 1886, 1892 to 1896, and in 1901.[40] In 1902, the league joined the NAPBL and was classified as a Class B league through the 1904 season. It was elevated to Class A in 1905 and to Class A1 in 1936, and was again upgraded to Class AA in 1946. The league also was referred to as the Southern Association prior to 1920.[41]

The current Southern League is the successor of the South Atlantic (SALLY) League, which operated from 1946 through 1963 in many of the same towns as the original Southern League.[42] Prior to 1946, the SALLY had been in operation on and off since 1904. First organized as a Class C league, the league operated from 1904 to 1917, and again from 1919 to 1920. It was upgraded to Class B in 1921 and remained in operation until 1930. After a six-year break, the league resumed play from 1936 to 1942.[43]

In 1964, the SALLY changed its name to the Southern League in recognition of its new higher classification of Class AA. In 1971, the Southern League and the Texas League, each with only seven teams, joined together in the Dixie Association. The association lasted for one season, as both leagues added additional teams in 1972 to even out their divisions.[44]

Over the years, the league earned its nickname the "Major Minor League," from *The Sporting News*.[45] In 2002, the Southern League had teams in Hoover, Huntsville, and Mobile, Alabama; Greenville, South Carolina; Zebulon, North Carolina; Chattanooga, Kodak, and Jackson, Tennessee; and Jacksonville and Kissimmee, Florida (see Table 2.5).

Texas League

Everything about Texas is big, and the Texas League is no different. Throughout its history, the league has covered twenty-six cities in Texas, and has reached from New Mexico to Arkansas and Missis-

TABLE 2.5. Southern League Teams, 2002

Team	Location of Home Stadium	Major League Affiliate	Years in League
Birmingham Barons	Hoover, AL	Chicago White Sox	1964-1965, 1967-1975, 1981-present
Carolina Mudcats	Zebulon, NC	Colorado Rockies	1991-present
Chattanooga Lookouts	Chattanooga, TN	Cincinnati Reds	1964-1965, 1976-present
Greenville Braves	Greenville, SC	Atlanta Braves	1984-present
Huntsville Stars	Huntsville, AL	Milwaukee Brewers	1985-present
Jacksonville Suns	Jacksonville, FL	Los Angeles Dodgers	1970-present
Mobile BayBears	Mobile, AL	San Diego Padres	1966, 1970, 1997-present
Orlando Rays	Kissimmee, FL	Tampa Bay Devil Rays	1973-present
Tennessee Smokies	Kodak, TN	Toronto Blue Jays	1964-1967, 1972-present
West Tenn Diamond Jaxx	Jackson, TN	Chicago Cubs	1998-present

Source: Compiled from *Baseball America 2002 Directory*, Nineteenth Edition (Durham, NC: Baseball America, Inc., 2002); Southern League Web Site, <http://www.southernleague.com>.

sippi.⁴⁶ The wide expanses of the Texas landscape made for long road trips for the teams, and even longer trips for players moving up to the major leagues. However, prior to the expansion of the National League in 1962 and the arrival of the Houston Colt .45s, Texas League baseball was the only game in town for most of the early twentieth century in the Lone Star State.

The history of the Texas League dates back to 1888, when the league included five teams in Texas (Dallas, San Antonio, Galveston, Houston, and Fort Worth) and one in Louisiana (New Orleans). The fledgling league did not fare well, with four teams disbanding before the completion of the season. The league tried again the following year with teams in Houston, Dallas, Austin, Galveston, Fort Worth, and Waco. Three teams survived that season.⁴⁷ Nonetheless, the Texas League has been in operation continuously since its start over a century ago.

With the creation of the NAPBL, the Texas League became a Class D league for the 1902 season. It was upgraded to Class C in 1907, to Class B in 1911, and to Class A in 1920. The league was again upgraded—to Class A1—in 1936. The league has been a Class AA league since 1946.⁴⁸ It briefly entered into the Pan-American Association with the Mexican League in 1959, and was part of the Dixie Association in 1972.⁴⁹

Two of the teams currently on the Texas League circuit—San Antonio and Shreveport—are in cities that have had teams in the Texas League almost continuously since the late 1800s. Little Rock, El Paso, and Tulsa have had Texas League teams since the 1960s. Rounding out the Texas League roster for the 2002 season were Midland, Round Rock, and Wichita (see Table 2.6).

Class A Leagues

California (Cal) League (Advanced A)

Hampered by its distance from the East Coast, the California League traditionally has partnered with major league affiliates such as the Anaheim Angels, the Los Angeles Dodgers, the Oakland Athletics, the San Francisco Giants, and the Seattle Mariners. The league has also had to contend with major league expansion and relocation

TABLE 2.6. Texas League Teams, 2002

Team	Location of Home Stadium	Major League Affiliate	Years in League
Arkansas Travelers	Little Rock, AR	Anaheim Angels	1966-present
El Paso Diablos	El Paso, TX	Arizona Diamondbacks	1962-1970, 1972-present
Midland RockHounds	Midland, TX	Oakland Athletics	1972-present
Round Rock Express	Round Rock, TX	Houston Astros	2000-present
San Antonio Missions	San Antonio, TX	Seattle Mariners	1888, 1892, 1895-1999, 1907-1942, 1946-1964, 1968-present
Shreveport Swamp Dragons	Shreveport, LA	San Francisco Giants	1895, 1908-1910, 1915-1932, 1938-1942, 1946-1957, 1968-present
Tulsa Drillers	Tulsa, OK	Texas Rangers	1933-1942, 1946-1965, 1977-present
Wichita Wranglers	Wichita, KS	Kansas City Royals	1987-present

Source: Compiled from *Baseball America 2002 Directory*, Nineteenth Edition (Durham, NC: Baseball America, Inc., 2002); Texas League Web Site, <http://www.texas-league.com>.

into its territories. Nonetheless, the league has expanded from its primarily northern California roots, located in towns such as Modesto and Visalia, to now spanning the entire state.[50]

The California League has been in operation since 1941, though it was shut down during World War II. Prior to the league restructuring of 1963, the California League played Class C ball. In 1963, Class C leagues were reclassified as Class A; the California League has operated as an Advanced Class A league since then. Over the years, the league has fluctuated between operating with six and ten teams.[51] Today, the league has both a Northern and a Southern division, operating from Stockton to Lake Elsinore (see Table 2.7).

The Carolina League (Advanced A)

After the 1988 release of the movie *Bull Durham*, the Carolina League was perhaps the most widely recognized minor league, and the Durham Bulls were one of the most well-known minor league teams. The movie, which depicts life in a minor league town and on the road with the team, provides a glimpse into Minor League Baseball that, until then, few people had seen. Although the Durham Bulls are no longer part of the Carolina League circuit, after moving into a new stadium in 1995 and moving up to the AAA International League in 1998, their role in a major motion picture has often been attributed to the increase in popularity of Minor League Baseball and the rising minor league attendance figures of the 1990s.[52]

The Carolina League was formed in 1945, with six teams in North Carolina and two teams in southern Virginia.[53] Although founded during wartime, the Carolina League was the only Class C league in operation in 1945, guaranteeing major league support for that season.[54] The league weathered the war, and from the 1940s through the 1950s, operated primarily in North Carolina. Although the Carolina League was not the only league in the area, it is the one that has survived until today. At the height of the minor league boom in the late 1940s and early 1950s, several leagues operated in the Carolinas, including: the Tar Heel League, the North Carolina State League, the Western Carolina League, the Eastern Carolina League, the Tobacco

TABLE 2.7. California League Teams, 2002

Team	Location of Home Stadium	Major League Affiliate	Years in League
Bakersfield Blaze	Bakersfield, CA	Tampa Bay Devil Rays	1941-1942, 1946-1975, 1978-1979, 1982-present
High Desert Mavericks	Adelanto, CA	Milwaukee Brewers	1991-present
Lake Elsinore Storm	Lake Elsinore, CA	San Diego Padres	1994-present
Lancaster JetHawks	Lancaster, CA	Arizona Diamondbacks	1996-present
Modesto A's	Modesto, CA	Oakland Athletics	1946-1964, 1966-present
Rancho Cucamonga Quakes	Rancho Cucamonga, CA	Anaheim Angels	1993-present
San Bernardino Stampede	San Bernardino, CA	Seattle Mariners	1941, 1987-present
San Jose Giants	San Jose, CA	San Francisco Giants	1942, 1947-1958, 1962-1976, 1979-present
Stockton Ports	Stockton, CA	Cincinnati Reds	1941, 1946-1972, 1978-present
Visalia Oaks	Visalia, CA	Oakland Athletics	1946-1962, 1968-1975, 1977-present

Source: Compiled from *Baseball America 2002 Directory*, Nineteenth Edition (Durham, NC: Baseball America, Inc., 2002); California League Web Site, <http://www.californialeague.com>.

State League, and the Coastal Plain League.[55] Jim Sumner speculates on the reasons for the Carolina League's survival:

> It's not clear why the Carolina League survived when so many other leagues didn't. Many knowledgeable observers believe a critical factor was the compactness of the league, which kept travel expenses at a minimum. Furthermore, the league had gained a reputation for solid baseball by the early 1950s. Most of the league's cities were traditionally good minor league cities with large-enough populations to support the professional game.[56]

Whatever the reasons for the league's success, it is found in eight cities as far north as Wilmington, Delaware, and as far south as Myrtle Beach, South Carolina (see Table 2.8).

Florida State League (FSL) (Advanced A)

The cities hosting teams of the Florida State League (FSL) enjoy the position of hosting both Minor League Baseball and Major League Baseball between February and September, as many of the minor league ballparks also serve as spring training camps. Known as the Grapefruit League, major league teams arrive in late February and stay through March to get ready for the upcoming baseball season. For example, Ed Smith Stadium in Sarasota, Florida, is home to both the Cincinnati Reds for spring training and the Sarasota Red Sox during the FSL season. Likewise, the Los Angeles Dodgers hold spring training at Holman Stadium in Vero Beach, Florida, where the Vero Beach Dodgers play during the regular season.[57]

The Florida State League was established in 1919. The league operated as a Class D organization from 1919 to 1920, and was upgraded to Class C in 1921. However, after the 1924 season, the league was again reclassified as Class D. A series of hurricanes and economic downturns shut down the league from 1928 until 1936. The league again ceased operations for the duration of World War II.[58]

Over the years, thirty-one different cities in Florida have been home to FSL teams. Several cities have been part of the league for a large part of its more than eighty-year history, including Daytona Beach, Lakeland, and Tampa. The league also has teams in Melbourne, Port Charlotte, Clearwater, Dunedin, Fort Myers, Jupiter,

TABLE 2.8. Carolina League Teams, 2002

Team	Location of Home Stadium	Major League Affiliate	Years in League
Frederick Keys	Frederick, MD	Baltimore Orioles	1989-present
Kinston Indians	Kinston, NC	Cleveland Indians	1956-1957, 1962-1974, 1978-present
Lynchburg Hillcats	Lynchburg, VA	Pittsburgh Pirates	1966-present
Myrtle Beach Pelicans	Myrtle Beach, SC	Atlanta Braves	1999-present
Potomac Cannons	Woodbridge, VA	St. Louis Cardinals	1978-present
Salem Avalanche	Salem, VA	Colorado Rockies	1968-present
Wilmington Blue Rocks	Wilmington, DE	Kansas City Royals	1993-present
Winston-Salem Warthogs	Winston-Salem, NC	Chicago White Sox	1945-present

Source: Compiled from *Baseball America 2002 Directory*, Nineteenth Edition (Durham, NC: Baseball America, Inc., 2002); Carolina League Web Site, <http://www.carolinaleague.com>.

Port St. Lucie, Sarasota, and Vero Beach (see Table 2.9). The league's Web site proclaims the FSL to be "Where the Major League Stars of Tomorrow Play Today."[59]

South Atlantic (SALLY) League

The South Atlantic League is home to many of the grand old stadiums of the minor leagues. Like the rest of Minor League Baseball, the SALLY league has enjoyed its share of new stadiums, such as Perdue Stadium in Salisbury, Maryland, which opened in 1996, and Applebee's Park, where the Lexington (Kentucky) Legends have played since 2001. However, there is much history to be learned in other SALLY stadiums, including Luther Williams Field, built in Macon, Georgia, in 1929; Hagerstown (Maryland) Municipal Stadium, constructed in 1931; Charleston, West Virginia's Watt Powell Park, built in 1949; and Golden Park, located in Columbus, Georgia, since 1951.[60]

In 2002, the South Atlantic League fielded teams in sixteen cities (see Table 2.10). As currently configured, the South Atlantic League began operations in 1980, though it can be traced back several decades to the Western Carolina League, which operated as a Class D league from 1948 to 1952. In 1953, the Western Carolina League was combined with the North Carolina State League to form the Class D Tar Heel League which played for only two seasons. Resuming operations in 1960, the league was known as the Western Carolina League through the 1962 season, after which it changed its name to the Western Carolinas League to accommodate the inclusion of teams from both North and South Carolina. The league operated as the Western Carolinas League until 1979.[61] (Although a league known as the South Atlantic League was founded in 1904, it was the predecessor of the current Southern League and not the South Atlantic League.)

Midwest League

Thinking about baseball in the midwestern United States might conjure up visions of the farm in Dyersville, Iowa, which was the setting of the baseball-themed movie *Field of Dreams*. Since the 1800s, baseball has been played throughout the Midwest in locations such as Belleville, Illinois; Clear Lake, Iowa; Terre Haute, Indiana; and many

TABLE 2.9. Florida State League Teams, 2002

Team	Location of Home Stadium	Major League Affiliate	Years in League
Brevard County Manatees	Melbourne, FL	Montreal Expos	1994-present
Charlotte Rangers	Port Charlotte, FL	Texas Rangers	1987-present
Clearwater Phillies	Clearwater, FL	Philadelphia Phillies	1985-present
Daytona Cubs	Daytona Beach, FL	Chicago Cubs	1920-1924, 1928, 1936-1941, 1946-1973, 1977-1987, 1993-present
Dunedin Blue Jays	Dunedin, FL	Toronto Blue Jays	1978-1979, 1987-present
Fort Myers Miracle	Fort Myers, FL	Minnesota Twins	1926, 1978-1987, 1991-present
Jupiter Hammerheads	Jupiter, FL	Florida Marlins	1998-present
Lakeland Tigers	Lakeland, FL	Detroit Tigers	1919-1926, 1953-1955, 1960, 1962-1964, 1967-present
St. Lucie Mets	Port St. Lucie, FL	New York Mets	1988-present
Sarasota Red Sox	Sarasota, FL	Boston Red Sox	1927, 1961-1965, 1989-present
Tampa Yankees	Tampa, FL	New York Yankees	1919-1927, 1957-1988, 1994-present
Vero Beach Dodgers	Vero Beach, FL	Los Angeles Dodgers	1980-present

Source: Compiled from *Baseball America 2002 Directory*, Nineteenth Edition (Durham, NC: Baseball America, Inc., 2002); Florida State League Web Site, <http://www.fslbaseball.com>.

TABLE 2.10. South Atlantic League Teams, 2002

Team	Location of Home Stadium	Major League Affiliate	Years in League
Asheville Tourists	Asheville, NC	Colorado Rockies	1976-present
Augusta GreenJackets	Augusta, GA	Boston Red Sox	1988-present
Capital City Bombers	Columbia, SC	New York Mets	1960-1961, 1983-present
Charleston Alley Cats	Charleston, WV	Toronto Blue Jays	1987-present
Charleston RiverDogs	Charleston, SC	Tampa Bay Devil Rays	1973-1978, 1980-present
Columbus RedStixx	Columbus, GA	Cleveland Indians	1991-present
Delmarva Shorebirds	Salisbury, MD	Baltimore Orioles	1996-present
Greensboro Bats	Greensboro, NC	New York Yankees	1979-present
Hagerstown Suns	Hagerstown, MD	San Francisco Giants	1993-present
Hickory Crawdads	Hickory, NC	Pittsburgh Pirates	1952, 1960, 1993-present
Kannapolis Intimidators	Kannapolis, NC	Chicago White Sox	1995-present
Lakewood BlueClaws	Lakewood, NJ	Philadelphia Phillies	2001-present
Lexington Legends	Lexington, KY	Houston Astros	2001-present
Macon Braves	Macon, GA	Atlanta Braves	1962-1963, 1980-1987, 1991-present
Savannah Sand Gnats	Savannah, GA	Texas Rangers	1962, 1984-present
South Georgia Waves	Albany, GA	Los Angeles Dodgers	2002-present

Source: Compiled from *Baseball America 2002 Directory,* Nineteenth Edition (Durham, NC: Baseball America, Inc., 2002); South Atlantic League Web Site, <http://www.southatlanticleague.com>.

others. For example, Clear Lake participated in the Class D Central Association in 1917. Belleville fielded a team in the Class D Illinois State League from 1947 to 1948, and a team in the Class D Mississippi-Ohio Valley League in 1949. Before the end of the nineteenth century, Terre Haute hosted many minor league baseball teams in leagues such as the Northwestern League, the Central Interstate League, and the Two-I League. In 1900 and again from 1903 to 1916, Terre Haute fielded a team in the Class D Central League. However, the city has not had a minor league team since 1956, when it was a member of the Class B Three-I League.[62]

The Midwest League can be traced back to the Class D Illinois State League, which was in operation for the 1947 and 1948 seasons. The Illinois State League had teams in seven different Illinois cities: Belleville, Centralia, Marion, Mattoon, Mount Vernon, Murphysboro, and West Frankfort. In 1949, a team from Paducah, Kentucky, joined the league and its name was changed to the Mississippi-Ohio Valley League. From 1949 until 1955, the league included teams primarily from Illinois, but also from Clinton and Dubuque, Iowa; Hannibal, Missouri; Paducah, Kentucky; and Lafayette, Kokomo, and Vincennes, Indiana.[63]

The name was again changed when the league moved farther into Iowa in 1956. The newly named Midwest League ultimately would include teams from Indiana to Wisconsin. Today, the Midwest League is comprised of fourteen teams in Wisconsin, Iowa, Ohio, Indiana, Illinois, and Michigan (see Table 2.11).

According to the league's Web site: "Although the teams are as diverse as the cities they play in, one thing remains constant: Tomorrow's Major League stars get their start in the Midwest League today."[64]

New York-Penn League (Short Season A)

The New York-Penn League is located in the heart of baseball history country and has been the training ground for several baseball hall of famers—even Babe Ruth barnstormed through Oneonta, New York, in 1920. Located in the league's territory are the National Baseball Hall of Fame and Museum in Cooperstown (which is approximately twenty miles from Oneonta, home of the Oneonta Tigers) and the Little League Baseball Museum (located in Williamsport, Pennsylvania, home of the Williamsport Crosscutters and the Little

TABLE 2.11. Midwest League Teams, 2002

Team	Location of Home Stadium	Major League Affiliate	Years in League
Beloit Snappers	Beloit, WI	Milwaukee Brewers	1982-present
Burlington Bees	Burlington, IA	Kansas City Royals	1962-present
Cedar Rapids Kernels	Cedar Rapids, IA	Anaheim Angels	1962-present
Clinton LumberKings	Clinton, IA	Montreal Expos	1956-present
Dayton Dragons	Dayton, OH	Cincinnati Reds	2000-present
Fort Wayne Wizards	Fort Wayne, IN	San Diego Padres	1993-present
Kane County Cougars	Geneva, IL	Florida Marlins	1991-present
Lansing Lugnuts	Lansing, MI	Chicago Cubs	1996-present
Michigan Battle Cats	Battle Creek, MI	Houston Astros	1995-present
Peoria Chiefs	Peoria, IL	St. Louis Cardinals	1983-present
Quad City River Bandits	Davenport, IA	Minnesota Twins	1960-present
South Bend Silver Hawks	South Bend, IN	Arizona Diamondbacks	1988-present
West Michigan Whitecaps	Comstock Park, MI	Detroit Tigers	1994-present
Wisconsin Timber Rattlers	Appleton, WI	Seattle Mariners	1962-present

Source: Compiled from *Baseball America 2002 Directory*, Nineteenth Edition (Durham, NC: Baseball America, Inc., 2002); Midwest League Web Site, <http://www.midwestleague.com>.

League World Championship).[65] The history and lore of baseball are kept alive through the old-fashioned stadiums: Bowman Field in Williamsport, Centennial Field, home of the Vermont Expos, which opened in 1922; and Oneonta's Damaschke Field, built in 1940. In addition, the Auburn Doubledays, in Auburn, New York, pay tribute to the mythical founder of baseball, Abner Doubleday.[66]

The predecessor of the New York-Penn League was the PONY League, or the Pennsylvania-Ontario-New York League, which was in operation from 1939 to 1956. The name of the league was changed to the New York-Penn League in 1957 after the Hamilton, Ontario, team withdrew from the league. An Ontario team did not return to the league until 1986, when the St. Catharines Blue Jays were added to the circuit.[67] Today, the league operates in fourteen cities in six states (see Table 2.12).

Northwest League (Short Season A)

The Northwest League occupies a section of the country virtually ignored by Major League Baseball until it added Seattle to its roster of cities in 1969 and again in 1977. The 1969 Seattle Pilots stayed in the Northwest only one year before moving to Milwaukee; the Seattle Mariners arrived in 1977 and have remained in the area since then. However, the northwestern part of the United States from Idaho to Washington and its Canadian neighbors have a long tradition of playing baseball.

The Northwest League began play in 1955, with teams in Lewiston, Idaho; Eugene and Salem, Oregon; and Wenatchee, Tri-City, Yakima, and Spokane, Washington. However, the Northwest League is part of a long tradition of baseball in the Pacific Northwest. The league is the successor to the Pacific Coast International League, which was in operation from 1918 to 1921, and the Western International League, which operated for several different periods: 1922, 1937 to 1942, 1946 to 1951, and 1952 to 1954. Cities represented in the league have roots as far back as the Pacific Northwest League, one of the earliest leagues in the region. The Pacific Northwest League was in operation in 1902, and was renamed the Pacific National League in 1903. The Pacific National League ceased operations in 1905.[68] In 2002, the Northwest League fielded eight teams from Idaho, Oregon, Washington, and British Columbia (see Table 2.13).

TABLE 2.12. New York-Penn League Teams, 2002

Team	Location of Home Stadium	Major League Affiliate	Years in League
Aberdeen IronBirds	Aberdeen, MD	Baltimore Orioles	2002-present
Auburn Doubledays	Auburn, NY	Toronto Blue Jays	1958-1980, 1982-present
Batavia Muckdogs	Batavia, NY	Philadelphia Phillies	1939-1953, 1957-1959, 1961-present
Brooklyn Cyclones	Brooklyn, NY	New York Mets	2000-present
Hudson Valley Renegades	Wappingers Falls, NY	Tampa Bay Devil Rays	1994-present
Jamestown Jammers	Jamestown, NY	Florida Marlins	1939-1957, 1961-1973, 1977-present
Lowell Spinners	Lowell, MA	Boston Red Sox	1996-present
Mahoning Valley Scrappers	Niles, OH	Cleveland Indians	1999-present
New Jersey Cardinals	Augusta, NJ	St. Louis Cardinals	1994-present
Oneonta Tigers	Oneonta, NY	Detroit Tigers	1996-present
Staten Island Yankees	Staten Island, NY	New York Yankees	1999-present
Tri-City ValleyCats	Troy, NY	Houston Astros	2002-present
Vermont Expos	Winooski, VT	Montreal Expos	1994-present
Williamsport Crosscutters	Williamsport, PA	Pittsburgh Pirates	1968-1972, 1994-present

Source: Compiled from *Baseball America 2002 Directory,* Nineteenth Edition (Durham, NC: Baseball America, Inc., 2002); New York-Penn League Web Site, <http://www.nypennleague.com>.

TABLE 2.13. Northwest League Teams, 2002

Team	Location of Home Stadium	Major League Affiliate	Years in League
Boise Hawks	Boise, ID	Chicago Cubs	1975-1976, 1978, 1985-present
Eugene Emeralds	Eugene, OR	San Diego Padres	1955-1968, 1974-present
Everett AquaSox	Everett, WA	Seattle Mariners	1984-present
Salem-Keizer Volcanoes	Keizer, OR	San Francisco Giants	1997-present
Spokane Indians	Spokane, WA	Kansas City Royals	1972, 1983-present
Tri-City Dust Devils	Kennewick, WA	Colorado Rockies	1955-1974, 1983-1986, 2001-present
Vancouver Canadians	Vancouver, British Columbia	Oakland Athletics	2000-present
Yakima Bears	Yakima, WA	Arizona Diamondbacks	1955-1966, 1990-present

Source: Compiled from *Baseball America 2002 Directory*, Nineteenth Edition (Durham, NC: Baseball America, Inc., 2002); Northwest League Web Site, <http://www.northwestleague.com>.

Rookie Leagues

Appalachian League (Advanced Rookie)

Nestled among the Blue Ridge Mountains and into the Shenandoah Valley are the towns of the Appalachian (Appy) League, where many players take their first steps in professional baseball. John Thorn and Bob Carroll, the editors of *The Whole Baseball Catalog,* note that when you arrive at an Appy League ballpark

> you'll quickly realize you've reached the entry level of professional baseball. Most of the players look barely old enough to shave. The umpires look like they might be some of the players' older brothers. Some of the ballparks even double as high school fields. Take away the hand-me-down major league uniforms, and you could be at an American Legion game. But even as the walks and errors pile up, stick around for a while.[69]

In contrast to the youth of the players is the historic charm of the Appalachian League's ballparks. Only three of the Appy's ten stadiums have been built in the last twenty years: Hooker Field in Martinsville, Virginia, and Hunnicutt Field in Princeton, West Virginia, both built in 1988, and Hunter Wright Stadium in Kingsport, Tennessee, built in 1995. The remaining ball fields in the league were built between 1935 (Calfee Park in Pulaski, Virginia) and 1974 (Joe O'Brien Field in Elizabethton, Tennessee). Adding to their charm is the size of the Appy League's stadiums, which range from a seating capacity of 1,500 fans in Elizabethton to a seating capacity of 3,000 in Burlington, North Carolina. In comparison, AAA ballparks seat between 8,000 and 24,000 fans, and full-season single A parks seat between 3,000 and 11,000 fans, with the exception of stadiums found in Clinton, Iowa (2,500 seats); Lakeland, Florida (1,000 seats); and Visalia, California (1,800 seats).[70]

The Appalachian League has been in operation since 1911. Originally classified as a Class D League, it ceased operation in 1955. Returning in 1957, the league has been active ever since. In 1963, during the minor league restructuring, the Appalachian League was reclassified as a Rookie League.[71] Today, the league operates in West Virginia, Virginia, North Carolina, and Tennessee (see Table 2.14).

TABLE 2.14. Appalachian League Teams, 2002

Team	Location of Home Stadium	Major League Affiliate	Years in League
Bluefield Orioles	Bluefield, WV	Baltimore Orioles	1946-1955, 1957-present
Bristol White Sox	Bristol, VA	Chicago White Sox	1921-1925, 1940-1955, 1969-present
Burlington Indians	Burlington, NC	Cleveland Indians	1986-present
Danville Braves	Danville, VA	Atlanta Braves	1993-present
Elizabethton Twins	Elizabethton, TN	Minnesota Twins	1937-1942, 1945-1951, 1974-present
Johnson City Cardinals	Johnson City, TN	St. Louis Cardinals	1911-1913, 1921-1924, 1937-1955, 1957-1961, 1964-present
Kingsport Mets	Kingsport, TN	New York Mets	1921-1925, 1938-1952, 1957, 1960-1963, 1969-1982, 1984-present
Martinsville Astros	Martinsville, VA	Houston Astros	1988-present
Princeton Devil Rays	Princeton, WV	Tampa Bay Devil Rays	1988-present
Pulaski Rangers	Pulaski, VA	Texas Rangers	1946-1950, 1952-1955, 1957-1958, 1969-1977, 1982-1992, 1997-present

Source: Compiled from *Baseball America 2002 Directory*, Nineteenth Edition (Durham, NC: Baseball America, Inc., 2002); Appalachian League Web Site, <http://www.appyleague.com>.

Pioneer League (Advanced Rookie)

The Pioneer League occupies another territory that has been overlooked by Major League Baseball. Idaho, Montana, and Utah, in the United States, and Alberta, in Canada, have been actively involved in baseball since the 1800s. However, until recently they were isolated from the rest of professional baseball. In the first part of the 1900s, Idaho, Montana, and Utah were on their own in the baseball world, playing in leagues such as the Inter-Mountain League, which fielded teams in 1901 and 1909, the Montana State League, in operation only in 1900, the Union Association, which was in existence between 1911 and 1914, and the Utah-Idaho League, which operated from 1926 to 1928. During this period, teams in Alberta, Canada, played against teams in Manitoba and Saskatchewan in the Western Canada League, which operated on and off between 1907 and 1921. Other leagues, such as the Pacific Northwest (Class B, 1892, 1896, 1901 to 1902) and the Western Tri-State leagues (Class D, 1912 to 1914), operated in larger territories, encompassing teams and cities from Portland, Oregon, to Vancouver, British Columbia, and as as far east as Lewiston, Idaho.[72]

The Pioneer League was established in 1939 as a Class C league, with six teams in Idaho and Utah. The league suspended operations for the duration of World War II, from 1942 to 1945, and returned in 1946. In 1948, the league expanded into Montana.[73] During the 1950s and 1960s, Pioneer League teams played in Montana, Idaho, and Utah. The league was reclassified a Class A league after the restructuring of the minor leagues in 1964. The next year it was reclassified again as a Rookie League.[74]

In 1977, the league expanded into Calgary and Medicine Hat in Alberta, Canada. Today, the league operates in eight cities, including Casper, Wyoming, and Provo, Utah, which entered the league in 2001. Several other cities currently in the Pioneer League have been part of the league for several decades (see Table 2.15).

Other Rookie and Lower Leagues

The rookie leagues are the lowest classification in minor league baseball. This is where a player often starts his career, either after completing high school or during the summers while still playing

TABLE 2.15. Pioneer League Teams, 2002

Team	Location of Home Stadium	Major League Affiliate	Years in League
Billings Mustangs	Billings, MT	Cincinnati Reds	1948-1963, 1969-present
Casper Rockies	Casper, WY	Colorado Rockies	2001-present
Great Falls Dodgers	Great Falls, MT	Los Angeles Dodgers	1948-1963, 1969-present
Idaho Falls Padres	Idaho Falls, ID	San Diego Padres	1940-1942, 1946-present
Medicine Hat Blue Jays	Medicine Hat, Alberta	Toronto Blue Jays	1977-present
Missoula Osprey	Missoula, MT	Arizona Diamondbacks	1956-1960, 1999-present
Ogden Raptors	Ogden, UT	Milwaukee Brewers	1939-1942, 1946-1955, 1966-1974, 1994-present
Provo Angels	Provo, UT	Anaheim Angels	2001-present

Source: Compiled from *Baseball America 2002 Directory,* Nineteenth Edition (Durham, NC: Baseball America, Inc., 2002); Pioneer League Web Site, <http://www.pioneerleague.com>.

college ball. The advanced rookie leagues, the Appalachian League and the Pioneer League, operate like the other minor league classifications, focusing on marketing, sales, and promotions. However, the lower rookie leagues usually focus less on ticket sales and more on player development. Currently, Major League Baseball operates two rookie leagues, the Arizona League and Gulf Coast League. Other developmental leagues, such as the Dominican Summer League and the Venezuelan Summer League, also are associated with Minor League Baseball and Major League Baseball.

INDEPENDENT LEAGUES

Independent baseball leagues are not aligned with Major League Baseball teams, and they do not participate in the minor league umbrella organization, Minor League Baseball. They are free to hire their own players and develop their own product. They also are solely responsible for the management and fiscal well-being of their organizations. In his description of the Northern League, an independent league created in 1993, author Steve Perlstein declares:

> This was going to be baseball the way it was supposed to be, and the fans were about to take it back for their own.
>
> If it wasn't enough inducement for folks to go out and watch the St. Paul Saints of the Northern League, maybe they could be enticed by what the league wasn't. It was not an affiliated minor league. There were no major-league parent organizations.... It was an operation slipping under the radar of big-league baseball.
>
> That would mean no commissioner of baseball telling the league, its officials, and its owners what they could and could not do. No farm directors instructing managers which players to put in the lineup when—for the good of the eventual needs of the major-league club, not out of any concern over whether the minor-league club wins or loses.[75]

Although some independent leagues and teams always have been in existence, the creation of the Northern League and the Frontier League in 1993 marked a new era in independent baseball. From 1902 to 1993, only nine independent leagues had existed, and few lasted for more than one year (see Table 2.16). Most of those leagues joined the NAPBL after one year as an independent league. The exceptions to this rule were the California League (1902, 1907-1909), the United States League (1912), and the Federal League (1913-1915). Another league, the Colonial League, was a member of the NAPBL in 1914, became independent the following year, then went out of business after the 1915 season (see Table 2.16).

The California League seems to have suffered the fate of many minor leagues, regardless of whether they were part of the NAPBL. In 1902, the league fielded teams in Oakland, Los Angeles, San Francisco, and Sacramento. The league returned in 1907 with additional teams in Stockton, San Jose, and Alameda, but without its team in Los Angeles. The next year, Santa Cruz and Fresno were added to the California League circuit. In 1909, the Alameda Encinals did not take the field. By midseason, the Santa Cruz Sand Crabs and the San Jose Prune Pickers had disbanded. The San Francisco Orphans moved to Sacramento and were renamed the Senators in July 1909. The Stockton Tigers refused to participate in a playoff, so the Oakland Invaders were awarded the pennant. The league did not return in 1910.[76]

The United States League did not fare so well. This independent league did not even complete the 1912 season. In May of its ill-fated season, teams in Washington, DC, and New York City withdrew from the league. A few days later, in the beginning of June, the Reading and Cleveland teams also withdrew. The league disbanded on June 24.[77]

Between 1914 and 1947, there were no leagues operating independently. Then, in 1948, the Provincial League was established. At first, the league operated exclusively in Quebec, Canada, in the towns of Sherbrooke, St. Jean, St. Hyacinthe, Granby, Drummondville, and Farnham. The league joined the NAPBL in 1950 as a Class C league and played for six more seasons.[78] This pattern was similar to earlier independent leagues that went it alone at first, then joined the other teams in the NAPBL.

In the 1990s, however, a new breed of independent minor leagues appeared. Since 1993, sixteen leagues have been established. By the close of the 2001 season, six were still in operation—the majority of which had been around for seven or more years. Leagues no longer transferred to the NAPBL; they either succeeded or failed on their own (see Table 2.16).

TABLE 2.16. Independent Minor Leagues, 1902 to 2002

League	Number of Years Independent	Dates As Independent League	Dates Member of NAPBL
American Association	1	1902	1903-1962, 1969
California League	4	1902, 1907-1909	n/a
Northern League	1	1902	1903-1905, 1908, 1913-1917, 1933-1942, 1946-1971
Pacific Coast League	1	1903	1904-2001
Tri-State League	3	1904-1906	1907-1914
United States League	1	1912	n/a
Federal League	1	1913	**
Colonial League	1	1915	1914
Provincial League	2	1948-1949	1950-1955
Frontier League	9*	1993-2001	n/a
Northern League	9*	1993-2001	n/a
Great Central League	1	1994	n/a
North Central League	2	1994-1995	n/a
Texas-Louisiana League	8****	1994-2001	n/a
Atlantic Coast League	1	1995	n/a
Golden State League	1	1995	n/a
Mid-America League	1	1995	n/a
North Atlantic League	2	1995-1996	n/a

45

TABLE 2.16 (continued)

League	Number of Years Independent	Dates As Independent League	Dates Member of NAPBL
Prairie League	3	1995-1997	n/a
Northeast League	4	1995-1998***	n/a
Western League	7*	1995-2002	n/a
Big South League	2	1996-1997	n/a
Heartland League	3	1996-1998	n/a
Atlantic League	4*	1998-2002	n/a
All-American Association	1	2001	n/a
Central League	1	2002	n/a

*Signifies leagues that were still active after the 2002 season.
**The Federal League operated as a major league from 1914 to 1915.
***The Northeast League became part of the Northern League in 1999.
****The Texas-Louisiana League became the Central League in 2002.

Sources: Compiled from *The Encyclopedia of Minor League Baseball*, *Baseball America Directories*, and league Web sites. See Lloyd Johnson and Miles Wolff, eds., *The Encyclopedia of Minor League Baseball*, Second Edition (Durham, NC: Baseball America, Inc., 1997); *Baseball America 1993 Directory* (Durham, NC: Baseball America, Inc., 1993); *Baseball America 1994 Directory* (Durham, NC: Baseball America, Inc., 1994); *Baseball America 1995 Directory* (Durham, NC: Baseball America, Inc., 1995); *Baseball America 1996 Directory* (Durham, NC: Baseball America, Inc., 1996); *Baseball America 1997 Directory* (Durham, NC: Baseball America, Inc., 1997); *Baseball America 1998 Directory* (Durham, NC: Baseball America, Inc., 1998); *Baseball America 1999 Directory* (Durham, NC: Baseball America, Inc., 1999); *Baseball America 2000 Directory* (Durham, NC: Baseball America, Inc., 2000); *Baseball America 2001 Directory* (Durham, NC: Baseball America, Inc., 2001); *Baseball America 2002 Directory* (Durham, NC: Baseball America, Inc., 2002); Atlantic League Web Site, <http://www.atlanticleague.com>; Central League Web Site, <http://www.centralleague.com>; Frontier League Web Site, <http://www.frontierleague.com>; Northern League Web Site, <http://www.northernleague.com>; Western League Web Site, <http://www.westernleague.com>.

According to Lloyd Johnson and Miles Wolff, the 1992 Professional Baseball Agreement between the majors and the minors, with its stadium specifications and tougher revenue requirements, spurred the growth of independent leagues:[79]

> Several long-time minor league operators, worried and tired of major league control, became part of a revived Northern League. . . . Independent baseball had not been successful on a league-wide basis since the late 1940s, and most expected this latest attempt to fail. But it was a success in its first season, and within three years a dozen other independent leagues had started. Few enjoyed the total success of the Northern, but independent baseball proved that many cities had a hunger for professional baseball that the 150 major league working agreements could not satisfy.[80]

At the same time, there were fewer opportunities for aligning with a major league team. Major League Baseball had made it clear in the 1992 PBA that they wanted fewer minor league teams.[81]

Nonetheless, with the reestablishment of independent leagues, a new crop of teams with a new attitude toward community baseball, was introduced to the United States and Canada. Located from New Hampshire to South Dakota, from Mississippi to California, and even in Ontario, Canada, these teams have brought baseball to many towns that hadn't enjoyed Minor League Baseball in decades. During the 1990s, ten of the new leagues either failed or were rolled into other leagues. For example, seven leagues began play in 1995; three disbanded after their first season. The North Atlantic League survived two seasons, and the Prairie League was around for three seasons. The Northeast League became the Eastern Division of the Northern League in 1999. Only the Western League survived intact into the twenty-first century. Neither of the leagues founded in 1996 lasted until the 1999 season (see Table 2.16).

The most recent addition to the ranks of independent minor leagues was the All-American Association, which began play in 2001. The league's mission summed up the nature of Minor League Baseball:

> The All-American Association's mission is to establish a winning tradition that embodies the genuine spirit of baseball; an organization to which all residents in league cities will point

with pride, which conducts its business with integrity and community responsibility; so that children in our league cities will grow up knowing the rich tradition that has made baseball America's national pastime.[82]

In 2001, the All-American Association fielded teams in Alabama, Georgia, Louisiana, Tennessee, and Texas, but with the migration of two of its teams to the Central League after the 2001 season, it was unable to operate during 2002. Thus, only six independent leagues played the 2002 season.

Northern League

The Northern League was the first independent minor league to be established in recent years. It has been called "*the* pre-eminent modern era independent league."[83] Founded in 1992 by minor league mogul Miles Wolff (former owner and general manager of the Durham Bulls as well as publisher of *Baseball America*), the league was premised on the idea that "town-based teams rather than organization-grounded clubs could flourish in the right communities."[84] The first season of play commenced in 1993 with teams in Duluth, Minnesota; St. Paul, Minnesota; Sioux Falls, South Dakota; Sioux City, Iowa; Thunder Bay, Ontario; and Winnipeg, Manitoba.

The Northern League brought baseball to many communities that had formerly hosted minor league teams. Prior to 1993, there had been three other leagues with the name "Northern League," in addition to other leagues operating in the northwestern United States. The first Northern League was an independent league established in 1902.[85]

In 1999, the Northern League merged with another independent league, the Northeast League, creating "a new class of Super-Independent baseball."[86] The Northeast League had been in operation in the northeastern United States since 1995. The philosophy of the league was "to provide high caliber professional baseball entertainment packages in a friendly atmosphere."[87] Today the Northeast League operates as the Northern League East and is comprised of teams from New York, Pennsylvania, New Jersey, and Quebec. The Northern League Central has teams in Minnesota, North Dakota, Nebraska, Illinois, Iowa, South Dakota, and Manitoba (see Table 2.17).

TABLE 2.17. Northern League Teams, 2002

Team	Location of Home Stadium	Years in League (Years in Northeast League)
Central Division		
Duluth-Superior Dukes	Duluth, MN	1993-present
Fargo-Moorhead RedHawks	Fargo, ND	1996-present
Gary Southshore RailCats	Gary, IN	2002-present
Joliet JackHammers	Joliet, IL	2002-present
Lincoln Saltdogs	Lincoln, NE	2001-present
Schaumburg Flyers	Schaumburg, IL	1999-present
Sioux City Explorers	Sioux City, IA	1993-present
Sioux Falls Canaries	Sioux Falls, SD	1993-present
St. Paul Saints	St. Paul, MN	1993-present
Winnipeg Goldeyes	Winnipeg, Manitoba	1994-present
Eastern Division		
Adirondack Lumberjacks	Glens Falls, NY	1999-present (1995-1998)
Albany-Colonie Diamond Dogs	Albany, NY	1999-present (1995-1998)
Allentown Ambassadors	Allentown, PA	1999-present (1997-1998)
Berkshire Black Bears	Pittsfield, MA	2002-present
Brockton Rox	Brockton, MA	2002-present
Elmira Pioneers	Elmira, NY	1999-present (1996-1998)
New Jersey Jackals	Little Falls, NJ	1999-present (1998)
Capitales de Quebec	Quebec City, Quebec	1999-present

Source: Compiled from *Baseball America 1993 Directory* (Durham, NC: Baseball America, Inc., 1993); *Baseball America 1994 Directory* (Durham, NC: Baseball America, Inc., 1994); *Baseball America 1995 Directory* (Durham, NC: Baseball America, Inc., 1995); *Baseball America 1996 Directory* (Durham, NC: Baseball America, Inc., 1996); *Baseball America 1997 Directory* (Durham, NC: Baseball America, Inc., 1997); *Baseball America 1998 Directory* (Durham, NC: Baseball America, Inc., 1998); *Baseball America 1999 Directory* (Durham, NC: Baseball America, Inc., 1999); *Baseball America 2000 Directory* (Durham, NC: Baseball America, Inc., 2000); *Baseball America 2001 Directory* (Durham, NC: Baseball America, Inc., 2001); *Baseball America 2002 Directory* (Durham, NC: Baseball America, Inc., 2002); Northern League Web Site, <http://www.northernleague.com>.

Frontier League

The Frontier League fielded its first teams in 1993. The original teams were found in Chillicothe, Lancaster, Portsmouth, and Zanesville, Ohio; Parkersburg and Wayne County, West Virginia; and Pikeville and Ashland, Kentucky.[88] In the mid-1990s, the league experienced some franchise shifts. In 1996, for example, the Portsmouth, Ohio, team moved to Springfield, Illinois. In 1997, the Zanesville team moved to Canton, Ohio, taking up residence in Thurman Munson Memorial Stadium, which had been vacated by the Akron Aeros of the Eastern League as they moved to a new stadium.[89] Then, in 1999, the league absorbed several of the teams that had played in the independent Heartland League, which was established in 1993, but was unable to complete the 1998 season.[90]

Today the Frontier League is comprised of twelve teams in two divisions. The East Division has teams in Canton and Chillicothe, Ohio; Johnstown, Pennsylvania; Kalamazoo, Michigan; Richmond, Indiana; and London, Ontario. The West Division covers Crestwood, Collinsville, and Springfield, Illinois; Huntingburg and Evansville, Indiana; and O'Fallon, Missouri (see Table 2.18).[91]

Central League

The Central League began play in 1994 as the Texas-Louisiana League, comprised of teams in Alexandria, Louisiana; Mobile, Alabama; and Amarillo, Beaumont, Corpus Christi, Edinburgh/ McAllen, San Antonio, and Tyler, Texas. After the 2001 season, the league underwent several changes, including changing its name to the Central League and aligning with the Northern League, another independent league. In March 2002, the Central League appointed Miles Wolff, commissioner of the Northern League, as its commissioner as well.[92]

In addition, the league picked up two teams that were formerly in the All-American Association, an independent league that disbanded after the 2001 season. For the 2002 season, the Ft. Worth, Texas, team became as member of the Central League, as did the Tyler, Texas, team, which moved to Jacksonville, Mississippi.[93] Since its inception in 1994, the league has expanded well beyond its Texas and Louisiana roots and in 2002 hosted teams in Louisiana, Texas, Mississippi, and Missouri (see Table 2.19).

TABLE 2.18. Frontier League Teams, 2002

Team	Location of Home Stadium	Years in League
Canton Coyotes	Canton, OH	1993-present
Chillicothe Paints	Chillicothe, OH	1993-present
Cook County Cheetahs	Crestwood, IL	1999-present
Dubois County Dragons	Huntingburg, IN	1999-present
Evansville Otters	Evansville, IN	1996-present
Gateway Grizzlies	Collinsville, IL	1999, 2001-present
Johnstown Johnnies	Johnstown, PA	1995-present
Kalamazoo Kings	Kalamazoo, MI	1997-1998, 2001-present
Richmond Roosters	Richmond, IN	1995-present
River City Rascals	O'Fallon, MO	1999-present
Rockford RiverHawks	Rockford, IL	2002-present
Washington Wild Things	Washington, PA	2002-present

Source: Compiled from *Baseball America 1993 Directory* (Durham, NC: Baseball America, Inc., 1993); *Baseball America 1994 Directory* (Durham, NC: Baseball America, Inc., 1994); *Baseball America 1995 Directory* (Durham, NC: Baseball America, Inc., 1995); *Baseball America 1996 Directory* (Durham, NC: Baseball America, Inc., 1996); *Baseball America 1997 Directory* (Durham, NC: Baseball America, Inc., 1997); *Baseball America 1998 Directory* (Durham, NC: Baseball America, Inc., 1998); *Baseball America 1999 Directory* (Durham, NC: Baseball America, Inc., 1999); *Baseball America 2000 Directory* (Durham, NC: Baseball America, Inc., 2000); *Baseball America 2001 Directory* (Durham, NC: Baseball America, Inc., 2001); *Baseball America 2002 Directory* (Durham, NC: Baseball America, Inc., 2002); Frontier League Web Site, <http://www.frontierleague.com>.

Western League

The Western League was founded in 1994 by Portland businessman Bruce L. Engel; its first season was 1995. That year, teams were located in Bend, Oregon; Grays Harbor, Washington; Surrey, British Columbia; Tri-City, Washington; and Long Beach, Palm Springs, Salinas, and Sonoma County, California. The next year, the Surrey team was replaced by a team in Reno, Nevada. The league continued to experience growing pains. In 1997, Palm Springs did not field a team as ownership was working to move the team to Oxnard, California. In

TABLE 2.19. Central League Teams, 2002

Team	Location of Home Stadium	Years in League
Alexandria Aces	Alexandria, LA	1994-present
Amarillo Dillas	Amarillo, TX	1994-present
Edinburg Roadrunners	Edinburg, TX	1994-1999, 2001-present
Fort Worth Cats	Fort Worth, TX	2002-present
Jackson Senators	Jackson, MS	2002-present
Springfield/Ozark Mountain Ducks	Ozark, MO	1999-present
Rio Grande Valley White Wings	Harlingen, TX	1995-present
San Angelo Colts	San Angelo, TX	2000-present

Source: Compiled from *Baseball America 1994 Directory* (Durham, NC: Baseball America, Inc., 1994); *Baseball America 1995 Directory* (Durham, NC: Baseball America, Inc., 1995); *Baseball America 1996 Directory* (Durham, NC: Baseball America, Inc., 1996); *Baseball America 1997 Directory* (Durham, NC: Baseball America, Inc., 1997); *Baseball America 1998 Directory* (Durham, NC: Baseball America, Inc., 1998); *Baseball America 1999 Directory* (Durham, NC: Baseball America, Inc., 1999); *Baseball America 2000 Directory* (Durham, NC: Baseball America, Inc., 2000); *Baseball America 2001 Directory* (Durham, NC: Baseball America, Inc., 2001); *Baseball America 2002 Directory* (Durham, NC: Baseball America, Inc., 2002); Central League Web Site, <http://www.centralleaguebaseball.com>.

their place, the Chico Heat was added, which ended up winning the championship that year.[94]

In 1998, the Palm Springs Suns returned as the Pacific Suns (playing in Oxnard), and the Salinas Peppers sat out the year. Also in 1998, the Grays Harbor team ceased operation and the league took over the club, which became primarily a traveling club. By 1999, the league had been reduced to six teams, though league management approved expansion for the next year. After the 1999 season, several changes were made, including the Sacramento and Reno teams moving to Vacaville and Marysville, respectively. In addition, two teams were added in Arizona: the Valley Vipers in Scottsdale and the Yuma Bullfrogs.[95] In 2002, the Western League celebrated its eighth season, fielding six teams (see Table 2.20).

TABLE 2.20. Western League Teams, 2002

Team	Location of Home Stadium	Years in League
Chico Heat	Chico, CA	1995-present
Long Beach Breakers	Long Beach, CA	1995-1997, 2001-present
Solano Steelheads	Vacaville, CA	2000-present
Sonoma County Crushers	Rohnert Park, CA	1995-present
Yuma Bullfrogs	Yuma, AZ	2000-present
Yuma-Sutter Gold Sox	Marysville, CA	2002-present

Source: Compiled from *Baseball America 1995 Directory* (Durham, NC: Baseball America, Inc., 1995); *Baseball America 1996 Directory* (Durham, NC: Baseball America, Inc., 1996); *Baseball America 1997 Directory* (Durham, NC: Baseball America, Inc., 1997); *Baseball America 1998 Directory* (Durham, NC: Baseball America, Inc., 1998); *Baseball America 1999 Directory* (Durham, NC: Baseball America, Inc., 1999); *Baseball America 2000 Directory* (Durham, NC: Baseball America, Inc., 2000); *Baseball America 2001 Directory* (Durham, NC: Baseball America, Inc., 2001); *Baseball America 2002 Directory* (Durham, NC: Baseball America, Inc., 2002); Western League Web Site, <http://www.westernleague.com>.

Atlantic League

One of the newest independent leagues, the Atlantic League was established in 1998. The mission of the league is "to bring a high level of professional baseball and affordable family entertainment to selected communities not presently being served by Major League or Minor League teams."[96] The league currently has teams in Atlantic City and Somerset County, New Jersey; Bridgeport, Connecticut; Long Island, New York; and Nashua, New Hampshire (see Table 2.21).

CONCLUSION

Minor League Baseball has thrived across the United States, Canada, and Mexico in a variety of locales. Each team has developed a unique relationship with its community, and as the communities have changed, so has minor league baseball. Because Minor League Baseball teams are found in smaller communities than their major league

TABLE 2.21. Atlantic League Teams, 2002

Team	Location of Home Stadium	Years in League
Atlantic City Surf	Atlantic City, NJ	1998-present
Bridgeport Bluefish	Bridgeport, CT	1998-present
Camden Riversharks	Camden, NJ	2001-present
Long Island Ducks	Central Islip, NY	2000-present
Nashua Pride	Nashua, NH	1998-present
Newark Bears	Newark, NJ	1998-present
Pennsylvania Road Warriors	operated as a road team in 2002	2002-present
Somerset Patriots	Bridgewater, NJ	1998-present

Source: Compiled from *Baseball America 1998 Directory* (Durham, NC: Baseball America, Inc., 1998); *Baseball America 1999 Directory* (Durham, NC: Baseball America, Inc., 1999); *Baseball America 2000 Directory* (Durham, NC: Baseball America, Inc., 2000); *Baseball America 2001 Directory* (Durham, NC: Baseball America, Inc., 2001); *Baseball America 2002 Directory* (Durham, NC: Baseball America, Inc., 2002); Atlantic League Web Site, <http://www.atlanticleague.com>.

counterparts, they have been more vulnerable to the social and economic fortunes of their hometowns. Thus, over the years, there have been many and frequent changes within the leagues as teams have come and gone. Nonetheless, Minor League Baseball teams have represented many of the smaller cities and towns in North America, and have developed their own unique character and special brand of entertainment.

In addition to geographic diversity, Minor League Baseball encompasses several levels of professional play—from the developmental rookie leagues to the AAA leagues, the last stop before the majors. This organization of leagues and its association with Major League Baseball has been vital to the success and development of the major league players that are known worldwide by baseball fans. The relationship between the two organizations, Minor League Baseball and Major League Baseball, provides the foundation for the national pastime, and as such, minor league teams can have a strong impact on their communities.

The independent leagues, which are not affiliated with either Minor League Baseball or Major League Baseball, provide even more opportunities for communities to enjoy the benefits of professional baseball. Moving into a market that was hungry for baseball, several independent leagues have cropped up since 1993. Many of these leagues have become the home of towns cast aside by minor league teams that moved elsewhere and of players rejected by major league teams, providing a baseball outlet for both. Although they have suffered growing pains similar to upstart corporations, independent leagues are establishing their niche in the baseball industry and are bringing baseball to communities in need of teams.

Chapter 3

The Lure of Minor League Baseball

There is a symbiotic relationship between the minor league team and the city or town that it represents. In the case of major league sports, the relationship is often fueled by economic outcomes. At the minor league level, however, the relationship appears to go beyond mere money and prestige. Minor league teams occupy a special place in our hearts. Fans are more forgiving when these teams lose, and are extremely proud of them when they win.

THE NATION AWAKENS

I first learned of Minor League Baseball relatively late in life, I was in my twenties and had been a baseball fan for years. I had always liked baseball, even had a Hank Aaron notebook when I was in second grade. Growing up I'd attended a few major league games with my dad. I remember being glued to the television, watching Eddie Murray, Cal Ripken Jr., and the rest of the Orioles win the 1983 World Series. Yet even though my dad and I are huge baseball fans, he didn't introduce me to the minor leagues until I was in college— I never even knew he had been a minor league pitcher until somewhere around my sophomore year in college.

Of course, not many people become interested in Minor League Baseball until it comes to their town. In fact, it wasn't until the 1990s that Minor League Baseball finally gained its place in the national spotlight. No longer the stepchild of Major League Baseball, minor league teams came into their own as legitimate businesses and sources of local pride. Of course, avid baseball fans and others were aware of the minors all along. But thanks to the 1988 movie *Bull Durham*, and more sophisticated marketing of the teams, the average citizen was introduced to the hometown game.

As with many other Americans, I attended my first minor league game in the late 1980s. It was a Prince William Cannons (now the Potomac Cannons) game. Back then they were a farm team for the New York Yankees. We got to see Bernie Williams as a Yankee-in-training. It was at this Carolina League game that I became hooked on Minor League Baseball, and I began to notice the differences between the majors and the minors. There was a sense of community at the game that I had never quite felt in major league stadiums. Inside jokes and local quirks were celebrated with a lighthearted abandon that was welcome and refreshing. I felt at home, and there was a certain sense of pride and a connection to the players that I hadn't felt elsewhere.

Perhaps because of this feeling of connectedness, growing disenchantment with Major League Baseball, or new marketing strategies employed by minor league teams, the minors enjoyed a resurgence in popularity that ensures continued success into the twenty-first century. But are there other ingredients to the Minor League Baseball recipe for success? What is it that cements the bond between the community and its team? Is there indeed a local population of loyal supporters, or is there something else that bonds the community to its minor league team?

ACADEMICS TAKE NOTICE

The concomitant rise in awareness of Minor League Baseball and the legitimization of sports studies in academia provided scholars with the opportunity to take in a few games. Not only was it in style for regular folks to attend minor league games, but the game itself was such an important part of American culture that it was high time to study it.

The fields of sports history, sports sociology, and other sports studies grew enormously in the latter part of the twentieth century. In the 1990s in particular, studies of Minor League Baseball were added to the growing literature. Minor League Baseball was studied not only from a historical perspective, but also as an economic and social phenomenon.[1]

When I began my journey to become a baseball sociologist in 1991, I wanted to understand the communal aspects of Minor League

Baseball. I began reading research studies on community identity, fan attraction to the game, and attendance. In looking for studies on Minor League Baseball in particular, I noticed that it was often the subject of community economic-impact studies and used in planning economic-development strategies. I believed there had to be a connection, so I undertook an in-depth review of several areas of sports literature.

Although most scholars and supporters of sports agree that sports are a key institution in the United States, there have been few systematic studies of the relationship between communities and their sports teams. Many authors allude to an inherent connection between a sports team and the community.[2] Other researchers claim that a professional sports team has an insignificant impact on the community, or even a negative economic impact.[3] Many of these authors suggest that there are intangible benefits of hosting a professional team, such as increased community pride, but argue that such effects are not significant enough to justify expenditures for stadiums, tax breaks, or other economic subsidies to team owners.[4] Nonetheless, no close examination of such benefits has been made. A brief review of such studies, however, suggests that three areas of research come close to explaining the relationship between town and team: fan attachment and attendance studies, studies on the "intangible" benefits of sports, and analyses of the economic impact of sports.

Fan Attachment and Attendance

On the way to my family reunion in the summer of 2000, I decided to spend the night in Durham, North Carolina, and catch a game at the Durham Bulls Athletic Park. They were playing the Richmond Braves that night. I took the downtown Durham exit, drove around town awhile, and finally found the stadium. Being a newcomer, I drove around the block a few times trying to figure out where to park. Eventually, I followed a few cars that were parking in what appeared to be a vacant lot. Cars were parked in an organized fashion, their occupants hopping out and heading toward the stadium; naturally, I followed them.

Confident that there would be seats available, I strode up to the window when it was my turn and asked for box seats. The ticket seller gave me an odd look and informed me that only the "Diamond View" seats—situated above right field—were available. Sheepishly, I took what was available, and got in line to enter through the gates and find my seat.

Sports researchers offer several suggestions as to why attendance ebbs and flows. Most studies measure attendance with socioeconomic variables such as population, per capita income, and ticket price, as well as sports-related factors of demand including number of star players, number of other professional teams in the area, age of stadium, recent pennant wins, and games behind. For example, Scully found that ticket price, team quality, and population variables explain 68 percent of the variance in attendance.[5] But that doesn't necessarily explain why it is that people such as me (and there *are* others like me out there) plan vacation stops around baseball schedules. Although most attendance is probably from local residents, there must be other factors involved to explain what it is that draws the crowds.

Other studies attempt to expand on the independent variables included in the model, but do not include variables that would represent the "romantic attachment of the fans."[6] Marcum and Greenstein include demographic variables, factors concerning accessibility to the event (including seating, location, and weather), and performance.[7]

In a similar study, Baade and Tiehen examine stadium capacity and real per capita income. They found that city population, age of stadium, number of stars, attendance in the previous season, competition from other local sports, team standings, and real per capita income have an effect on attendance.[8] In fact, they claim that "during the 1970s and 1980s a portion of the change observed in baseball attendance is explained by the growing interest in baseball."[9] However, they do not try to explain what caused this increase in interest, which could be related to a positive effect of sports on civic identity. Although they express the concern that "current and projected measures of city support and loyalty are necessary for deliberations about whether a team's nomadic pursuit of profit is coming at the expense of loyal fans,"[10] they do not focus on measuring fan loyalty.

The estimation of "home court advantage" comes close to considering community attachment. The major contribution of such research is its use of Durkheimian theory. Schwartz and Barsky's discussion of the "invigorating influence of supportive social congregation"[11] borrows from Emíle Durkheim's thoughts on the collective conscience. This suggests that if we turn to other realms of sociology, such as classical sociological theory, we may find more of a theoretical background for the idea that communities are tied to their teams.

Schwartz and Barsky demonstrate that there is a home court advantage (HCA) in sports. HCA is defined as home wins divided by road wins; if this percentage is greater than 50 percent, the authors consider the team to have a positive, significant HCA. Thus, in their study, baseball has a positive HCA because the home/road win percentage is 53 percent. The authors discount performance differentials and the effect of team quality, and determine that "the home advantage is socially determined."[12] Their conclusion summarizes what much of the other researchers have assumed:

> ... if residents invest themselves in favor of their local athletic teams, it is partly because those teams are exponents of a community to which they feel themselves somehow bound and in whose destiny they find themselves in some way implicated. The connection, however, is by no means a simple one. A local team is not only an expression of the moral integrity of a community; it is also a means by which that community becomes conscious of itself and achieves its concrete representation.[13]

Mizruchi suggests that the fans determine the outcome of the game, to the extent that fan support is determined by "the social context within which the game is played."[14] Mizruchi offers several hypotheses concerning community support. For example, "The extent to which a local sports team is viewed as a source of civic pride is expected to be inversely related to the size of a city."[15] Mizruchi measures fan support similarly to Schwartz and Barsky's HCA, and thus the conclusions of both studies are the same.

Although attendance provides an estimate of community support, it does not explain the source or consequences of this support. If an estimator of actual home court advantage could be developed, Mizruchi's method would be helpful in determining the consequences of community support. These studies, as other studies in sports sociology, indicate that a positive connection between communities and their teams exists, but cannot be supported because the models do not appropriately measure the independent variables affecting team loyalty. However, these studies are significant because they provide many of the variables that will be used in the model employed in this study.

The Intangible Benefits of Sports

Many would agree that there are some intangible benefits of sports. The camaraderie felt at the ballpark and the sense of pride in one's hometown team are felt in all corners of the world. There's nothing quite as exciting as being on vacation or away from home for other reasons and seeing someone walk by sporting a cap with your hometown team's logo. All of a sudden, you feel at home, as though you are connected to someone and some place.

For "fanatics" like me, just being in a stadium or among other fans can feel like home. I recall being at Toronto's SkyDome for an Orioles-Toronto Blue Jays game. I'm a pretty quiet baseball fan, but at the game a friend encouraged me to yell "O!" in the middle of the U.S. National Anthem, which is an Oriole fan tradition (when the singer of the anthem says "O say does that star spangled banner yet wave," fans yell "O" along with him or her). The stadium was rather empty where we sat, and my bright orange Oriole shirt was quite visible as I yelled "O." A group of other O's fans not too far from us quickly spotted me, and we formed and instant bond and enjoyed the game together.

Whenever I was homesick when I was living in Ohio, all I had to do was get in my car and drive to a stadium, and I'd feel a little better. I recall driving from Kent, Ohio, to Canton, Ohio, to see old Thurman Munson Memorial Stadium. It was the off season, and no one was there, but it made me feel safe. Maybe that's why I like to stop at minor league stadiums en route to other destinations. They are like a home away from home.

Scholars have made many attempts to explain the link between sport, society, and culture. Janet Lever's study on soccer is one of the most systematic attempts at showing the importance of sports within a certain culture. Through interviews and questionnaire results, Lever attempts to show the importance of soccer in the everyday lives of Brazilians. She uses the typical generalizations about sports and communities, e.g., a sport team is a community's "most visible representative to the outside world" or a "collective symbol of the town."[16]

Lever's general conclusions for Brazil can be applied to Minor League Baseball as well:

> People are social animals. The tribal instinct—the need to belong to something larger than ourselves—is apparent in all soci-

eties. In advanced societies sports teams are perfect recipients for human loyalty. Fans identify themselves with their teams and with other fans who share their concern. Threats from challenging teams rally our sense that we are needed, which in turn reassures us that we belong. Perceiving the team "tribe" as our own makes us proud when it wins, ashamed when it loses, and hopeful it will win again.[17]

Lever's observation suggests that sports teams are more than organizations and economic entities. They are considered to be culturally significant.

Similarly, Smith tells us that sports act as an agent of socialization and add to social integration by providing recreation, entertainment, and escape, stating that "the existence of elite sports teams in a community is deemed a major positive factor in determining whether or not an area is a desirable place to live."[18] Similarly, by observing and interviewing fans and employees during the final homestand at Old Comisky Park and Arlington Stadium, Trujillo and Krizek conclude that the local baseball team "engenders a powerful sense of identification and identity for fans and franchise employees alike."[19]

Riess's research on the simultaneous growth of cities and sports demonstrates how sports became an important part of cities and the lives of the residents. According to Riess, as cities grew, each ethnic community retained its identity through sports, and socioeconomic divisions were reinforced by the different types of games the various groups brought to the cities and could afford to play. As such, certain sports became identified with certain communities. As clubs and professional sports became entrenched in a community, they would come to represent their city and its people in games against rival towns and in championship series.

However, by the 1950s, community leaders began to realize the commercial and civic advantages of hosting professional sports franchises. Communities realized the risks they were dealing with when franchise owners, operating out of their monopolistic interests, began to move teams in search of bigger profits. Societal response clearly shows how important a team can be to a town. According to Riess:

> The single most important franchise shift in the 1950s, and surely the most shocking, was that of the Dodgers in 1958 from Brooklyn to Los Angeles. No professional sports franchise had

been as closely identified with its host city as the Dodgers were with Brooklyn. The club was by a wide margin the most important institution in the borough and for all Americans it symbolized the character, culture, and ethnic diversity of Brooklyn, whose population was outnumbered by only four other cities.[20]

This shows the perceived importance of sports to the community. The Brooklyn Dodgers were seen as a social institution and as a symbol of the community itself. The departure of the team had a significant impact on fans and the community.

Sullivan suggests that the "romantic attachment of fans"[21] develops over many generations and becomes a part of the community itself. This attachment is extended to other communities where people from the original town have moved, which perpetuates the attachment. As in the case of Brooklyn, those memories have been passed on from generation to generation and "have become a part of baseball folklore."[22]

Kuklick analyzes the importance of a team to its community and the growth of traditions surrounding that team. In his analysis of Shibe Park and the Philadelphia Athletics, Kuklick discusses urban renewal, ethnic subcultures, economics, and community politics. Built in 1909, by the 1920s a "definite community" had grown around the ballpark.[23] Community was also felt within the ballpark:

> The unique aspect of Shibe Park baseball was not the failures and successes of management or the feats or defeats on the field. The unique element was that the sport magically taught people about excellence and joined them communally to something not available in day-to-day experience.[24]

Further, Kuklick states that the "integrity of the souls of urban Philadelphians depended on a semisacred collection of beliefs, handed-down stories, and recollections about sports, politics, and mass entertainment."[25] He argues that humans attach meanings to objects; without such attachment, the objects are meaningless.[26] Yet eventually the "ecological niche of Philadelphia baseball" changed, the neighborhoods and communities around the ballpark disintegrated, and Shibe Park no longer provided or represented communal life to the city[27]—which, perhaps, explains the need for new stadiums as teams and communities continue to grow and evolve.

Studies of the Negro Leagues in baseball and African-American experiences in sports show a definite link between community and team. Rob Ruck's study of sports in the African-American community of Pittsburgh emphasizes the role sports played in the lives of both the players and fans:

> Sport helped bring forth black Pittsburgh's potential for self-organization, creativity, and expression in [the first half of the twentieth century]. . . . Through identification with teams and players, sport fostered a sense of pride in black Pittsburgh that often transcended divisions between migrant and Pittsburgh-born blacks and among those of different social classes.[28]

In addition, sports provided "a pleasant cultural counterpoint to the often grim experiences encountered at work and in the neighborhood."[29] Home games provided an opportunity for families and neighbors to get together and be a part of the game itself. In particular, the success of the Homestead Grays, Pittsburgh Crawfords, and other Negro League teams tied together the larger African-American community as prominent entertainers became supporters of the Negro League teams.[30]

Perhaps providing the strongest link to sociological theories of community, these studies often show how sports developed as the city itself grew and how these sports became symbolic of the city. Yet these studies are unable to show why this relationship occurs today when, for example, a new team moves to an already-established city. Although they provide us with numerous examples of communities that are emotionally tied to their teams, they leave us with few answers as to why.

Ingham, Howell, and Schilperoot call for a theory of the relationship between professional sports and communities that considers the logic of capital accumulation and capital mobility. Similar to Johnson, they recognize the competition in communities between material and cultural capital. They also recognize that "How the investment/disinvestment decisions (including those of sport firms) influence a city's/community's sense of itself requires further research."[31]

The authors analyze franchise investment decisions in the "trial-and-error" period of entrepreneurial sports, in the early period of franchise relocation, and in recent transactions. They suggest that the conflict between communities and professional teams lies in the consumer-monopolist relationship that is typical of today's sports. Franchise owners' decisions are made not with the consumer in mind, but "now articulate more with the capital investment/disinvestment decisions of the hegemic fractions of the dominant class and with the tax abatement/public subsidy decisions of substate (city and county) officials."[32]

Ingham, Howell, and Schilperoot conclude that sports can provide a sense of collective identity and continuity in a "discontinuous and increasingly atomized society," and can be used to assert a "cultural reformation."[33] But this function is in danger as professional sports move into the "abstract" economy. That is, as sports become the model for capital investment and accumulation schemes, communities are in danger of losing their identities.

Gregory Stone deals with the question of the extent to which sports can represent a community. He suggests that sports teams have become symbols of their communities, similar to historic buildings or other regional specialties. Using examples from earlier community studies, Stone attempts to prove that "Sport as a source of solidarity can be found wherever it is a representation of the collective community,"[34] and wherever it is an integral part of the community.

Stone feels that television contracts and business tycoons have led to a decline in the community representation function of sports. However, he relies on community studies that rarely focused on sports. In his conclusion, Stone offers his guess that "high school sports cannot compete with professional sports for the attention of spectators, though the attention to them may well be more intense."[35] Although Stone tries to imbed his analysis of sport and community representation in the sociological theory of Weber and Durkheim, his method (analysis of community studies done in the 1950s and 1960s and discussion of personal experience) does not include an analysis of empirical data, and his conclusions are based on generalizations. Thus, much research in this area is still needed.

The Economic Impact of Sports

An economic development specialist for a local community may be tempted to lure a minor league team to the community. Teams seem to crop up in up-and-coming towns. Development seems to spur more development and having a minor league team move to town can be an exciting prospect. Besides, you get to attend a lot of Minor League Baseball games as part of your research on the phenomenon.

In my own hometown, I have seen many changes in recent years. The Bowie Baysox came to town at the same time the community was on the verge of a major transformation. Two shopping centers have come to town since 1995, and a new mall opened in 2001. Just a few short years ago the housing development in which I live was still a farm, and the road in front of my house was only two lanes—not the six-lane road linking shopping centers that it has become. The opening of Prince George's Stadium concurrent with new restaurants directly across the highway from Ballpark Road is just another example of the relationship between economic development and stadium construction.[36]

This trend has continued into the twenty-first century. Shortly after Ripken Stadium opened its doors in Aberdeen, Maryland, local officials were heralding it and Cal Ripken's IronBirds as an economic boon to the city, county (Harford), and state. In addition to the new ballpark, new hotel construction is planned and local economic development planners are trying to lure a major retail and/or entertainment complex to the area. It has been estimated that the stadium and its new team will generate an annual $265 million for Aberdeen, Harford County, and the surrounding areas.[37]

Indeed, the heart of the matter of communities and their teams is most apparent in the literature concerning economic-development strategies, such as stadium subsidies and franchise relocation issues. It is in this area that owners are pitted against fans and civic leaders must balance the economic needs of the community, the demands of the owners, the desires of the fans, and the interests of the nonfan voting population.

Okner points out that "when the social benefits of production are greater than the private benefits, production in the private sector will be less than socially optimal."[38] Thus, public ownership of stadiums is justifiable "if extensive social benefits arise from public provision of sports facilities."[39] After discussing the theory of facility pricing and various subsidies for sports facilities, Okner concludes, "it is impossible to generalize about whether the local subsidy of a sports facility is 'worth it' to any particular community."[40] Although he fails to generate a model for testing the potential worth of hosting a sports team, his work suggests that the existence of sports teams must be of some importance to a community.

Frank Hefner attempts to provide a theoretical background for the logic of using economic-impact models in determining the importance of a sports team to the local economy. He notes that there are four values that can be included in such an analysis: direct revenue projections, indirect multiplier effects, booster benefits, and intangible benefits. Since intangible benefits are "unmeasurable by definition,"[41] they are usually left out. Thus, all such studies fail to accurately measure the impact of sports on the local economy.

Hefner does point out the dangers of the variables used in economic-impact studies, and also cautions that there are problems associated with the survey data that most of these studies employ. Much of the information is taken from interviews and questionnaires, to which people may give inaccurate responses. It is also difficult to obtain sales data. Hefner concludes that if such studies are done correctly they can provide useful information. However, the omission of intangible benefits is not addressed.

Baade and Dye argue that direct municipal revenues, multiplier benefits (including increased personal income or retail sales in the area), and the attraction of new business is not large enough to justify stadium subsidies. Because of this, many municipalities argue that the intangible benefits justify the cost. Baade and Dye state that intangibles come in two forms: immeasurable and measurable.[42] Immeasurable intangibles include fan identification and civic pride; measurable intangibles include media exposure and commercial endorsements. Again, the immeasurable intangibles are dropped from the analysis; although, based on my research, they are precisely the factors needed for a model of community representation.

In another study, Baade and Dye describe the use of professional sports as an economic-development tool as "naive public policy."[43] They conclude that the greatest contribution a sports team makes is the intangible benefits it generates:

> The image of a city is certainly affected by the presence of professional franchises. Professional sports serve as a focal point for group identification. Sports contests are part of civic culture.[44]

If group identification is the greatest contribution a team makes to its community, then it should be studied more rigorously.

Johnson echoed Baade and Dye's conclusion. In a survey of ninety-five Minor League Baseball teams, Johnson found that the main benefits of having a team were identified as entertainment (98.9 percent of the respondents); community identity (84.2 percent); economic benefits (83.2 percent); regional prestige (82.1 percent); civic pride (77.9 percent); and the attraction of nonresidents to their communities (72.6 percent).[45] Despite these findings, Johnson analyzed the economic benefits and concluded that "a minor league team's economic impact is insignificant relative to a community's total economy and should not be used to justify a public investment of several millions of dollars."[46] He noted, however, that a minor league team does offer intangible benefits, such as image enhancement, which can be conducive to growth. How these intangible benefits come to be and how they lead to growth are not explored by Johnson.

Johnson describes sports as "a cultural resource of a community or region."[47] He notes that

> It is not the nature of sports leagues that attracts our attention, but the enthusiasm, interest and identity that a team provokes within its locale. Many of the fans do view a team as theirs, and owners encourage that.[48]

As such, communities have a "legal as well as moral right"[49] to prevent a team from relocating or to attract a team to the area, despite the economic costs. This right extends beyond questions of monopoly, antitrust, or private ownership. Public subsidy of teams "creates a partnership between city and team."[50]

Johnson tested the idea of a partnership between cities and teams in a later study. He examined Minor League Baseball to determine whether the same political and economic dynamics that affected major league teams were present in minor league agreements. He found that although few towns had actually documented the economic impact of the presence of a minor league team in their community, almost one-third believed that having a team was part of an explicit development plan. Most of the towns in the survey said their team aided the local economy, promoted the city's image, and added to the quality of life.[51]

Pelissero, Henschen, and Sidlow recognize that community pride in a team plays an important role in economic-development plans. Their study follows the franchise relocation issues that faced various "urban regimes" (governing coalitions) in Chicago. Different regimes will follow different agendas and strategies, and will form different relationships with the private sector. Policy decisions will be made based on these agendas and relationships, and will represent "a mediation between private and public needs."[52]

They point out that in each of the regimes studied, the mayor "did not want to answer to fans for losing a team to the suburbs or another state. After all, fans vote, and fans spend money on sports-related businesses in Chicago."[53] Thus, another intangible benefit, at least to those making the policy decisions, is the perceived acceptance by the fans of the franchise decisions made by the local government.

Johnson suggests some public-policy solutions to the problem of franchise relocation. Since expansion teams are rare and new teams in new leagues are even more uncommon, communities are forced to compete with one another to obtain a sports franchise. Current practices of self-regulation and exemption from antitrust laws have allowed the various sports leagues to act as they please with regards to franchise relocations. Congress, on the other hand, has been reluctant to pass any type of restrictive legislation. One reason is that relocation restrictions are not placed on other businesses. Another is that restricting the movement of franchises bestows "major league" status on certain towns (i.e., maintains the status quo) and denies other areas the opportunity to obtain a team.[54]

Johnson suggests solutions such as reduced barriers to entry and use of eminent domain laws. The argument for eminent domain laws is based on the idea that the "sports franchises serve a public purpose and constitute a public use that is important, if not essential, to the communities' economic and social well-being,"[55] which gives the city the right to purchase the team and resell it to local investors that pledge to keep it in that city. Johnson also suggests that the host city's state, the neighboring communities, and the private sector should share in the cost of retaining a team.

Colclough, Daellenbach, and Sherony use a model for estimating the economic impact of Minor League Baseball on a community. Along with regional multipliers compiled by the Bureau of Economic Analysis, they test their model on La Crosse County, Wisconsin. By analyzing both the short-term impact (of constructing the stadium) and the long-term impact (of annual operations and tourist and visiting team expenditures), they find that although the economic effect is positive, it is not nearly as large as predicted by proponents of stadium construction. Thus, it is concluded that "communities might consider other factors, e.g. entertainment value, community identity and quality of life,"[56] when deciding whether to finance a stadium project to attract a minor league team.

In contrast, other researchers find little evidence of an impact of these so-called intangible benefits. Euchner notes that health care, roads, utilities, recreation facilities, and good schools are the "fundamental building blocks of urban prosperity and a good quality of life."[57] According to him, sports teams can only add to community sentiments if other social services and activities (such as parks, libraries, schools, community theaters, neighborhood associations, street festivals, etc.) are already well established in the community. Using case studies of various franchise relocations, Euchner concludes that although franchise movements or stadium proposals evoke much emotion, the current nature of sports does not have much of an effect at the community level. Teams are often marketed regionally or to fans that do not live in the same neighborhood as the stadium. Although sports teams serve as symbols that "make city life understandable," only a small percentage of city residents (i.e., taxpayers) may derive identity from the team.[58]

This could suggest, however, that the model should, in fact, be extended to a larger area (such as to the county) to measure the real impact of a team. It must also be noted that many of Euchner's examples were of major league sports. The differences between major league and minor league cities may represent a difference in quality of life as suggested by classical sociological theorists.

Whitson and Macintosh conclude that the benefits from investing in sports and tourism are often overstated.[59] Profits may accrue to the more visible members of a city, but there are many others who are unlikely to benefit. Although sports franchises and hallmark events bring recognition, and perhaps bestow the status of "world class" or major league to a city, local interest may not be enough for the team to generate communal sentiments or monetary benefits. As with Euchner's analysis, Whitson and Macintosh are considering only hallmark events in Canada, which may not be comparable to the unit of analysis (Minor League Baseball in the United States) employed in many of the other economic-development studies.

Rosentraub and Swindell question how much a team can really define a city's image. They note that having a team provides escapism and publicity.[60] Thus, the city will be mentioned in many newspapers every day. Rosentraub and Swindell, however, are doubtful that this exposure is of much value:

> ... given the level of economic data regarding labor, land, capital, and utilities that companies can access, it seems difficult that one needs a baseball team to supplement the economic image available from Standard and Poor's, or Moody's. Further, it is this actual economic identity, and not the sports image of a city, which drives locational decision-making by private firms.[61]

According to the authors, the idea of bringing publicity and commerce to a city holds up as well as the economic-development argument did, particularly in the case of Minor League Baseball, which is not always in the business of winning a pennant, and is often not going to even make it into anything but the local paper.

These consenting views represent the minority. Most researchers conclude that sports teams bring civic pride, group identification, community identity, and an improvement to the quality of life. Such studies conclude that economic effects alone do not justify stadium construction;[62] yet the existence of stadium subsidies make it obvious that intangible benefits of hosting a sports franchise for a community must exist.

SOCIOLOGY AND MINOR LEAGUE COMMUNITIES

As previously discussed, research in the sociology of sports suggests that a significant relationship exists between sports organizations and their communities, yet such a relationship has not been studied systematically nor estimated empirically. Numerous studies of the impact of sports teams on communities refer to intangible benefits but measure only economic benefits, and therefore fail to find any impact on the community. Further, many studies fail to define the term *community,* further complicating the analysis.

However, classical sociology and other sociological theories of community provide some insight into this issues. In fact, sometimes I think the classical sociologists must have been baseball fans—either that, or the inventors of baseball were armchair sociologists. In particular, community theory in classical sociology provides much understanding of the phenomenon of Minor League Baseball.

As discussed in the following, the term *community* has many different connotations and can be applied to Minor League Baseball in a variety of ways. The concepts of system and interaction, found in the systems and network approaches to community discussed here, are particularly relevant to this analysis of Minor League Baseball. The most important use of the term *community,* and that which is most relevant to the study at hand, is found in Ferdinand Tonnies' theory of Gemeinschaft and Gesellschaft, which is compared to Durkheim's theory of mechanic and organic solidarity.

Sociological Theories of Community

Community encompasses more than the geographical limitations of an area. Communities comprise systems and networks of ideas, persons, and relationships. In many cases, community also refers to the quality of such relationships. There are many different theories of community, including: (1) systems and networks, (2) traditionalism and attachment, (3) social construction, (4) human ecology, and (5) classical sociological theory. In addition, some of the literature on the psychology of community is applicable to Minor League Baseball. All of these views are important as together they provide a rich framework for understanding the concept of community and the role of sports within it.

Systems and Networks

Systems theorists argue that community is more than territoriality or interdependence. Communities are marked by common interests and shared beliefs. MacIver stated that the "mark of a community is that one's life may be lived within it, that all one's social relationships may be found in it."[63] Such a definition comes from the systems approach, which argues that a community comprises smaller subsystems within a larger "total" system.64 Warren's discussion of the "great change" echoes this use of community:

> The term "community" implies something both psychological and geographical. Psychologically, it implies shared interests, characteristics, or association. . . . Geographically, it denotes a specific area where people are clustered. Sociologically, the term combines these two connotations. It relates to the shared interests and behavior patterns which people have by virtue of their common locality.65

The great change that Warren refers to is the increasing interaction of the local community with institutions outside of it. Warren identifies seven developments in modern society that have resulted in a decrease in community autonomy and cohesion:

1. Increasing division of labor, which has weakened community
2. Differentiation of interests and association, which changes the focus of participation from locality based to interest based
3. An increase in the number of "systematic" relationships to the larger society
4. Bureaucratization and impersonalization
5. Transfer of functions to government and private enterprises
6. Urbanization and suburbanization
7. Changing values

These changes are taking place throughout all levels of society, not only at the community level. Changes at all levels are interrelated.66 Such phenomena are discussed by many community sociologists and are applicable to this study of Minor League Baseball.

Another approach to the definition of community is the network approach, in which community is seen as a network of interaction.67 Within the community, individuals, groups, and institutions interact with one another. Key concepts to this approach are the vertical and horizontal patterns within the community. The vertical pattern is the set of relationships the community has with organizations outside of the community. The horizontal pattern is the relationships the community units have with one another, such as the relationships between the church and the school, or government and business.68

This system of interconnectedness is quite apparent in the sports world, particularly in Minor League Baseball. Minor league teams and stadiums provide a great community forum—community events are often held in minor league stadiums and are often hosted by the team. For example, every year the Bowie Baysox and Prince George's Stadium host the Congressional Baseball Game for Charity in which members of Congress play against one another with the proceeds going to local charities. In 2002, over $100,000 was raised as the Republican squad under manager Representative Mike Oxley (R-OH) beat the Democrats, managed by Representative Martin Olav Sabo (D-MN), 9-2. The Grand Old Party Elephants lead the series having won twenty-seven games against the Dems Donkeys.[69] Another event is Prince George's County Reading Night, for which fans are encouraged to bring new or used children's books to benefit literacy programs in the county. Local businesses advertise on outfield billboards and host special giveaway nights and other stadium events. The chamber of commerce holds a "business mixer" at the stadium; local parents appreciate the entertainment it provides for the entire family; and even the mayor has season tickets and meets with the fans. Essentially, there is a network of interaction that occurs not only within the ballpark, but within the community itself.

Traditionalism and Attachment

For many, community connotes tradition, or the opposite of rationalistic (i.e., calculating), bureaucratic organizations. Nisbet, for example, takes a more humanist approach in describing community, using words such as "Personal intimacy, emotional depth, moral commitment, social cohesion, and continuity in time."[70] As state and national governments take over many of the functions of society, the remaining issues left to be handled within the local community become less important. Having fewer things of importance in common, local people have less reason for mutual association. Locality becomes irrelevant to the important issues in society.[71] Thus, individuals do not derive security and fulfillment from the community as they once did.[72] According to Nisbet, "neither moral values, nor fellowships, nor freedom can easily flourish apart from the existence of diverse communities each capable of enlisting the loyalties of its members."[73] Nisbet was particularly concerned with the loss of community and the resulting alienation and isolation that earlier theorists had predicted.

This book examines the ability of Minor League Baseball to combat such ills as alienation and isolation. Indeed, such sentiments are often found in the current literature on the minor leagues. One cannot escape the allusions to innocence, renewal, and history in the popular press. For example, Coleman McCarthy, a *Washington Post* writer, noted that "Imagination and whimsy are found in the minors."[74] David Lamb, a writer who traveled throughout the minor leagues for an entire season, said that he found "a refreshing honesty and innocence" in Minor League Baseball.[75] Minor league towns are considered to be communities in the traditional sense:

> The small-town atmosphere many people seem to want is to be found not in the huge, million-dollar, cookie-cutter sports complexes of the majors, but in the tiny old bandbox stadiums of the minors, with their outfield walls painted over with advertising signs, real grass, wooden seats, badly painted ticket booths, and uneven fields.[76]

Writers often compare the profit-oriented major leagues to the minors. The *Sporting News* referred to the minors as "sites where players and clubs seemed to care. . . ."[77] *The Washington Post* contrasts the business aspects of both: "This [Minor League Baseball] is baseball in it simplest form—just balls, bats and gloves. There are no Diamond Vision scoreboards, no seven-figure salaries. No lawsuits. No trade demands."[78]

Minor League Baseball is associated with families and children, and has been called the "sport that belongs to the fans."[79] In other words, sportswriters seem to be suggesting that Major League Baseball has an alienating quality, and Minor League Baseball provides the fulfillment of community. The more than 200-day Major League Baseball strike of 1994-1995 seems to have furthered that conception.

Social Construction

Gusfield discusses the symbolic and social construction of tradition and community. It is through this process that relationships are seen as communal. Symbolic construction requires the definition of certain aspects of interaction as being symbolic of community. In Gusfield's words, it is "a process of creating and signifying the existence and character of persons and objects by the ways in which human beings conceptualize, talk about and define them."[80]

In this way, Minor League Baseball has become symbolic of the close-knit, "traditional" community in which everyone participates fully. Through it, communities develop a sense of pride and cohesion. The presence of a minor league team is believed to represent a strong economy and a high quality of life.

Human Ecology

Another approach to the concept of community is found in theories of human ecology, which is the basis of organizational theories of population ecology. According to sociologist Dennis Poplin, the goal of human ecology is to explain spatial organization and the growth of communities.[81] Just as plants and animals occupy common habitats and form competing and reciprocal relationships with one another and their environments, so too do humans.[82]

Park notes that the dichotomy between community and society is unique to human organization. Society is a collective phenomenon based on consensus and common purpose. This does not exist in the plant and animal worlds. Community, on the other hand, is the biotic, competitive counterpart of society that all species experience. Park refers to it as the "web of life" in which "all living organisms, plants and animals alike, are bound together in a vast system of interlinked and interdependent lives."[83]

Given this framework, Park defines community as being territorially limited, geographically rooted, and, most important, comprising interdependent individuals.[84] Within the community the number of members can be regulated such that competition can be balanced among the members of the community. Thus, for example, zones could be identified within communities wherein the use of land in each zone was determined by competition.[85]

Following this framework, Burgess identifies five concentric zones of a city: the central business district (the cultural and economic center of the city, characterized by high property values), the industrial/factory zone (to which business and light manufacturing have moved that cannot afford the prices of the central business district), the transitional zone (which is inhabited by lower- to middle-class workers who work in the industrial/factory zone but who cannot afford to live in the central business district or the higher-class residential area), the residential zone (where more expensive apartments and single-family homes are located), and the commuters' zone (the suburban areas and satellite cities, usually within an hour from the central business district).[86] Each zone reflects the characteristics of the group that inhabits it, the group that most efficiently utilizes the resources found within it.[87] This theory views the city "as a dynamic adaptive system that relates various population groups, commercial institutions, and local industries to each other and the outside world."[88]

An example of this type of spatial organization can be seen in the literature on urban sports. Riess, for example, discusses the various neighborhoods in the developing cities of the nineteenth and early-twentieth centuries. Different sports developed in the different zones of the city, and eventually the various socioeconomic, racial, and ethnic groups adopted different sports that subsequently came to be identified as belonging to those particular groups. Baseball, for example, was a game for middle class, office workers. Boxing and pugilism were associated with the poorer neighborhoods.[89] Such differentiation served to distinguish groups, and provide the positive functions of sports to the community.

Alternatively, Hawley views human ecology as broader than spatial interdependence. His focus is the community: human ecology attempts "to determine the nature of community structure in general, the types of communities that appear in different habitats, and the specific sequence of change in community development."[90] Community is defined by Hawley as the "structure of relationships through which a localized population provides its daily requirements."[91] Community structure thus consists of the mechanisms through which a population organizes itself for survival.

Hawley notes that "the collective life of man . . . revolves simultaneously about two axes, one of which is symbiotic, the other commensalistic."[92] The symbiotic aspect pertains to the interdependence of the community members who perform different functions. By commensalistic, Hawley is referring to cooperation among those who perform the same functions. These two characteristics of society are "a peculiar and complementary integrative force and together, therefore, they constitute the basis of community cohesion."[93]

As previously discussed, sports sociologists have noted an integrative function of sports. For example, Lever concludes that sports fans come to identify with their teams and their fellow fans.[94] Kuklick also suggests that sports join fans "communally."[95] Given that minor league teams are found in smaller locations, and that Minor League Baseball has been labeled as more family oriented, it follows that communities that host minor league teams may be more integrated, and may possess a higher quality of life than other communities.

Classical Theorists

The classical theorists, such as Karl Marx and Max Weber, took notice of the loss of community associated with the rise of urbanism, capitalism, and bureaucratization. Marx and Weber were concerned with the development of modernity and the resulting effects on society, such as class conflict, rationalization, and alienation. Associated with these problems is the breakdown of community.[96]

According to classical sociologists, urbanization, capitalism, and industrialization brought about a decline in the traditional authority of the church and the family. Because of the increasingly complex division of labor, communities that were once isolated became dependent upon each other, linked to the larger economic system.[97] Cities were impersonal and individuals were often left to themselves to discern what was right and wrong. According to Durkheim, the result of such individualism is anomie: a sense of normlessness, or a loss of community.[98]

This loss was brought about by a decline in the collective conscience or "the totality of beliefs and sentiments common to average citizens of the same society."[99] Though this force was weakened, social bonds would not be entirely lost:

> The material neighborhood will always constitute a bond between men; consequently, political and social organization with a territorial base will certainly exist. Only, they will not have their present predominance, precisely because this bond has lost its force.[100]

Sport is one of the cultural/societal elements that can strengthen those bonds.

Another work that has had a great influence on students of community, and that may be most relevant to a discussion of the effects of sports on the community, is Ferdinand Tonnies's *Gemeinschaft und Gesellschaft*,[101] or as I like to call it, *Minor League Towns and Major League Cities*. Tonnies is primarily concerned with how people relate to one another. The two basic forms of human relationship, for him, are *gemeinschaft* and *gesellschaft*. Although both types exist simultaneously, the concept of *gemeinschaft* can be applied to small, rural communities, and *gesellschaft* is characteristic of larger ones.[102]

Gesellschaft, roughly translated as "society," is found in economic and professional relationships. Persons in such relationships are independent of one another; there are no strong, communal bonds in *gesellschaft*. *Gesellschaft* is characterized by rationality and calculation, similar to Weber's industrialized, capitalistic society. The laws governing *gesellschaft* are rational, calculated, and scientific. Faith, trust, and tradition are irrelevant.

Gemeinschaft, translated as "community," comprises kinship, place, neighborhood, and friendship. It encompasses "All intimate, private, and exclusive living together."[103] Tonnies identifies various types of *gemeinschaft*: *gemeinschaft* of blood, locality, and mind. The *gemeinschaft* of mind "represents the truly human and supreme form of community."[104] Examples of *gemeinschaft*, aside from the family, include guilds, churches, and holy orders.

Gemeinschaft relationships are formed by natural will, and are therefore based on unity, sentiment, and mutual understanding. Individuals in such relationships take direct interest in each other's welfare. Those in *gemeinschaft* relationships share traditions and a spirit of brotherhood that is strengthened by bonds of kinship and locality; goals, values, and beliefs rest upon common traditions and experiences. Thus, a relationship based on natural will is an end in itself and not a means to another end. Natural will is found in families and in the thinking of artisans, peasants, women, and young people.[105] Natural will and *gemeinschaft*-like relationships can be found in a minor league ballpark and, often, throughout minor league communities.

Tonnies argues that eventually *gesellschaft* relationships will replace *gemeinschaft* relationships. In other words, rational will will triumph over natural will. This will come about because of the rapid expansion of capitalism.[106] Society will suffer as a result: "here everybody is by himself and isolated, and there is a condition of tension against all others."[107]

Tonnies's argument is similar to that of Durkheim: as societies modernize and adopt capitalism, the organization of society changes, and people are unsure of their roles in society. Skills become specialized, such that individuals must depend on others to perform the basic tasks of living. People are also dependent upon money, and conflicts arise over money, territory, and time. Faith and trust are lost. All of this leads to a tendency for persons to be individualistic, self-centered, and isolated.

This line of thinking has been unconsciously reflected in many of the musings about baseball as the national pastime. As with the classical theorists, many writers "mourn" the loss of a traditional, simpler period when baseball was the nation's game. In today's fast-paced, rationalized society, according to these theorists, baseball is no longer the national pastime. Baseball is a "pastoral" sport where time has no meaning: there are no "time-outs" and no game clock. According to Ross,

> Baseball evokes for us a past which may never have been ours, but which we believe was, and certainly that was enough. . . . But now the . . . dream is no longer our preeminent national pastime and now this myth is being replaced by another more appropriate to the new realities (and fantasies) of our time.[108]

Following such reasoning, many sports sociologists in the 1970s and 1980s proclaimed football as the new national pastime, the game that reflected changes in technology and in the pace of society.[109] Football reflects a more "outer-directed" urban society. Similarly, the growth in the popularity of the National Basketball Association in the 1990s has led many writers to conclude that basketball is the new national pastime of a society "with shorter attention spans brought on by television, with a need for quicker, metropolitan gratification."[110]

The simpler world of baseball has been replaced in a fast-paced rationalized world with games that are more television friendly, and by individuals that have lost the sense of community. However, the increasing interest in Minor League Baseball may be an indicator of a societal desire to return to *gemeinschaft*.

Community Psychology

The sense of attachment that many writers and researchers claim is absent from modern-day communities and community studies has recently emerged in psychological studies of community. The psychological sense of community was introduced by Sarason in 1974.[111] The literature of community psychology is relevant to this discussion because it includes an important ingredient of community that is often referred to by the inhabitants of the communities, and which is alluded to in the sociological literature. That is, community is often concerned with the "quality of character of human relationship, without reference to location."[112]

As such, community psychologists McMillan and Chavis include four elements in their definition of community: membership, influence, integration and fulfillment of needs, and shared emotional connection.[113] It is the shared emotional connection that is often overlooked or, rather, merely assumed in much of the sociological literature of the past. It is this connection that one finds in Minor League Baseball.

Conclusion

Community can be defined and experienced many ways. For many, community is measured by a sense of belonging and the quality of life. However, Warren notes that increases in interdependence and bureaucratization, growth of the cities and suburbs, and changing values combine to "transform the structure and function of American communities."[114]

Warren's words echo the debate over the evolution from *gemeinschaft* to *gesellschaft,* the growth of the division of labor, and the resulting alienation and anomie. The failure to "identify" with community has become a social problem.[115] However, some researchers find such claims to be unfounded. What is important, they conclude, is how one defines community.[116] Thus, other variables, such as community services, migration, length of residence, and other social and demographic variables, are important to the measurement of community.

As Durkheim, Tonnies, and others point out, society has changed greatly since the Industrial Revolution. Tonnies' distinction between *gemeinschaft* and *gesellschaft* provides a starting point for comparing communities (e.g., one can compare large cities to smaller towns, communities with minor league teams to communities without, or major league towns to minor league ones). Such a perspective, which can provide measures of community bonds and emotions, can be combined with the ecological approach and investigated using population and organizational data.

Although data do not always exist for measuring concepts such as "emotional attachment" or "brotherhood," sociologists must take care not to underspecify a model of community. Geographical location and availability of social services are not sufficient for capturing the spirit of community. It may also be true that different combinations of individuals and changes over time will have an effect on how we define community. Yet the continuation of studies analyzing community, no matter how it is defined, is vital to our understanding of how society is organized. As such, Minor League Baseball provides the perfect focus for a sociological study of community.

In their book, *Winning Is the Only Thing,* Randy Roberts and James Olson suggest that

> Blessed with money but deprived of community in the 1970s and 1980s, Americans began to use sports to rebuild their sense of community and fitness to define individual happiness and individual pleasure, creating a culture of competitive narcissism . . .[117]

Sports came to be seen as an expression of identity in the nineteenth and twentieth centuries. Sports teams represented schools, towns, and even nations. With many choices for membership in the urbanized age, sports became a replacement for family, church, and other institutions to which people traditionally reached for identity and a sense of belonging.

A sense of community, or feelings of solidarity, is often the basis for the support of sporting groups and teams. Furthermore, many have felt a loss of community through the impact of big business on sports, and wish to return to the past when teams did not migrate to other towns and when players did not hold out for more money. A sociological definition of community, which includes all of the elements suggested by the theorists previously discussed, can be utilized to understand the importance and popularity of sports in the United States.

Many of the recent studies concerning franchise relocation and the expenditure of public funds for sports arenas have discussed the intangible benefits of hosting a sports team for the local community. The relationship between a community and its team is based on unity, sentiment, and mutual understanding. The team brings these benefits to the community. Faith and tradition are an important aspect of fan loyalty to a team. In the case of Minor League Baseball, the team itself often plays an important role in the community. Owners often are local businessmen who become personally involved with the fans, the players, and other community members.[118]

The research presented attempts to measure the extent of community in minor league towns using the following framework: Foremost, the classical concepts of alienation and anomie are apparent in many levels of sports; the increase in the business aspects of professional sports alienates fans and the community. The loss of a team leaves a community in a state of anomie, much of its identity stripped away.

Second, the concepts of territory and mutual interdependence, employed by human ecologists, may prove useful to understanding how small communities are organized around sporting activities. A review of articles and stories about Minor League Baseball in the press indicates a strong connection between the team and its community. The team ownership relies on business connections and residents of the area for advertising and business. The residents rely on a team for entertainment and a wholesome, affordable place for a family outing.

Third, the differentiation between small communities and larger communities is particularly relevant to minor league sports. Minor League Baseball towns can be likened to *gemeinschaft*. Major league towns may exhibit more *gesellschaft*-like characteristics. Indeed, as in the response to the Major League Baseball strike of 1994-1995, many fans now see the major leagues as alien, as big business, and the players as selfish and unconcerned with the fans. Minor league teams still seem to care about their fans.

Finally, McMillan and Chavis's four components of community can be seen in the case of small-town sports or Minor League Baseball. Particularly important is the fulfillment of needs and the shared emotional connection, as suggested by Lever. When one is made to feel part of the organization, and not just a spectator, the need for belonging is fulfilled, and the recognition that an individual who shares sentiments for a team (which is representing the town and its inhabitants) with others must also serve to enforce communal bonds.

For many fans, the issues of what their team means to them and whether their community has derived any economic benefits from having a minor league team are moot issues—they just want to enjoy the game and support their team. In rooting for the hometown team, they are also expressing notions of community pride and cohesiveness. For the few hours they are at the stadium, they are joined in a common mission. They celebrate the successes and mourn the failures of their team, and bask in the glory of a win. They are similar to a family, supporting each other and sharing their experiences. Friendships can be formed in the season ticket holders' section, or at the concession stand. Local traditions are cherished and replicated in the stadium.

When the game is over, the feeling of community spirit lingers. Strangers can form a bond over discussing the trials and tribulations of their local team. When far away from home, wearing something that expresses pride in your team and your city can be a link to your community. Encountering another fan of the hometown team often arouses a feeling of connection and strength.

At the minor league level, these feelings may be even more intense. Although most people have heard of the major league teams, few have heard of the smaller communities in which Minor League Baseball is played. Thus, in many ways, the local minor league team becomes an ambassador of our hometown, helping to spread the word about what makes us special and unique. We love Minor League Baseball because it is an expression of ourselves, and a part of who we are.

Hagerstown Municipal Stadium, Hagerstown, Maryland—Home of the Hagerstown Suns (photo by Rebecca Kraus)

Safe at home, Hagerstown Municipal Stadium (photo by Rebecca Kraus)

Major hopes in the minor leagues, Hagerstown Municipal Stadium (photo by Rebecca Kraus)

Press box at Hagerstown (photo by Rebecca Kraus)

The Baysox pay tribute to our fallen heroes (photo by John Beyer)

Prince George's Stadium, Bowie, Maryland—Home of the Bowie Baysox (photo by John Beyer)

Outfield at Prince George's Stadium (photo by John Beyer)

Chapter 4

The Evolution of Minor League Baseball

Minor League Baseball has its own special character that sets it apart from Major League Baseball and other sports. The community aspect of the game is only one of its unique characteristics. Its special relationship with the major leagues, its turbulent history, and the frequent minor league franchise relocations and name changes are all a part of the uniqueness of Minor League Baseball.

HISTORICAL OVERVIEW

In 1946, Minor League Baseball was made up of fifty-eight leagues and over 400 teams. Since then, it has experienced its share of ups and downs. Attendance declined throughout the 1950s and 1960s, and the number of teams and leagues diminished. Despite increases in attendance in 1969, 1970, and 1971 (primarily due to major league expansion and, thus, the addition of new minor league teams), attendance experienced another drop in the early 1970s. The number of teams reached a low point in 1975 with 106 minor league teams operating in the United States.

Since the 1980s, the number of leagues has stabilized while the number of teams has increased. Between 1980 and 1990, the number of teams grew from 125 to 150, while attendance was also on the rise (see Appendix A). By 2002, 160 teams were associated with Minor League Baseball and another twenty-eight belonged to independent baseball leagues. Minor League Baseball, once "an isolated organization, fighting for the preservation of its rights" has grown "into a formidable partner of Major League Baseball."[1]

The fate of the minor leagues is intertwined with the social and economic history of the United States, as well as with the fortunes of Major League Baseball, and thus can be viewed in light of changes experienced within the country. As the United States enjoyed post–World War II prosperity in the 1950s, so too did baseball. However, in the late 1950s, and throughout the 1960s and 1970s, as Major League Baseball was facing competition from other professional sports leagues and other forms of entertainment (such as television), its popularity declined somewhat, thus affecting the minor leagues as well.

The migration of people away from extended family or into the suburbs changed the relationship between baseball and communities, often causing teams to disband or relocate. Team movement and the need for new facilities also altered the relationship between teams and local governments.[2] In addition, changing economic conditions in the United States also affected attendance and interest in sports. With less community attachment and more disposable income in the 1970s and 1980s, sports became a substitute and a symbol of community in America.[3] According to Roberts and Olson, "In an age when television, movies, and mass culture threatened distinctiveness, sports emerged as the single most powerful symbol of localism and community loyalty."[4]

Over the years, society has viewed Minor League Baseball differently. The 1980s' vision of Minor League Baseball as an economic-development tool, for example, gave way to viewing the organization as a symbol of community and solidarity in the 1990s. With this evolution in mind, I analyze the history of Minor League Baseball in the following seven eras.[5]

- The Early Years, prior to 1946
- Prosperity, 1946-1950
- Decline, 1951-1962
- Subsidization, 1963-1967
- Indifference, 1968-1977
- Renaissance, 1978-1990
- Legitimization, 1991-1999

The Early Years, Prior to 1946

In the latter part of the nineteenth century, baseball was characterized by fierce competition for players. Often, players were enticed to leave their teams midseason to sign with other teams, sometimes resulting in teams and leagues folding before they could complete the season. In 1883, eighteen years prior to the creation of the National Association of Professional Baseball Leagues, the first formal agreement between the major and minor leagues was signed. Known as the National Agreement, this document provided a framework for peaceful existence among the American League, the National League, and a minor league called the Northwestern League. The agreement established territories for each league, described how contracts would be handled for players as they moved among the leagues, and set up an arbitration committee to hear disputes. By 1890, sixteen additional minor leagues had joined the National Agreement. With the establishment of this agreement, attendance, salaries, and profits increased, and the teams and leagues found stability.[6]

According to minor league historians, the National Agreement had become ineffective by 1900; there was little cooperation among teams and competition for players had grown. The various minor leagues reorganized under the National Association of Professional Baseball Leagues (NAPBL) on September 5, 1901, and began play in 1902. This reorganization reinstated salary limits and the reserve clause, which tied players to a particular team indefinitely.[7] The NAPBL was also recognized as the official minor leagues for the American and National Leagues.

Threatened by the Federal League (a new major league) and World War I, the minor leagues experienced a slight decline in popularity between 1914 and 1919. However, after the war, the minors experienced a boom that lasted until the Great Depression of the 1930s. With the innovation of nighttime baseball and growth of the major league farm system, the minors survived the Depression and were stronger than ever by 1941.[8]

In the 1920s, the minor leagues became structured as the training ground for players who hoped to eventually make it to the major leagues. The current minor league system, or farm system, was developed by Branch Rickey, the general manager of the St. Louis Cardinals. Rickey was concerned with the high cost and difficulty of acquiring quality players from the minor leagues. Rickey determined that if the Cardinals owned the minor league teams and players outright, players could be developed and sent to the major league team at a great cost savings. By the late 1920s, the Cardinals owned seven minor league teams and had greatly improved the quality of the major league team, having won the World Series in 1926.[9] By 1946, Major

League Baseball teams were affiliating with approximately twelve minor league teams each. St. Louis had peaked in 1940 with thirty-two affiliated teams.[10] (Under the current farm system, major league teams do not generally own their farm teams, but own the players.)

Prosperity, 1946-1950

The minor leagues benefited from a postwar boom that gave people more time and money for leisure activities, including Minor League Baseball. With a change in leadership in the National Association, expansion was encouraged in the minor leagues. Semipro and textile league teams were added to minor league circuits.[11] Overall, the leagues were relatively stable during this time. Of 458 communities that hosted teams during this period, 247 had a team for the entire period, a retention rate of 54 percent (see Table 4.1).

During this time of prosperity, teams were located in more than fifty leagues and in almost every state in the country. Teams were found in small towns, such as Lincolnton, North Carolina, as well as larger locales, such as Baltimore, Maryland. This era represents a time when towns and cities across the country could enjoy a sense of community and pride. Unfortunately, it did not last.

Decline, 1951-1962

The postwar boom could not be sustained throughout the 1950s. Although the Korean War may have had some impact on attendance,[12] the minor leagues faced competition from television, new leisure activities, other professional sports such as football, improved and affordable air conditioning that kept people indoors, and major league expansion and relocation.[13] Between 1951 and 1962, 404 communities had minor league teams. However, only forty-eight communities, or 12 percent, retained their team for all twelve years during this era of decline. In comparison, sixty-five communities saw their teams leave after the 1951 season (see Table 4.1).

Particularly devastating was the movement of major league teams to traditionally minor league towns. Minor league teams in Los Angeles, Baltimore, Milwaukee, Kansas City, and San Francisco were displaced as major league teams took over their territories. Many of

TABLE 4.1. Number of Years Teams Remained in Communities, by Period

No. of Years	Era 1 1946-1950	Era 2 1951-1962	Era 3 1963-1967	Era 4 1968-1977	Era 5 1978-1990
1	39	65	15	19	8
2	28	36	12	17	6
3	56	29	21	9	10
4	88	33	15	13	10
5	247	35	76	7	10
6	0	33	0	7	11
7	0	32	0	13	7
8	0	19	0	7	6
9	0	27	0	19	6
10	0	22	0	56	6
11	0	25	0	0	9
12	0	48	0	0	7
13	0	0	0	0	80
Total	458	404	139	167	176
% Retaining Team Entire Period	54%	12%	55%	34%	45%

Source: Rebecca Susan Kraus, "Sport and the Community: The Case of Minor League Baseball, 1950s-1990s" (Doctoral dissertation, The Catholic University of America, 1998), p. 74.

Note: The total represents the number of communities that had a team at any point in the era. For example, thirty-nine teams remained in their counties for only one year during Era 1 (1946-1950), and 247 teams remained in the county all five years of this period. Throughout the entire era, 458 communities had a team at any point in time. Thus, in Era 1, of the 458 communities that had a team at any point, 247 had a team all five years. In other words, 54 percent of the counties with teams retained a team during the entire period. This retention rate declined severely in the 1950s, as the total number of teams declined.

the remaining teams played in deteriorating stadiums built during the Depression by the Works Projects Administration or quickly but poorly constructed during the 1950s. With little government funds for improvements, many of these stadiums were torn down and cities, owners, and leagues found it difficult to field teams and complete their seasons.[14]

Between 1950 and 1951, the number of teams dropped from 440 to 371, and attendance fell by almost seven million fans (see Appendix A). The number of teams and attendance continued to fall throughout the 1950s. By the end of the decade, the major leagues realized that something had to be done to protect their source of players.

In 1957, a 500,000-dollar stabilization fund was established to subsidize the low minors. In 1959, the fund was replaced by the Player Development and Promotion program, which provided one million dollars to the minor leagues. However, the minor leagues continued to struggle until the Player Development Plan was created in 1962. This plan reorganized the minor leagues and called for the affiliation of minor league teams with major league teams. Major league teams would now pay a portion of player salaries and provide other assistance to their minor league affiliates.[15]

Subsidization, 1963-1967

The existence of at least 100 minor league teams had been guaranteed by the Player Development Plan of 1962. After the collapse of the American Association and the Georgia-Florida League following the 1963 season, the number of minor leagues remained steady at fifteen in the United States, until the demise of the Northern League in 1971.[16] Although both the minor and major leagues expanded in 1969, all of baseball suffered from national disinterest during this time.[17]

The number of teams continued to fall, from 118 in 1963 to 112 in 1967. Total attendance bottomed out in 1967 at a mere 6.9 million— a far cry from the nearly 40 million fans that had attended games at the end of the 1940s (see Appendix A). With assistance from their major league partners, communities were able to improve the team retention rate during this period. Seventy-six of the 139 communities that had a team in 1963 (55 percent) still had a team in 1967 (see Table 4.1).

Indifference, 1968-1977

The minors continued a lackluster existence during the 1970s, serving primarily as a training ground for future major leaguers, as they had done throughout the 1960s. In 1971, the Northern League folded, and by 1975 the Carolina League and the Western Carolina League were each down to only four teams. Teams began to turn to promotions and giveaways to attract spectators to the ballpark. Although teams were operated more as a business, many owners continued to rely on major league affiliates for support. Ownership was a "sometime thing" where there was little money to be made, and little money put into the team: owners and investors often pulled their money out in the middle of a season.[18]

During this period, minor league teams were a losing proposition, and teams were being given away or sold for extremely low sums of money, such as the Reading Phillies, who, as noted earlier, were sold for one dollar. Shortly thereafter, Joe Buzas, the purchaser of the Reading team, obtained the Bristol Red Sox for free—after agreeing to assume the $50,000 in debt the team owed to its creditors.[19]

In this era, the number of teams changed from year to year. It began with 113 teams and ended with 116. The number of teams reached a high in 1970 with 123, and a low in 1975 with only 106. Attendance was unstable as well. However, by the end of the period, a long-term increase in attendance began, jumping from 7.6 million fans in 1976 to nearly 9.1 million fans in 1977 (see Appendix A).

Although owners and fans were rather indifferent to the minor leagues in the 1970s, the team retention rate was somewhat lower than during the previous period as teams changed hands and moved to new areas. Thirty-four percent of the communities hosting Minor League Baseball during this period had the team for the entire ten years. Attendance was on the rise in 1977, thus marking the end of this period. An increase in the number of teams fueled the increase in attendance, which continued throughout the 1980s and into the early 1990s.

Renaissance, 1978-1990

The resurgence of Minor League Baseball that began in the late 1970s was in full swing by 1980. Cities were once again spending money to build new stadiums or refurbish old ones. Cities such as Buffalo, New York, and Frederick, Maryland, contributed millions of dollars toward the construction of new stadiums; over thirty new facilities were built during this time.[20] In the 1980s, Buffalo committed over 7.7 million dollars (from their operating budget and through the sale of bonds) to the construction of Pilot Field, which opened in 1988. The total cost of the project was over 44 million dollars.[21] Nonetheless, the new stadium has been viewed as an economic-development success story, and almost attracted a major league expansion franchise to the city.

A "new breed" of minor league owners also began to surface during this time, as those who had operated clubs in the 1940s and 1950s left the game.[22] Many minor league teams were now operated strictly as businesses. Teams in the 1950s, 1960s, and 1970s had often been operated as hobbies or as marketing tools for other products, with owners relying on their cities or major league affiliates for financial support.[23] Today, minor league front office staff are more often trained in sports administration,[24] and owners seek local investors and commitments from their communities.[25] However, teams have recognized the importance of including community members in the game through marketing efforts and promotions, and other events held at the stadium.

The new philosophy of Minor League Baseball (that of economic development and box office success, as opposed to on-field success) is reflected in the selling prices of minor league teams during this time. For example, in 1980 the Durham Bulls were purchased for approximately 2,500 dollars. One major motion picture and eleven years later, the team was sold for four million dollars.[26] By 1991, single-A teams were valued around one million dollars, and AAA teams were worth five million dollars.[27]

Attendance grew continuously throughout the 1980s, reaching near-record highs in the 1990s. In 1994, it was 33,355,199, the second-highest attendance ever, and the highest since 1949, when the record was set at 39.7 million[28] (see Appendix A). By 1992, attendance had broken the million mark five times in a row in Buffalo alone.[29]

The team-retention rate improved during the 1980s as well. Forty-five percent of the communities hosting a team at any point throughout this period kept it for all thirteen years. Thus, by the 1990s, the minors were entering a period of relative stability (see Table 4.1).

Legitimization, 1991-1999

By the 1990s, Minor League Baseball had achieved its place on the national scene. No longer in fear of falling profits and shrinking attendance, it had proven itself to be a legitimate business endeavor and focal point of the community. Attendance at minor league ballparks was high throughout the 1990s, and communities continued to compete fiercely with one another to acquire minor league teams.[30] One reason for the increased interest in Minor League Baseball is its focus on entertainment and the family.[31] Another is the belief that it embodies the values of simplicity, honesty, and community.[32] As such, Minor League Baseball represents the opposite of Major League Baseball and other institutions, which have fallen prey to an alienating modern world. According to David Lamb, "America and the minor leagues, [are] each a metaphor for the other."[33]

Between 1991 and 1999, Minor League Baseball reclaimed its position as one of the most thriving entertainment options for small cities and midsized towns. During the decade, new teams located to places such as Bowie, Maryland, and Wilmington, Delaware. New stadiums were built in historically thriving baseball towns such as Norfolk, Virginia, and Durham, North Carolina.

The New Minor League Millennium, 2000 and Beyond

The prosperity of the minor leagues in the 1990s appears to be continuing into the twenty-first century. In 2000, minor league attendance was up 7.3 percent over the previous year. Over 37 million fans attended games, the third highest total since 1949. Several new ballparks, including the 84-million-dollar AutoZone Park in Memphis, Tennessee, helped increase attendance throughout the minors. Further, the Sacramento River Cats, newcomers to the minor leagues in 2000, had the largest season attendance for the year at 861,808, and the Round Rock Express, located near Austin, Texas, broke the Texas League attendance record with 660,110.[34] The minors definitely appear to be here to stay.

MINOR LEAGUE BASEBALL AS A DIFFERENT KIND OF BUSINESS

Minor league teams represent a unique form of business venture. Not only do they operate as a business, but as part of a league of teams that rely on one another for competition. Further, as junior partners in the Major League Baseball player development process, they cannot rely on the standard business formulas for sales and success.

Complying with the Professional Baseball Agreement

The Professional Baseball Agreement (PBA) and the corresponding Player Development Contracts (PDCs), discussed in Chapter 2, have a significant impact on the costs of running a minor league team. For example, the 1990 PBA required major league teams to pay the minor league players' salaries and provide equipment.[35] However, that PBA expired on September 30, 1997. Whenever a new PBA is negotiated, the costs for minor league owners may change, depending on the agreement reached between the owners and Major League Baseball. According to Johnson and Wolff, the nature of Minor League Baseball in the 1990s was shaped by the PBA that was signed in 1990. In the agreement, Major League Baseball demanded 5 percent of minor league ticket-sales revenue, the control of team logos to be transferred to Major League Baseball Properties, and higher stadium standards. Johnson and Wolff suggest that these changes, which seemed extra burdensome to many minor league owners at the time, have produced positive results for the minor league baseball industry.[36]

The 5 percent ticket revenue tax resulted in better record-keeping systems for most minor league teams. Still in a transition from "mom and pop" operations to profitable businesses, minor league franchises had to quickly improve their accounting systems to comply with this requirement. Similarly, with trademarks under the control of Major League Baseball Properties, minor league teams were able to take advantage of new marketing opportunities and a new source of revenue.[37]

Most important, the new facility requirements caused Minor League Baseball teams to upgrade and abandon ailing facilities, and fueled a "stadium boom."[38] Many requirements could not be met with simple stadium upgrades. For example, single-A stadiums must have at least 4,000 seats (10,000 for AAA). At least 10 percent of the seats have to be box seats (separate seats with backs) or reserved seats (benches with backs). The home clubhouse must be a minimum of 1,000 square feet; the visitors' clubhouse must be at least 750 square feet. Specifications for equipment, plumbing facilities, parking, turnstiles, ticket windows, scoreboards, pressrooms, etc., are specified in the PBA.[39] Local and state governments provided much of the funding for the new stadiums, which include major league amenities such as skyboxes, electronic scoreboards, state-of-the-art clubhouses, etc.

Attracting Customers

Another feature of the minor league business is how it attracts and keeps fans. Since minor league players can be "called up" to the major league team or promoted to the next level at any time during a season, the mix of players on the team during a season, and in future seasons, is constantly changing. Fans, therefore, cannot form strong attachments to players or rely on a set roster. Standard business variables such as costs and team success also factor into the club's overall success.

To counteract this potentially devastating aspect of the game, minor league teams rely on promotions and antics to keep their fans. This feature has been called a link to a "naive, young, easily excited and entertained, if a bit unsophisticated, America that knew how to have a good time without all the trappings and hype of the 1990s."[40] Since most of a team's revenue comes from gate receipts, minor league teams market their product as a family-oriented social occasion to attract fans to the games.[41] This adds to the communal atmosphere in the ballpark.

Fans have come to expect entertainment as part of the aura of Minor League Baseball. Between innings the fans are often entertained with an assortment of games and contests—from watching other fans spin around a bat then race around the bases, to the announcement of the winner of the "dirtiest car in the parking lot award," usually sponsored by a local car wash. Nightly renditions of "YMCA," scoreboard messages urging fans to participate, inexpensive food, and various contests keep the fans coming back. Examples include:

- Elvis Presley look-alike contests[42]
- "Instant suitcase night" for which fans come to the ballpark packed and ready to go on a vacation (usually to an unspecified location) if picked as the winner[43]
- "Move of the game" in which fans can win the chance to upgrade their seats from general admission to box seats[44]

- The "diamond dig" for which fans (sometimes women only) are given a spoon and let loose on the field to dig for a diamond
- The "toilet toss," in which fans attempt to win prizes by tossing plungers into a toilet that has been brought onto the field
- The "T-shirt toss" during which team employees sling shot T-shirts into the stands and fans catch them

Other, more ambitious, promotions have been attempted. For example, in 1989, the Charleston Wheelers held "Noah Night." After nine consecutive rainouts, the owner declared that fans who came to the game dressed as Noah or ark animals, or who came "two by two," would be let into the game for free. Those bringing toy boats were charged only one dollar. According to one report, the owner commented, "We had a couple hundred crazies come with horns on. One guy wore a rhinoceros nose. Some came in with antlers they got off their father's gun rack."[45] Other promotions include the "Great Banana Split" created during a doubleheader in Nashville, Tennessee, in 1982, and the "Greased Pig Contest" in Gastonia, North Carolina, in 1974 during which younger fans were invited to try to catch a pig covered with cooking grease. After the main event, the pig got loose and was eventually trapped in the ladies room.[46]

Giveaways are another important ingredient. The key is to get sponsorship from local businesses. Fans readily come for free fare such as seat cushions, baseball caps, and umbrellas.

Other attractions are planned for the season such as fireworks and special appearances by minor league favorites, such as Morganna the Kissing Bandit, and the San Diego Chicken.

FRANCHISE RELOCATION AND NAME CHANGES

Franchise relocation and reaffiliation is commonplace among the minor leagues. Teams move to new locations, often to improved stadium facilities. Sometimes, a community can replace a team by luring another team to the vacated stadium—but not always. Upon the completion of a PDC with a major league team, a minor league team may sign with a different affiliate, changing its name in the process. A brief discussion of the minor leagues in Maryland, illustrates these changes in the location, league, affiliation, and name that occur often, sometimes at a dizzying pace.

For example, seventeen cities in Maryland have been home to minor league baseball franchises. Due to franchise shifts, league disbandings, and other changes, at least twelve leagues and forty-one teams played in Maryland between 1903 and 2002. There had been four minor league teams in Baltimore prior to the reorganization of the leagues in 1901.[47] In 1903, Baltimore became a member of the Eastern League when Jack Dunn purchased a team in Montreal, Quebec, Canada, and moved it to Baltimore. Dunn moved the team to Richmond for the 1915 season, when the newly formed Federal League fielded a Baltimore team. At the end of the season, the team was sold and remained in Richmond. Dunn then purchased a franchise that was located in Jersey City and moved it to Baltimore for the 1916 season. The minor league Orioles played in Baltimore for another thirty-eight years until the major league St. Louis Browns moved to Baltimore in 1954. The minor league team was then sold and moved, again, to Richmond.[48]

Cumberland, Maryland, was a stop on the minor league circuit for at least a short time in 1906 and again in 1907. The Cumberland Rooters played in the Pennsylvania-Ohio-Maryland League in 1906, and in the Western Pennsylvania League in 1907. The Rooters remained in Cumberland through June 1907, when they moved to Piedmont, West Virginia, before finally settling in Somerset, Pennsylvania. In 1916, Cumberland, Frostburg, and Lonaconing were homes to teams in the Potomac League, which disbanded on August 16 without completing the season.[49]

The Eastern Shore League of Maryland went through similar changes during its three phases (1922-1928, 1937-1941, and 1946-1949). Eastern Shore cities hosted the following teams:

- The Cambridge Canners (1922-1928), Cardinals (1937-1939), Canners (again, 1940-1941), and Dodgers (1946-1949)
- The Centreville Colts (1937-1939), Red Sox (1940-1941), and Orioles (1946)
- The Crisfield Crabbers (1922-1928, 1937)
- The Easton Farmers (1924-1928), Browns (1937), Cubs (1938), and Yankees (1939-1941, 1946-1949)
- The Federalsburg Athletics (1937-1938), A's (1939-1941, 1946-1948), and Feds (1949)

- The Pocomoke City Salamanders (1922-1923), Red Sox (1937-1939), and Chicks (1940)
- The Salisbury Indians (1922-1928, 1937-1938), Senators (1939), and Cardinals (1940-1941, 1946-1949)[50]

Most of the name changes were caused by changes in major league affiliation.

The latter part of the century also brought many franchise relocations and name changes to Maryland. In 1981, the Rocky Mount (North Carolina) Pines disbanded, leaving an opening in the Carolina League,[51] which was filled with the Baltimore Orioles' single-A team, who became the Hagerstown Suns. In 1989, the Orioles moved their Carolina League team to Frederick, and the team became known as the Frederick Keys. The Orioles moved their AA team from Charlotte, North Carolina, to Hagerstown that same year. In 1993, the Oriole's Hagerstown team was moved to Bowie, Maryland, and the Toronto Blue Jays moved their South Atlantic League team from Myrtle Beach, South Carolina, to Hagerstown (the team kept the name Hagerstown Suns). In 1996, the Albany (Georgia) Polecats moved to Salisbury and became the Delmarva Shorebirds.[52]

In addition to teams moving from one city to another, names often change regardless of whether a team has relocated. Name changes often occur with affiliation changes. Names also have been changed when a team moved into a new stadium. For example, the Tidewater Tides of Norfolk, Virginia, became the Norfolk Tides when the team moved into a new stadium downtown on the Norfolk waterfront. The Canton-Akron Indians became the Akron Aeros when the team moved from Thurman Munson Stadium in Canton, Ohio, to Canal Park in Akron, Ohio, in 1997.[53]

In addition, during the 1990s, minor league teams began to recognize the profits to be made from selling merchandise with the team logo. With the popularity of the Carolina Mudcats name and logo, other teams followed suit. Mid-1990s name changes include such catchy names as the New Britain Red Sox becoming the Hardware City Rock Cats, the Bakersfield Dodgers becoming the Bakersfield Blaze, and the Madison Hatters becoming the Battle Creek Golden Kazoos.[54] (The name changes did not stop there, however. The Hardware City team changed its name again to the New Britain Rock Cats in 1997, and the Battle Creek Golden Kazoos became the Michigan

Battle Cats in 1996.[55]) To keep up with the trend, newer teams have been given comparably trendy names, such as the Bowie Baysox, the Lansing Lugnuts, and the Lancaster JetHawks, with interesting mascots and symbols that entertain children and entice fans to purchase merchandise bearing the logos. *Baseball America* reported that such changes are not necessarily viewed favorably by Major League Baseball, which pays for new uniforms under the PBA.[56]

For the 2001 season, there were many franchise shifts among the leagues. The Albuquerque Dukes of the Pacific Coast League moved to Portland, Oregon, and became the Portland Beavers. This move prompted the Portland team in the Northwest League to relocate to Pasco, Washington, as the Tri-City Dust Devils. In addition, the South Atlantic League welcomed expansion teams in Lexington, Kentucky, and Wilmington, North Carolina. Also in the SALLY League, the Cape Fear Crocs moved from North Carolina to New Jersey and are now known as the Lakewood BlueClaws.[57]

In the Florida State League, two teams were abolished—Kissimmee and St. Petersburg, Florida, no longer host FSL teams. In the New York-Penn League, the Queens Kings moved to their new stadium in Brooklyn, New York, and became the Brooklyn Cyclones. Finally, in the Pioneer League, teams in Butte and Helena, Montana, relocated to Casper, Wyoming, and Provo, Utah.[58]

Change has been a constant part of Minor League Baseball. As previously discussed, when teams were faced with greater competition from other leagues and when teams and leagues began disbanding as the boom years of the 1940s and 1950s ended, there was constant reshuffling among the leagues. In a way, the same holds true today. Leagues and teams that have been in operation for a long time tend to be more stable, but changes still occur.

Tables 4.2 through 4.4 provide examples of franchise shifts, name changes, and affiliation changes. Between 1995 and 2002, three teams in the California League changed their names and one team moved to a new location (see Table 4.2a). During the same time there were eleven changes in affiliation with major league teams (see Table 4.2b). For example, in 1996 the Bakersfield team changed its name to the Bakersfield Blaze, since it was no longer affiliated with the Los Angeles Dodgers, and the Riverside Pilots relocated to Lancaster, California, becoming the Lancaster JetHawks. Also that year, the Visalia Oaks switched from having no major league affiliate to being affili-

TABLE 4.2a. Name Changes and Franchise Relocations in the California League, 1995-2002

1995	1996	1997	1998	1999	2000-2001	2002
Bakersfield Dodgers	Bakersfield **Blaze**	Bakersfield Blaze	Bakersfield Blaze	Bakersfield Blaze	Bakersfield Blaze	Bakersfield Blaze
High Desert Mavericks	High Desert Mavericks	High Desert Mavericks	High Desert Mavericks	High Desert Mavericks	High Desert Mavericks	High Desert Mavericks
Lake Elsinore Storm	Lake Elsinore Storm	Lake Elsinore Storm	Lake Elsinore Storm	Lake Elsinore Storm	Lake Elsinore Storm	Lake Elsinore Storm
Modesto A's	Modesto A's	Modesto A's	Modesto A's	Modesto A's	Modesto A's	Modesto A's
Rancho Cucamonga Quakes	Rancho Cucamonga Quakes	Rancho Cucamonga Quakes	Rancho Cucamonga Quakes	Rancho Cucamonga Quakes	Rancho Cucamonga Quakes	Rancho Cucamonga Quakes
Riverside Pilots	**Lancaster JetHawks**	Lancaster JetHawks	Lancaster JetHawks	Lancaster JetHawks	Lancaster JetHawks	Lancaster JetHawks
San Bernardino Spirit	San Bernardino **Stampede**	San Bernardino Stampede	San Bernardino Stampede	San Bernardino Stampede	San Bernardino Stampede	San Bernardino Stampede
San Jose Giants	San Jose Giants	San Jose Giants	San Jose Giants	San Jose Giants	San Jose Giants	San Jose Giants
Stockton Ports	Stockton Ports	Stockton Ports	Stockton Ports	**Mudville Nine**	Mudville Nine	**Stockton Ports**
Visalia Oaks	Visalia Oaks	Visalia Oaks	Visalia Oaks	Visalia Oaks	Visalia Oaks	Visalia Oaks
Total name changes	2	0	0	1	0	1
Total team moves	1	0	0	0	0	0

Source: Compiled from: *Baseball America 1995 Directory* (Durham, NC: Baseball America, Inc., 1995); *Baseball America 1996 Directory* (Durham, NC: Baseball America, Inc., 1996); *Baseball America 1997 Directory* (Durham, NC: Baseball America, Inc., 1997); *Baseball America 1998 Directory* (Durham, NC: Baseball America, Inc., 1998); *Baseball America 1999 Directory* (Durham, NC: Baseball America, Inc., 1999); *Baseball America 2000 Directory* (Durham, NC: Baseball America, Inc., 2000); *Baseball America 2001 Directory* (Durham, NC: Baseball America, Inc., 2001); *Baseball America 2002 Directory* (Durham, NC: Baseball America, Inc., 2002).

Note: Changes are in bold.

TABLE 4.2b. Affiliation Changes in the California League, 1995–2002

Team	1995	1996	1997	1998	1999	2000	2001	2002
Bakersfield	Co-op	Co-op	**Giants**	Giants	Giants	Giants	**Devil Rays**	Devil Rays
High Desert	Orioles	Orioles	**Diamond-backs**	Diamond-backs	Diamond-backs	Diamond-backs	**Brewers**	Brewers
Lake Elsinore	Angels	Angels	Angels	Angels	Angels	Angels	**Padres**	Padres
Modesto	A's	A's	A's	A's	A's	A's	A's	A's
Rancho Cucamonga	Padres	Padres	Padres	Padres	Padres	Padres	**Angels**	Angels
Riverside/Lancaster	Mariners	Mariners	Mariners	Mariners	Mariners	Mariners	**Diamond-backs**	Diamond-backs
San Bernardino	Dodgers	Dodgers	Dodgers	Dodgers	Dodgers	Dodgers	**Mariners**	Mariners
San Jose	Giants	Giants	Giants	Giants	Giants	Giants	Giants	Giants
Stockton/Mudville	Brewers	Brewers	Brewers	Brewers	Brewers	Brewers	**Reds**	Reds
Visalia	Independent	**Tigers, Diamond-backs**	**A's**	A's	A's	A's	A's	A's
Total changes		1	3	0	0	0	7	0

Source: Compiled from: *Baseball America 1995 Directory* (Durham, NC: Baseball America, Inc., 1995); *Baseball America 1996 Directory* (Durham, NC: Baseball America, Inc., 1996); *Baseball America 1997 Directory* (Durham, NC: Baseball America, Inc., 1997); *Baseball America 1998 Directory* (Durham, NC: Baseball America, Inc., 1998); *Baseball America 1999 Directory* (Durham, NC: Baseball America, Inc., 1999); *Baseball America 2000 Directory* (Durham, NC: Baseball America, Inc., 2000); *Baseball America 2001 Directory* (Durham, NC: Baseball America, Inc., 2001); *Baseball America 2002 Directory* (Durham, NC: Baseball America, Inc., 2002).

Note: Changes are in bold.

ated with both the Detroit Tigers and the Arizona Diamondbacks. The following year, Visalia affiliated with the Oakland A's, High Desert became a Diamondbacks team, and Bakersfield signed on with the San Francisco Giants. The league maintained the status quo until 1999 when the Stockton team changed its name to the Mudville Nine. After a change in ownership, the team once again became the Stockton Ports for the 2002 season.

However, affiliation changes did not necessarily coincide with team moves or name changes. For the 2001 season, there was almost a wholesale affiliate swap in the California League, which was due primarily to a Major League Baseball requirement that teams make affiliation changes in even-numbered years. Therefore, after the 2000 season, many minor league teams signed new contracts with different Major League Baseball partners. In all, thirty minor league teams changed affiliation between 2000 and 2001.[59] There were no moves or affiliation changes for the 2002 season.

The New York-Penn League experienced a few more changes than did the California League. Between 1995 and 2002, a total of seven teams relocated. The Elmira Pioneers moved to Lowell, Massachusetts, in 1996. In 1999, the Erie team moved to Niles, Ohio, where they are known as the Mahoning Valley Scrappers. That same year, the Watertown, New York, team relocated to Staten Island. For the 2000 season, the St. Catharines team moved from its home in Ontario, Canada, to Queens, New York. The following year, the Queens Kings became the Brooklyn Cyclones after settling in a new facility in Brooklyn, New York. In 2002, two New York-Penn League teams moved. The Pittsfield, Massachusetts, team relocated to Troy, New York, and became the Tri-City ValleyCats. The Utica team was sold to Ripken Professional Baseball, LLC, which is owned by former Baltimore Oriole, Cal Ripken Jr. Ripken moved the team to his hometown, Aberdeen, Maryland, and named the team the Aberdeen IronBirds[60] (see Table 4.3a).

There were eight name changes during this time as well. The Auburn Astros changed their name to the Auburn Doubledays in 1996 and the Batavia Clippers became the Batavia Muckdogs in 1998. After affiliating with the Pittsburgh Pirates, the Williamsport Cubs became known as the Williamsport Crosscutters in 1999. In addition, when the New York Mets switched their New York-Penn League team affiliation to the new Brooklyn Cyclones for the 2001 season, the Pittsfield Mets

TABLE 4.3a. Name Changes and Franchise Relocations in the New York-Penn League, 1995-2002

1995	1996	1997	1998	1999	2000	2001	2002
Auburn Astros	Auburn **Doubledays**	Auburn Doubledays	Auburn Doubledays	Auburn Doubledays	Auburn Doubledays	Auburn Doubledays	Auburn Doubledays
Batavia Clippers	Batavia Clippers	Batavia Clippers	Batavia **Muckdogs**	Batavia Muckdogs	Batavia Muckdogs	Batavia Muckdogs	Batavia Muckdogs
Elmira Pioneers	**Lowell Spinners**	Lowell Spinners	Lowell Spinners	Lowell Spinners	Lowell Spinners	Lowell Spinners	Lowell Spinners
Erie SeaWolves	Erie SeaWolves	Erie SeaWolves	Erie SeaWolves	**Mahoning Valley Scrappers**	Mahoning Valley Scrappers	Mahoning Valley Scrappers	Mahoning Valley Scrappers
Hudson Valley Renegades	Hudson Valley Renegades	Hudson Valley Renegades	Hudson Valley Renegades	Hudson Valley Renegades	Hudson Valley Renegades	Hudson Valley Renegades	Hudson Valley Renegades
Jamestown Jammers	Jamestown Jammers	Jamestown Jammers	Jamestown Jammers	Jamestown Jammers	Jamestown Jammers	Jamestown Jammers	Jamestown Jammers
New Jersey Cardinals	New Jersey Cardinals	New Jersey Cardinals	New Jersey Cardinals	New Jersey Cardinals	New Jersey Cardinals	New Jersey Cardinals	New Jersey Cardinals
Oneonta Yankees	Oneonta Yankees	Oneonta Yankees	Oneonta Yankees	Oneonta **Tigers**	Oneonta Tigers	Oneonta Tigers	Oneonta Tigers
Pittsfield Mets	Pittsfield Mets	Pittsfield Mets	Pittsfield Mets	Pittsfield Mets	Pittsfield Mets	Pittsfield **Astros**	**Tri-City ValleyCats**
St. Catharines Stompers	St. Catharines Stompers	St. Catharines Stompers	St. Catharines Stompers	St. Catharines Stompers	**Queens Kings**	**Brooklyn Cyclones**	Brooklyn Cyclones
Utica Blue Sox	Utica Blue **Martins**	Utica Blue **Sox**	Utica Blue Sox	Utica Blue Sox	Utica Blue Sox	Utica Blue Sox	**Aberdeen IronBirds**
Vermont Expos	Vermont Expos	Vermont Expos	Vermont Expos	Vermont Expos	Vermont Expos	Vermont Expos	Vermont Expos

TABLE 4.3a (continued)

1995	1996	1997	1998	1999	2000	2001	2002
Watertown Indians	Watertown Indians	Watertown Indians	Watertown Indians	**Staten Island Yankees**	Staten Island Yankees	Staten Island Yankees	Staten Island Yankees
Williamsport Cubs	Williamsport Cubs	Williamsport Cubs	Williamsport Cubs	Williamsport **Crosscutters**	Williamsport Crosscutters	Williamsport Crosscutters	Williamsport Crosscutters
Total name changes	3	1	1	2	0	1	0
Total team moves	1	0	0	2	1	1	2

Source: Compiled from: *Baseball America 1995 Directory* (Durham, NC: Baseball America, Inc., 1995); *Baseball America 1996 Directory* (Durham, NC: Baseball America, Inc., 1996); *Baseball America 1997 Directory* (Durham, NC: Baseball America, Inc., 1997); *Baseball America 1998 Directory* (Durham, NC: Baseball America, Inc., 1998); *Baseball America 1999 Directory* (Durham, NC: Baseball America, Inc., 1999); *Baseball America 2000 Directory* (Durham, NC: Baseball America, Inc., 2000); *Baseball America 2001 Directory* (Durham, NC: Baseball America, Inc., 2001); *Baseball America 2002 Directory* (Durham, NC: Baseball America, Inc., 2002).
Note: Changes are in bold.

became a Houston farm team and changed its name to the Pittsfield Astros (see Tables 4.3a and 4.3b).

In the less-established independent leagues, franchise shifts appear to occur more often. The Frontier League has experienced many changes since its establishment in 1993. In ten seasons, there have been ten franchise relocations, four new teams (one from a disbanded league), and three name changes. The 2000 season was the only season in which no changes occurred (see Table 4.4).

During the league's first year in operation, the teams in Ashland, Kentucky, and Wayne County, West Virginia, disbanded before the end of the season. The next year, those teams were replaced with new teams, the Newark Buffalos and the Erie Sailors. However, the Erie team moved to Johnstown for the 1995 season, and the Newark team changed its name to the Newark Bison. Also in 1995, the Lancaster team moved to Evansville, Indiana, and the Kentucky Rifles were replaced by the Richmond Roosters. In 1996, two teams moved. The Portsmouth Explorers relocated to Springfield, Illinois, where they became the Springfield Capitals, and the Newark Bison moved to Michigan and changed their name to the Kalamazoo Kodiaks[61] (see Table 4.4).

In 1997, the Eastern League left Canton, Ohio, for a new stadium in Akron. Thus, Thurman Munson Memorial Stadium was available for a new team and the Frontier League approved the addition of a new franchise. To make room for the new team, the Zanesville team did not play that year or in 1998. In 1999 the Zanesville franchise was sold and relocated to O'Fallon, Missouri, as the River City Rascals.[62]

Two other Frontier League franchises relocated in 1999. The Ohio Valley Redcoats moved from Parkersburg, West Virginia, to Huntingburg, Indiana, to become the Dubois County Dragons. The Kalamazoo Kodiaks of Kalamazoo, Michigan, relocated to London, Ontario, and became the London Werewolves. Also in 1999, the league added two new teams in Illinois: the Gateway Grizzlies of Collinsville and the Cook County Cheetahs of Crestwood.[63]

There were no changes in the league for the 2000 season, and the only change in 2001 was the addition of a new team, the Kalamazoo Kings, as the league returned to Kalamazoo, Michigan. However, in 2002, there were several changes as one team changed its name and two teams relocated. The Canton Crocodiles became the Canton Coyotes for the 2002 season, while the Springfield Cardinals and the

TABLE 4.3b. Affiliation Changes in the New York-Penn League, 1995-2002

Team	1995	1996	1997	1998	1999	2000	2001	2002
Auburn	Astros	Astros	Astros	Astros	Astros	Astros	**Blue Jays**	Blue Jays
Batavia	Phillies	Phillies	Phillies	Phillies	Phillies	Phillies	Phillies	Phillies
Elmira/Lowell	Marlins	**Red Sox**	Red Sox	Red Sox	Red Sox	Red Sox	Red Sox	Red Sox
Erie/Mahoning Valley	Pirates	Pirates	Pirates	Pirates	**Indians**	Indians	Indians	Indians
Hudson Valley	Rangers	Rangers	Devil Rays	Devil Rays	Devil Rays	Devil Rays	Devil Rays	Devil Rays
Jamestown	Tigers	Tigers	Tigers	Tigers	**Braves**	Braves	Braves	**Marlins**
New Jersey	Cardinals	Cardinals	Cardinals	Cardinals	Cardinals	Cardinals	Cardinals	Cardinals
Oneonta	Yankees	Yankees	Yankees	Yankees	**Tigers**	Tigers	Tigers	Tigers
Pittsfield/Tri-City	Mets	Mets	Mets	Mets	Mets	Mets	**Astros**	Astros
St. Catharines/Queens/Brooklyn	Blue Jays	Blue Jays	Blue Jays	Blue Jays	Blue Jays	Blue Jays	**Mets**	Mets
Utica/Aberdeen	Red Sox	**Marlins**	Marlins	Marlins	Marlins	Marlins	Marlins	**Orioles**
Vermont	Expos	Expos	Expos	Expos	Expos	Expos	Expos	Expos
Watertown/Staten Island	Indians	Indians	Indians	Indians	**Yankees**	Yankees	Yankees	Yankees
Williamsport	Cubs	Cubs	Cubs	Cubs	**Pirates**	Pirates	Pirates	Pirates
Total changes	0	2	1	0	5	0	3	2

Source: Compiled from: *Baseball America 1995 Directory* (Durham, NC: Baseball America, Inc., 1995); *Baseball America 1996 Directory* (Durham, NC: Baseball America, Inc., 1996); *Baseball America 1997 Directory* (Durham, NC: Baseball America, Inc., 1997); *Baseball America 1998 Directory* (Durham, NC: Baseball America, Inc., 1998); *Baseball America 1999 Directory* (Durham, NC: Baseball America, Inc., 1999); *Baseball America 2000 Directory* (Durham, NC: Baseball America, Inc., 2000); *Baseball America 2001 Directory* (Durham, NC: Baseball America, Inc., 2001); *Baseball America 2002 Directory* (Durham, NC: Baseball America, Inc., 2002).
Note: Changes are in bold.

TABLE 4.4. Name Changes and Franchise Relocations in the Frontier League, 1993-2002

1993	1994	1995	1996	1997	1998	1999	2000	2001	2002
Chillicothe Paints	Chillicothe Paints	Chillicothe Paints	Chillicothe Paints	Chillicothe Paints	Chillicothe Paints	Chillicothe Paints	Chillicothe Paints	Chillicothe Paints	Chillicothe Paints
Kentucky Rifles	Kentucky Rifles	**Richmond Roosters**	Richmond Roosters	Richmond Roosters	Richmond Roosters	Richmond Roosters	Richmond Roosters	Richmond Roosters	Richmond Roosters
Lancaster Scouts	Lancaster Scouts	**Evansville Otters**	Evansville Otters	Evansville Otters	Evansville Otters	Evansville Otters	Evansville Otters	Evansville Otters	Evansville Otters
Ohio Valley Redcoats	Ohio Valley Redcoats	Ohio Valley Redcoats	Ohio Valley Redcoats	Ohio Valley Redcoats	Ohio Valley Redcoats	**Dubois County Dragons**	Dubois County Dragons	Dubois County Dragons	Dubois County Dragons
Portsmouth Explorers	Portsmouth Explorers	Portsmouth Explorers	**Springfield Capitals**	Springfield Capitals	Springfield Capitals	Springfield Capitals	Springfield Capitals	Springfield Capitals	**Rockford Riverhawks**
Tri-State Tomahawks*	**Newark Buffalos**	Newark **Bison**	**Kalamazoo Kodiaks**	Kalamazoo Kodiaks	Kalamazoo Kodiaks	**London Werewolves**	London Werewolves	London Werewolves	**Washington Wild Things**
West Virginia Coal Sox*	**Erie Sailors**	**Johnstown Steal**	Johnstown Steal	Johnstown Steal	**Johnstown Johnnies**	Johnstown Johnnies	Johnstown Johnnies	Johnstown Johnnies	Johnstown Johnnies
Zanesville Greys	Zanesville Greys	Zanesville Greys	Zanesville Greys	Did not play	Did not play	**River City Rascals**	River City Rascals	River City Rascals	River City Rascals
				Canton Crocodiles**	Canton Crocodiles	Canton Crocodiles	Canton Crocodiles	Canton Crocodiles	Canton **Coyotes**
						Gateway Grizzlies**	Gateway Grizzlies	Gateway Grizzlies	Gateway Grizzlies
						Cook County Cheetahs***	Cook County Cheetahs	Cook County Cheetahs	Cook County Cheetahs
								Kalamazoo Kings**	Kalamazoo Kings

109

TABLE 4.4 (continued)

Name changes	0	1	0	0	1	0	0	1
Team moves	0	3	2	0	0	3	0	2
New/returning teams	2	0	0	1	0	2	1	0
Teams leaving or not playing	2	0	0	1	0	0	0	0

Source: Compiled from: *Baseball America 1995 Directory* (Durham, NC: Baseball America, Inc., 1995); *Baseball America 1996 Directory* (Durham, NC: Baseball America, Inc., 1996); *Baseball America 1997 Directory* (Durham, NC: Baseball America, Inc., 1997); *Baseball America 1998 Directory* (Durham, NC: Baseball America, Inc., 1998); *Baseball America 1999 Directory* (Durham, NC: Baseball America, Inc., 1999); *Baseball America 2000 Directory* (Durham, NC: Baseball America, Inc., 2000); *Baseball America 2001 Directory* (Durham, NC: Baseball America, Inc., 2001); *Baseball America 2002 Directory* (Durham, NC: Baseball America, Inc., 2002).
Note: Changes are in bold.
*Disbanded July 12
**New team
***Expansion team (formerly in the Heartland League)

London Werewolves became the Rockford Riverhawks and the Washington Wild Things. The Springfield team remained in Illinois but moved to Rockford. The London, Ontario, team, however, emigrated from Canada to the United States, relocating in Washington, Pennsylvania.[64]

CORPORATE SPONSORSHIP

Corporate sponsorship has long been a part of baseball, from Little League to the major leagues. In the minors, outdoor advertising, particularly on the outfield fences, adds to the feeling of nostalgia deliberately created by owners and marketing experts. However, following major league professional sports, a recent trend in Minor League Baseball is corporate sponsorship in the form of naming rights for stadiums.

As new stadiums are being built, national corporations have partnered with minor league teams to help finance construction. Companies purchase the naming rights for a stadium for a set number of years, thus providing the needed funds to build new ballparks. For example, the Lansing Lugnuts of Lansing, Michigan, have played in the appropriately sponsored Oldsmobile Park since 1996. In 1999, AutoZone, Inc. entered into an agreement with the Memphis Redbirds of the Pacific Coast League to name their new downtown ballpark AutoZone Park. The company will pay a total of $4.3 million for exclusive naming rights to the stadium through the 2025 season.[65] In Buffalo, New York, the Bisons' ballpark, named Pilot Field when it opened in 1988, has changed its identity twice. The name of the stadium was changed in 1996 to North AmeriCare Park to reflect new sponsorship, and to Dunn Tire Park in 1999.[66]

CONCLUSION

The minor leagues have had a long and exciting history, and continue to play an important part in the community. The zaniness and quaintness of the minor leagues have added to the nostalgic quality of the aura surrounding the game. Each minor league town and stadium has its own flavor and rituals that keeps the fans, and tourists, coming:

the view of the Mississippi River in Cohen Stadium in Davenport, Iowa; the drive-in parking in Albuquerque, New Mexico; the guitar-shaped scoreboard in Nashville, Tennessee; and the ritual shaking of the keys at a Frederick, Maryland, Keys game, to highlight just a few.

Various writers have remarked on the unique attraction of Minor League Baseball. Lamb wrote that in minor league towns there is "an atmosphere of informality and intimacy, a sense of rediscovering a part of America you thought had disappeared with your youth."[67] Such sentiments have added to the lore of Minor League Baseball.

Because the standard measures of costs, salaries, and ticket sales used for other professional sports cannot be used for predicting the success and amount of fan support of a minor league team, other factors must be considered in developing a model of the impact of Minor League Baseball on the community. Quality of life and other social and economic variables could help explain the importance and survival of Minor League Baseball in the community.

The changes in the role of Minor League Baseball within the community may be reflected in the impact of teams on their communities over the years. In the years in which Minor League Baseball was most successful and popular, quality of life in minor league towns may have been relatively high. During the years in which Minor League Baseball had little following, quality of life may have been lower in minor league communities. The business orientation and financial success of teams in the 1980s may have had an alienating effect, thus suggesting a negative relationship to quality of life. However, the minor leagues' emphasis on community and family during the 1980s and 1990s may be related to a better quality of life.

Chapter 5

A Tale of Two Minor League Cities

Every minor league town has its own story to tell. Some cities have seen teams and leagues come and go throughout the years, and others are relatively new to the minors. All are different, reflecting the residents and the team itself. Each city has had a different social, cultural, and economic relationship with its team and a unique story to tell.

To show statistically that the presence of a minor league team has some special effect on a city, I created a database comprising not only demographic data, but baseball data: the number of years a team was in a community, the league it was in, whether it switched leagues, if a team left town and replaced another one, etc. (See Appendix B for a discussion of the data set used in this study.) I attempted to show statistically that there was more to Minor League Baseball than just ticket sales and merchandising profits, and to prove unequivocally that even if a town's investment in a stadium showed little profit, there was still a positive gain in terms of community spirit and quality of life.

I created an elaborate model and spent over a year running regressions to "prove" my theory. However, just as community spirit and quality of life are elusive concepts that are difficult to measure, so is Minor League Baseball. Baseball enthusiasts and owners collect all sorts of statistics—batting averages, earned run averages, annual attendance, etc.—but who measures community spirit and love of the game? Although my longitudinal model of baseball was a good start and provided a solid statistical understanding of minor league communities, there was still more to be learned. My study concluded that a statistical relationship exists between town and team. But, in some ways, this analysis led to more questions.

To measure the relationship between a city and its Minor League Baseball team, I chose two cities to analyze in detail—Hagerstown and Bowie, Maryland. The first has a long history with Minor League

Baseball, the latter is a relative newcomer. Both case studies, however, show how Minor League Baseball becomes intertwined in the history of the towns and a part of the community.

BASEBALL AS A MARYLAND TRADITION

To place the two teams in perspective, let's first look at their home state, Maryland. The Baltimore Orioles are not the only game in town, or the state, as the case may be. Maryland has hosted many teams. Even before the NAPBL, Baltimore was home to many semi-pro, major league, and minor league teams in the late 1800s, including the Maryland Base Ball Club, the Lord Baltimores, the Monumentals, and the Baltimore Orioles.[1] In 1903, a team from Montreal, Quebec, moved to Baltimore and became the Baltimore Orioles. The team played in American League Park on Greenmount Avenue, which would become known as Oriole Park. In 1908, the Orioles were upgraded to Class AA. (AA teams were reclassified as AAA in 1963.) Babe Ruth joined the team in 1914.[2]

Because of competition from the rival Federal League, the Baltimore Orioles owner, Jack Dunn, moved the team to Richmond for the 1915 season. Dunn sold the team, which would remain in Richmond, and purchased the Jersey City franchise and moved it to Baltimore in 1916. This new Oriole team played across the street from Oriole Park in Terrapin Park. From 1919 to 1925, the Orioles finished in first place, winning the Little World Series in 1920, 1922, and 1925. The team won the Little World Series again in 1944.[3]

The minor league Orioles moved to Memorial Stadium in 1950, which had been renovated to attract a major league team. In 1954, Baltimore became a major league town when the American League Browns moved from St. Louis to Charm City. The minor league team was sold and again moved to Richmond.[4] Baltimore briefly rejoined the minors in 1993 when it hosted the Bowie Baysox at Memorial Stadium.

Other leagues have called Maryland their home as well. The Class D Pennsylvania-Ohio-Maryland League fielded a team in Cumberland for the 1906 season. A Western Pennsylvania League (Class D) team briefly played in Cumberland the following season when the Cumberland Rooters moved to Cumberland after the start of the season. The Rooters remained in Cumberland through June when they moved to Piedmont, West Virginia, before finally settling in Somerset, Pennsylvania. In 1916 the ill-fated Class D Potomac League organized teams in Cumberland, Frostburg, and Lonaconing, Maryland (and Piedmont, West Virginia). The league disbanded on August 16, 1916, without completing the season.[5]

From 1915 to 1918, and again from 1920 to 1930, the Blue Ridge League, Class D, operated in Maryland, Pennsylvania, and West Virginia. The Frederick Hustlers played from 1915 to 1917, and returned in 1920, after the league's one-year hiatus in 1919. The team played in Frederick until 1930, when the league disbanded. The Cumberland Colts joined the Blue Ridge League in 1917 and disbanded with the league in 1918. The Piedmont (West Virginia)/Westernport (Maryland) Drybugs also played during the 1918 season. The Hagerstown Blues, Hubs, and Terriers played in the league in 1915, 1916, and 1917, respectively. Hagerstown hosted Blue Ridge League teams again from 1920 to 1930. Cumberland and Hagerstown also hosted Middle Atlantic League (Class C) teams in the 1920s and 1930s. The Cumberland Rooters played from 1925 to 1932. The Hagerstown Terriers joined the league for the 1931 season.[6]

The Class D Eastern Shore League (ESL) operated Maryland teams during three periods: 1922-1928, 1937-1941, and 1946-1949. Cambridge and Salisbury fielded teams during all sixteen years. The other Maryland cities hosting ESL teams were Centreville (1937-1941, 1946); Crisfield (1922-1928, 1937); Easton (1924-1928, 1937-1941, 1946-1949); Federalsburg (1937-1941, 1946-1949); and Pocomoke City (1922-1923, 1937-1940).[7] The teams showcased such future major league players as Frank "Home Run" Baker (Easton Yankees, 1949); Jimmy Foxx (Easton Farmers, 1924); Carl Furillo (Pocomoke City Chicks, 1940); and Don Zimmer (Cambridge Dodgers, 1949).[8]

In the 1940s and 1950s, the Class B Interstate League operated in Maryland. Hagerstown hosted a team from 1941 to 1952, and Salisbury hosted one from 1951 to 1952. When the league disbanded after the 1952 season, the Hagerstown Braves joined the Class B Piedmont League. The team was renamed the Packets in 1954 and disbanded with the league after the 1955 season.[9]

After almost thirty years, Minor League Baseball returned to Maryland in 1981, with the Hagerstown Suns of the Class A Carolina League, a Baltimore Orioles affiliate. The Suns were moved up to the Class AA Eastern League in 1989, when the Carolina League team moved to Frederick. The Frederick team was renamed the Keys in honor of Frederick native, Francis Scott Key. The Keys played in McCurdy Field in 1989 and moved to its new facility, Harry Grove Stadium, in 1990. The Keys have remained an Oriole affiliate ever since.[10]

In 1993, the Class AA Hagerstown team moved to Bowie. In the same year, a South Atlantic League (Class A) team relocated to Hagerstown and was renamed the Suns. Salisbury, Maryland, joined the South Atlantic League in 1996, with the Delmarva Shorebirds, an Orioles affiliate.[11] Table 5.1 presents a brief look at the Maryland cities that have hosted minor league teams over the years.

HAGERSTOWN, MARYLAND

When I first visited Municipal Stadium in Hagerstown, I was in awe. It is an old-fashioned stadium, with metal and wooden stands, complete with a mural of Babe Ruth in the outfield. It is nostalgic baseball at its best. As I sat in the stands I absorbed the excitement of the game. It reminded me why I love Minor League Baseball so much.

Hagerstown, Maryland, is a medium-sized town in Washington County in western Maryland, approximately seventy-five miles from Washington, DC, and six miles south of the Mason-Dixon Line. According to Fodor's *Ballpark Vacations* guide: "Hagerstown oozes old-time baseball and small-town charm."[12] Similarly, *Washington Post* writer Paul Hendrickson states that entering the stadium in Hagerstown is like "inhaling Cooperstown."[13]

Hagerstown, nicknamed the "Hub City," has always been known as a crossroads town. Formerly called Elizabethtown, the city was founded in 1762 by Jonathan Hager. Hager established his city at the intersection of two colonial roads in the Cumberland Valley. The city became the county seat in 1796 and was incorporated in 1813. By the end of the nineteenth century the railroad came to town and Hagerstown became a booming industrial city as well as an agricultural, trade, and government center.[14]

TABLE 5.1. Maryland Minor League Baseball Towns, 1902-Present

City	Leagues (Level)	Years
Aberdeen	New York-Penn League (A)	2002-present
Baltimore	Eastern League (A)	1903-1907
	Eastern League (AA)	1908-1911
	International League (AA)	1912-1914, 1916-1945
	International League (AAA)	1946-1953
Bowie	Eastern League (AA)	1993-present
Cambridge	Eastern Shore League (D)	1922-1928, 1937-1941, 1946-1949
Centreville	Eastern Shore League (D)	1937-1941, 1946
Crisfield	Eastern Shore League (D)	1922-1928, 1937
Cumberland	Pennsylvania-Ohio-Maryland League (D)	1906
	Western Pennsylvania League (D)	1907
	Potomac League (D)	1916
	Blue Ridge League (D)	1917-1918
	Middle Atlantic League (C)	1925-1932
Easton	Eastern Shore League (D)	1924-1928, 1937-1941, 1946-1949
Federalsburg	Eastern Shore League (D)	1937-1941, 1946-1949
Frederick	Blue Ridge League (D)	1915-1917, 1920-1930
	Carolina League (A)	1989-present
Frostburg	Potomac League (D)	1916
Hagerstown	Blue Ridge League (D)	1915-1918, 1920-1930
	Middle Atlantic League (C)	1931
	Interstate League (B)	1941-1951
	Piedmont League (B)	1953-1955
	Carolina League (A)	1981-1988
	Eastern League (AA)	1989-1993
	South Atlantic League (A)	1993-present
Hanover	Blue Ridge League (D)	1915-1917, 1920-1929
Lonaconing	Potomac League (D)	1916
Pocomoke City	Eastern Shore League (D)	1922-1923, 1937-1940
Salisbury	Eastern Shore League (D)	1922-1928, 1937-1941, 1946-1949
	Interstate League (D)	1951-1952
	South Atlantic League (A)	1996-present
Westernport	Blue Ridge League (D)	1918

Source: Compiled from Lloyd Johnson and Miles Wolff, eds., *The Encyclopedia of Minor League Baseball,* Second Edition (Durham, NC: Baseball America, Inc., 1997), p. 74.

Hagerstown was transformed "economically, architecturally and culturally" between 1880 and 1940.[15] During that time, the population of the city increased five times as the town transformed into

> a bustling industrial and manufacturing base, supporting machine shops, airplane, automobile, furniture and organ manufacturers, as well as home to a plethora of shops and hotels needed to serve passengers, crews and itinerant salesmen who plied their trade by rail.... The community changed structurally as well. Numerous new neighborhoods and additions to the town sprung up to accommodate the rapid population influx. Today, the city's predominant architectural styles echo the period representing the strongest influence of Hagerstown's railroad industry.[16]

Indeed, according to the city's Web site, "Hagerstown today is a window to turn-of-the-century America."[17] Yet by the 1980s, Hagerstown was struggling, trying to bounce back from economic recession.[18]

The changing fortunes of Hagerstown are reflected in its Minor League Baseball history. Given Maryland's rich baseball history, minor league ball was nothing new when the Blue Ridge League arrived in Hagerstown in 1915. Hagerstown hosted a Class D Blue Ridge League team from 1915 to 1918, and from 1920 to 1930 (the league disbanded during the 1919 season). The team was named the Hagerstown Blues in 1915, and renamed the Terriers in 1916.[19]

The Hagerstown Champs returned to the city when the league started up again in 1920.[20] The team was renamed the Hagerstown Terriers in 1922, and the Hubs in 1924. The Hagerstown Hubs moved up to the Class C Middle Atlantic League for the 1931 season. However, the team moved to Parkersburg, West Virginia, on June 28, 1931, and then to Youngstown, Ohio, on July 12, where it finished out the season.[21] (Blue Ridge Teams were located in Chambersburg, Gettysburg, and Waynesboro, Pennsylvania; Martinsburg and Piedmont, West Virginia; and Cumberland, Frederick, Hagerstown, Hanover, and Westernport, Maryland. See Table 5.2 for a summary of the Blue Ridge League teams from 1915 to 1930.)

From 1941 to 1949, the city hosted the Hagerstown Owls of the Class B Interstate League. The team was renamed the Braves in 1950, and remained in the Interstate League until the league disbanded after

TABLE 5.2. Teams in the Blue Ridge League, 1915-1930

Year	Chambersburg	Cumberland	Frederick	Gettysburg	Hagerstown	Hanover	Martinsburg	Piedmont/ Westernport	Waynesboro
1915	Maroons	—	Hustlers	Patriots	Blues	Hornets	Champs	—	
1916	Maroons	—	Hustlers	Ponies	Terriers	Raiders	Blue Sox	—	
1917	Maroons*	Colts*	Hustlers	Ponies	Terriers	Raiders	Blue Sox	—	
1918	—	Colts	—	—	Terriers	—	Mountaineers	Drybugs	
1920	Maroons	—	Hustlers	—	Champs	Raiders	Mountaineers	—	Red Birds
1921	Marooners	—	Hustlers	—	Champs	Raiders	Mountaineers	—	Villagers
1922	Maroons	—	Hustlers	—	Terriers	Raiders	Blue Sox	—	Villagers
1923	Maroons	—	Hustlers	—	Terriers	Raiders	Blue Sox	—	Villagers
1924	Maroons	—	Hustlers	—	Hubs	Raiders	Blue Sox	—	Villagers
1925	Maroons	—	Hustlers	—	Hubs	Raiders	Blue Sox	—	Red Birds
1926	Maroons	—	Hustlers	—	Hubs	Raiders	Blue Sox	—	Villagers
1927	Maroons	—	Hustlers	—	Hubs	Raiders	Blue Sox	—	Villagers
1928	Maroons	—	Hustlers	—	Hubs	Raiders	Blue Sox	—	Red Birds
1929	Young Yanks	—	Warriors	—	Hubs	Raiders	Blue Sox	—	Red Birds
1930	Young Yanks	—	Warriors	—	Hubs	—	—	—	Red Birds

Source: Compiled from Lloyd Johnson and Miles Wolff, eds., *The Encyclopedia of Minor League Baseball*, Second Edition (Durham, NC: Baseball America, Inc., 1997), p. 11.
*Chambersburg moved to Cumberland on June 30, 1917.

the 1952 season. During the 1950 season, Willie Mays made his minor league debut at Hagerstown for the visiting Trenton Giants.[22] Mays also broke the color barrier for the Interstate League that year, a situation for which many cities, including Hagerstown, were unprepared.[23]

Hagerstown joined the Class B Piedmont League in 1953. The team was renamed the Packets in 1954. The Piedmont league disbanded after the 1955 season,[24] and Hagerstown was left without a team until the Hagerstown Suns, an affiliate of the Baltimore Orioles, joined the Class A Carolina League in 1981. The 1981 team was a "co-op" team affiliated with six major league teams.[25] The return of Minor League Baseball to the city after a twenty-six-year absence drew a crowd of 2,463 on opening day, despite an incompletely renovated stadium.[26] To lure the new team, the city and the state invested $550,000 into the stadium, which covered the costs of renovating the stadium and adding new clubhouses, offices, and rest rooms.[27]

The Suns were moved up to the Class AA Eastern League in 1989, after the Baltimore Orioles moved their Class A Carolina League team down the road to Frederick, and transferred their AA team from Charlotte, North Carolina, to Hagerstown. After the 1992 season, the team moved to Bowie, where a new baseball facility was being built for them. In 1993, the Myrtle Beach Hurricanes of the Class A South Atlantic League relocated to Hagerstown and were renamed the Suns.[28] Between 1993 and 2000, the Suns were affiliated with the Toronto Blue Jays. For the 2001 season, the Suns became a Pittsburgh Pirates' farm team.[29]

Changes in the economic and demographic landscape of the city may explain some of the baseball transformations experienced by the city in the 1980s, as it struggled to hold on to its team. The population of Hagerstown increased by only 10.1 percent between 1980 and 1992, and the state average was 16.6 percent. The nearby city of Frederick, in Frederick County, experienced a population growth rate of 54.5 percent. In 1989, the median income in Hagerstown was only $27,912, compared to the statewide median income of $45,934. (Incidentally, median income in the city of Bowie that year was $61,844—no wonder they were ready for a minor league team just a few years later!) The unemployment and poverty rates were also somewhat high in Hagerstown at the end of the 1980s. The unemployment rate in the city was around 11 percent in the early 1990s, and 13 percent of all Hagerstown families lived in poverty. These rates were approximately double the state rates at the time—statewide, the unemployment rate was 5.9 percent and the poverty rate was 6 percent.[30]

Throughout the 1980s and 1990s there were rumblings about building a new stadium in Hagerstown to convince a team to stay in town or to attract another team to the area.[31] Despite attendance being higher in the 1980s and 1990s than it was in the 1950s, when attendance figures hovered between 50,000 and 80,000,[32] the aging—yet charming—Hagerstown Municipal Stadium, built in 1930, was no match for the newer stadiums cropping up in Maryland during the 1990s (see Figure 5.1 for a comparison of attendance in Hagerstown and Bowie).

Despite the ups and downs of both community and team, baseball and Municipal Stadium are an important part of Hagerstown's history and community.

With a population of 36,687 (see Table 5.3), Hagerstown remains a strong minor league town, not only because of its long history of Minor League Baseball, but also because it is just that type of smaller,

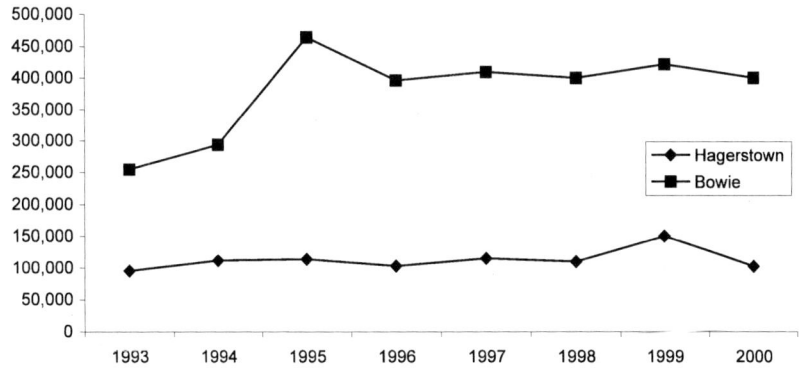

FIGURE 5.1. Attendance in Hagerstown and Bowie, 1993-2000. *Source:* Compiled from *Baseball America 1993 Directory* (Durham, NC: Baseball America, Inc., 1993); *Baseball America 1994 Directory* (Durham, NC: Baseball America, Inc., 1994); *Baseball America 1995 Directory* (Durham, NC: Baseball America, Inc., 1995); *Baseball America 1996 Directory* (Durham, NC: Baseball America, Inc., 1996); *Baseball America 1997 Directory* (Durham, NC: Baseball America, Inc., 1997); *Baseball America 1998 Directory* (Durham, NC: Baseball America, Inc., 1998); *Baseball America 1999 Directory* (Durham, NC: Baseball America, Inc., 1999); *Baseball America 2000 Directory* (Durham, NC: Baseball America, Inc., 2000).

TABLE 5.3. Hagerstown and Washington County Population, by Race and Ethnicity, 2000

Population Characteristic	Hagerstown		Washington County	
	Total	Percent	Total	Percent
Total Population	36,687	100.0	131,923	100.0
One Race	36,017	98.2	130,550	99.0
White	31,532	85.9	118,348	89.7
Black or African American	3,722	10.1	10,247	7.8
American Indian or Alaska Native	90	0.2	239	0.2
Asian	354	1.0	1,050	0.8
Native Hawaiian or Other Pacific Islander	15	0.0	55	0.0
Other	304	0.8	611	0.5
Two or More Races	670	1.8	1,373	1.0
Ethnicity				
Latino (any race)	649	1.8	1,570	1.2

Note: Due to rounding, percentages do not add up to 100.
Source: Compiled from U.S. Census Bureau, American Factfinder, Quick Tables, "DP-1. Profile of General Demographic Characteristics: 2000," for Hagerstown City, Maryland, and Washington County, Maryland, accessed at <http://factfinder.census.gov>.

independent town that we imagine a Minor League Baseball town to be. Though near the bottom in attendance in the South Atlantic League, the Hagerstown Suns continue to draw over 100,000 fans per season.[33]

BOWIE, MARYLAND

Baseball is an important part of community life in Bowie, Maryland. There used to be a mural of Prince George's Stadium in the Bowie Wal-Mart. Wendy's is decorated with baseball posters, and the grocery stores and dry cleaners proudly display Bowie Baysox schedules. Even a model home in a new development was decorated in a baseball motif.

In a sense, the Hagerstown Minor League Baseball tradition was continued in Bowie, when the Hagerstown Suns moved to a new stadium in Prince George's County and became the Bowie Baysox. In 1993, the team played in Baltimore's Memorial Stadium, former home of the Baltimore Orioles, as it awaited the completion of its new stadium, which opened in 1994.

The new stadium was only part of a recent economic boom experienced by the city in the 1990s, which is expected to continue into the new century. During the 1990s the city grew by almost 25 percent.[34] By 2000, it had become the fourth largest city in the state of Maryland.[35] It has come a long way from a small railroad community to a legitimate Minor League Baseball town.

Bowie was founded in 1870 and incorporated as Huntington in 1874. The town was originally subdivided into 500 housing lots to create a town at a junction of the Baltimore and Potomac Railroad's main line to southern Maryland. Later, the town changed its name in honor of Maryland Governor Ogden Bowie, also a president of the railroad.[36]

In 1957, the building firm of Levitt and Sons acquired nearby Belair Estate, which originally was a colonial plantation of Samuel Ogle. The Belair Estate also was known for the Belair Stable, which was one of the premier racehorse stables from the 1930s to the 1950s. It was there that Levitt and Sons developed the residential Levittown community known as "Belair at Bowie." In 1959, the Town of Bowie annexed the Belair community, and in 1963, the town was reincorporated as the city of Bowie.[37]

The city of Bowie stated that it "has the best that cities have to offer—responsive government, quiet neighborhoods, extensive parks and recreational activities, services for the young and old, municipal refuse collection and recycling, and its own water system."[38] (They forgot to include Minor League Baseball!) Bowie comprises an area of approximately sixteen square miles and is home to more than 50,000 residents.[39] During the 1990s, the communities witnessed not only the arrival of a new Minor League Baseball team and stadium, but the construction of several new shopping centers complete with restaurants, a movie theater, new office buildings, and residential housing from apartments to single-family homes. In 2000, the city opened a new senior center, and the following year a municipal gymnasium was opened next door to that. At the end of 2001, the city's new mall, Bowie Town Center, opened its doors. The mall covers 560,000 square feet and contains a variety of retail stores and restaurants including major department stores such as Sears and Hechts.[40] In 2002, construction was under way for a civic auditorium.[41]

Of course, all of Maryland has experienced economic and demographic growth. According to the Maryland Department of Business and Economic Development, the resident population of the state increased by 10.8 percent between 1990 and 2000. The population is expected to grow another 8 percent by the year 2010.[42] In addition, Prince George's County, which is home to the city of Bowie, is now one of the most populous counties in the state, second only to its neighbor, Montgomery County. The county has also grown more diverse, with the Hispanic population increasing by an astounding 90 percent, and the African-American population growing by 36 percent during the decade of the 1990s.[43] Table 5.4 presents the Census population data for the county and city.

TABLE 5.4. Bowie and Prince George's County Population by Race and Ethnicity, 2000

Population Characteristic	Bowie		Prince George's County	
	Total	Percent	Total	Percent
Total Population	50,269	100.0	801,515	100.0
One Race	49,111	98.2	780,631	97.4
White	31,492	62.6	216,729	27.0
Black or African American	15,500	30.8	502,550	62.7
American Indian or Alaska Native	150	0.3	2,795	0.3
Asian	1,482	2.9	31,032	3.9
Native Hawaiian or Other Pacific Islander	17	0.0	447	0.1
Other	470	0.9	27,078	3.4
Two or More Races	1,158	2.3	20,884	2.6
Ethnicity				
Latino (any race)	1,468	2.9	57,057	7.1

Note: Due to rounding, percentages do not add up to 100.
Source: Compiled from U.S. Census Bureau, American Factfinder, Quick Tables, "DP-1. Profile of General Demographic Characteristics: 2000," for Bowie City, Maryland, and Prince George's County, Maryland, accessed at <http://factfinder.census.gov>.

The city's motto of "Growth, Unity, and Progress" has been apparent in the changes being made around town. According to the city's Web site, Bowie "has grown from a small agricultural and railroad town to one of the largest and fastest growing cities in Maryland."[44] The city also proclaims that it "is a dynamic, family-oriented community whose residents enjoy an exceptional quality of life."

The team has done quite well in Bowie since its arrival in 1993 (see Figure 5.1). With attendance hovering around the 400,000 mark, the Bowie Baysox seem well integrated into the town and the league. In 2000, Bowie hosted the AA All-Star Game. Although it hasn't fared so well on the field recently, it has become a favorite place for city and county residents, as well as fans from nearby counties.

Chapter 6

The Impact of Minor League Baseball

In this book, I have attempted to present the theories on sports and community in light of the history and unique characteristics of Minor League Baseball, and I argue that it plays an important role within the community. My previous statistical analyses of the relationship between minor league teams and their towns (see Appendix B) provides some insight into the importance of the minors in the United States, yet more detailed data and further research are required to be able to determine the exact nature of the relationship between sports and community.

THEORY REVISITED

Recall from Chapter 3 that sociologists define community by the types of relationships and extent of interaction found within a system.[1] However, some theorists have suggested that in modern society people have become less tied to one another, resulting in a loss of community.[2] As government and other institutions take on many of the functions of society, people have fewer reasons to associate with or depend upon one another.[3] My theory, however, is that Minor League Baseball may counteract this trend by linking people together in communities. Minor league stadiums, as well as other stadiums, provide a common ground for local residents.[4] The *gemeinschaft*-like atmosphere of the stadium brings people together for a common purpose—the team and the community becoming a family. This symbiotic aspect of hosting a minor league team is an important element of community.[5]

At the stadium, people from a variety of backgrounds share a common purpose: to cheer for their team and enjoy the entertainment. Allies are made as people jointly support the team and either claim victory or comfort one another in defeat. People meet each other at the game and discuss it with those sitting around them. The traditions of the game and the sense of community are passed on from neighbor to neighbor and generation to generation as local residents support both team and community.

The games are relived in the local newspapers, and local businesses support the team with donations, discounts, and other forms of advertisement. Often team members and employees participate in community activities by making public appearances and meeting with community members and fans. All of these activities can integrate the community, as residents interact with the team and accept it as a representation of themselves and their community.

Further, the local stadium is often the site of many other community functions and community officials make public appearances at baseball games, which serves to link the team with the community. Community groups, such as youth sports teams and other youth groups, may be recognized or participate in the games in some way. In addition, many teams celebrate local events, such as the anniversary of a community's founding or the recognition of former players that are well known in the community. The team and the stadium also can become the focal point for the community in times of tragedy when residents are in need of comfort and support.

Such evidence is used by sports sociologists who argue that sports such as Minor League Baseball provide many positive functions for society, e.g., integration, and are important agents of socialization.[6] Many authors suggest that pride in one's community is reinforced through participating in and watching local sports.[7] The hometown team becomes symbolic of the community itself. Thus, supporting the team is an expression of community pride. As fans come together to cheer on their team, they are displaying community spirit as well.

Although this sense of community is recognized by sociologists and other scholars who have analyzed Minor League Baseball and other sports, it is not taken into consideration when measuring the impact of sports on the community.[8] However, social benefits such as increased community spirit and a high quality of life should be taken into consideration, along with economic benefits, when estimating the costs and benefits of hosting a minor league team. Further, given the small town, or *gemeinschaft,* atmosphere of many minor league communities, Minor League Baseball may have a greater impact than sports in large cities because a sense of community has already been established.

MINOR LEAGUE HISTORY

Any empirical data or statistical estimates of a team's contribution to the overall quality of life of a community must be analyzed in light of Minor League Baseball history. For example, during the first era of minor league history examined in this book—1946 to 1950—the minors experienced a postwar boom. The number of teams expanded rapidly. However, the industry could not sustain this level of prosperity and fell into a deep decline in the second era, which lasted from 1951 to 1962.

From 1963 to 1967, the minor leagues continued to experience a decline in attendance. During this time, however, the teams were largely subsidized by Major League Baseball teams, which owned minor league teams or operated them as farm teams for the development of players.

The minors fell into a period of indifference from 1968 to 1977. Although the number of teams, and therefore attendance, increased due to the addition of new major league teams, there was little interest in Minor League Baseball during that time. Many teams were sold or relocated throughout this period. As in the previous two periods, the unemployment rate was decreasing and the number of retail establishments was increasing in minor league communities.

The fifth era (1978 to 1990) saw a resurgence of popularity in Minor League Baseball. Teams became more valuable and attendance increased. Communities began to consider investment in minor league teams and facilities as economic-development tools. As the teams entered into the twenty-first century, the landscape of Minor League Baseball had changed dramatically, as had much of society. It may be too soon to evaluate the impact of the minors on today's society and communities, but it certainly seems to have taken hold and captivated the nation.

Although past statistical analyses of the impact of Minor League Baseball have shown contradictory results at best, specifying cause-and-effect relationships is not necessary to show a relationship between the minor leagues and quality of life. Regression results have shown a positive correlation between the presence of minor league teams and various measures of quality of life.

The relationship between Minor League Baseball and the quality of life of a community is more complex than a simple a cause-and-effect relationship, however.[9] The presence of a minor league team may add to an already high quality of life, as well as benefit from it. A team may provide more jobs and bring in more retail establishments, but perhaps not without an established, educated labor force to support economic development. Regardless, quality of life appears to be higher in communities with sports teams than in those without. It is not a coincidence that the majority of U.S. cities cosistently rated among the top places to live also host major league level professional sports and Minor League Baseball teams.[10]

HAGERSTOWN AND BOWIE: THEORY IN ACTION

The best way to examine the relationship between team and town is to experience firsthand the relationship between the two. When comparing the minor league experiences in Hagerstown and Bowie, Maryland, the first thing one notices is how different they are. Hagerstown has had a long history with Minor League Baseball, and Bowie has not. Hagerstown has gone through several of the Minor League Baseball eras: prosperity, decline, indifference, renaissance, and legitimization. Of note, the team that was in Hagerstown during the renaissance was the team that eventually moved to Bowie.

The baseball experience in both cities mirrors the economic times of each city. Hagerstown, once a booming, industrial city, has experienced a slight decline in recent years. At the same time, its stadium, built during the 1930s, is not in the same class as the newer and more modern facilities being used in other locales. In the past two decades, the city has lost both its Class A (Advanced) Carolina League franchise and its Class AA Eastern League franchise to cities with new stadiums (Frederick and Bowie). Today it hosts the Class A South Atlantic League Hagerstown Suns, yet every once in awhile there are intimations that the team may leave or the stadium will need to be renovated or other foreshadowings of doom. Nonetheless, Hagerstown remains a quiet, peaceful Western Maryland town with its Suns carrying on a long history of Minor League Baseball.

Bowie, on the other hand, appears to be on the move. Its population is booming, as is its economy. There is a lot in the city that is new, including its stadium and team; both have been there since 1993. As more families are drawn to the community, they are welcomed by wholesome, family entertainment in a state-of-the-art facility. Bowie was the perfect location for a minor league team during the era of legitimization, and it continues to be a good fit as the team and the community continue on into the twenty-first century.

CONCLUSION

Although questioned as an economic-development tool by various authors, the theories and examples highlighted in this book lend support to the assumption in the sociology of sports literature that sports provide intangible benefits to a community, such as improved community spirit and quality of life. Perhaps the cities themselves understand the impact better than the analysts. In a survey of cities that hosted Minor League Baseball teams in 1988, six benefits of having a team were noted: recreation for residents, economic benefits, regional prestige, community identity, civic pride, and the attraction of nonresidents to the community.[11]

The fans have known all along that the presence of a minor league team improves their quality of life. The stadium provides them with a place to relax and enjoy themselves. The hope of winning, and the hope that their players will someday make it to the major leagues, gives the community something to root for.

Further, the nature of Minor League Baseball itself adds to the quality of life in the community. The family atmosphere, the low prices, the promotions, and the genuine efforts of the players stand in marked contrast to Major League Baseball. Fans are often turned off by the perceived greediness of major league players and owners, the high cost of attending major league games, and the threat of franchise relocation and demands for bigger and better stadiums. Although communities compete to host major league teams, they also are often critical of the teams they host.

Of course, there are always community concerns about traffic, taxes, overdevelopment, and other issues when Minor League Baseball comes to town. There will always be those who argue that the town was just fine without a new stadium or a team with noisy or even undesirable fans. Ultimately, many residents dismiss the naysayers and flock to the stadium for old-fashioned fun in a newfangled package without having to drive a long distance or worry about where to park.

Overall, in minor league communities there is a sense of partnership between the community and the team. Residents are proud of the team whether it wins or loses, and the team management is viewed as making a genuine effort to support the community. This effect on community is supported, in part, by the results of this research.

Minor League Baseball has had a turbulent history, and will continue to change. Thus, it is important to study the effects of it over time as well as changes within it. The analysis of interaction effects between Minor League Baseball's presence and history has significantly added to the understanding of the nature of the minor league industry. Although times have changed, so too has Minor League Baseball, and it will always find a way to represent the spirit of community and join its fans together.

Epilogue

A Shelter in the Storm

In 2001, the Minor League Baseball playoffs were canceled for the first time since World War II in the aftermath of the devastating terrorist attacks perpetrated against the United States on the morning of Tuesday, September 11. As the entire nation mourned, individuals put aside their differences and bonded together to draw strength from one another and cope with the tragic events. In the days following the attacks, Americans struggled to regain a sense of normalcy, but with great difficulty. Because of the horrendous loss of life caused by the attacks, and out of respect for the victims and their families, professional sports games were postponed or suspended. Commissioner of Major League Baseball, Bud Selig, issued the following statement: "Given the continuing national horror and the many significant challenges faced by our government, our cities, and our citizens, I believe it is appropriate to postpone all Major League Baseball games for Wednesday, September 12, 2001."[1]

In workplaces and communities across the country, people did what they could to help their fellow Americans. Major league teams and players expressed their sympathy, and assisted in rescue and relief efforts. Major League Baseball and the Major League Baseball Players Association jointly established the MLB-MLBPA Disaster Relief Fund, and several players made special donations to various relief organizations.[2]

Minor League Baseball had its own role to play in the national recovery process. Although the regular season had ended before the terrorist attacks, the playoffs were still under way in many cities. Sharing the views of the other professional sports, minor league officials felt that it was more important for players to spend time with their families and to cope with their own sorrow.[3] The playoffs were canceled, with cochampions named in several leagues, and other leagues declaring the league champion to be the team that was ahead in the playoffs as of September 11.

However, minor league teams and employees did not simply close down for the off season. Within their own communities, many worked to help people cope with the tragedies that had befallen the country. Teams undertook a variety of efforts that displayed the full measure of their national patriotism and commitment to community.[4] The following are a few examples of Minor League Baseball's contributions during those trying days:

- Several Minor League Baseball Web sites—such as those representing businesses and organizations in every industry—displayed patriotic symbols and provided information on how fans could help the attack victims by donating time, money, and other items to charitable organizations.
- On September 13, the Brooklyn Cyclones announced that fans could donate refunds for canceled New York-Penn League Championship Series games to a relief fund for families and victims of the terrorist attacks. The team accepted donations from September 17 until November 2.
- On September 14, the Rochester Red Wings gave away 1,000 miniature American flags to fans who stopped by the team's offices at Frontier Field in Rochester, New York. The team also accepted donations of money and other needed items to assist American Red Cross relief efforts in Washington, DC, and New York City.
- A candlelight vigil was held at Durham Bulls Athletic Park on September 14, in remembrance of the victims of the terrorist attacks. The Durham Bulls and local media conducted a "Relief for America" campaign, which accepted monetary donations and pledges for blood donations from people who attended the vigil. In two days, over $500,000 was collected for the relief fund.
- On September 17, in Tucson, Arizona, the gates to Tucson Electric Park, home of the Tucson Sidewinders, were opened to approximately 15,000 people who entered the stadium to form a human American flag. The event was organized by several local businesses and organizations. Local firefighters were in attendance to collect donations for the New York Fire Department.
- In true minor league fashion, the Carolina Mudcats held a fundraiser aimed at breaking a world record. On October 1, Patrick

Kinas, the Mudcats' play-by-play broadcaster, broke the world record for marathon bowling. Additional donations to assist in relief efforts were collected during the event.

Throughout the days and weeks following September 11, Americans pulled together in a spirit of patriotism as they had not done since World War II. During this time of need, minor league teams proved that they are, indeed, an integral part of the national community. The team members opened their hearts to assist in the relief efforts, as did we all.

Appendix A

Minor League Attendance and Number of Teams, by Year and Era, 1947 to 1990

Era/Year	Attendance[1]	No. of Teams	Gained[2]	Lost[3]	New[4]	Counties with Teams[5]
Prosperity						
1947	37,825,894	388	85	2	9	354
1948	37,098,447	426	62	4	8	409
1949	39,670,065	448	26	13	10	409
1950	32,891,771	440	31	35	14	404
Decline						
1951	26,115,291	371	13	86	22	336
1952	23,950,135	324	24	63	8	296
1953	20,966,887	292	15	44	17	266
1954	18,720,556	269	21	41	9	244
1955	17,380,473	238	19	39	19	223
1956	15,024,767	205	24	26	24	192
1957	13,277,114	188	17	25	1	184
1958	11,565,156	167	17	40	7	158
1959	10,654,278	144	10	26	9	140
1960	9,133,911	140	18	20	0	135
1961	8,337,542	135	17	20	2	131
1962	8,023,076	122	19	33	5	119

Era/Year	Attendance[1]	No. of Teams	Gained[2]	Lost[3]	New[4]	Counties with Teams[5]
Subsidization						
1963	7,718,480	118	13	17	1	115
1964	7,341,221	110	5	13	1	106
1965	7,226,434	110	11	9	1	107
1966	7,112,315	112	15	18	3	106
1967	6,940,440	112	8	7	2	108
Indifference						
1968	7,075,682	113	10	9	3	110
1969	7,194,283	121	19	12	0	115
1970	8,495,358	123	13	7	0	119
1971	8,612,203	122	3	5	0	115
1972	8,364,075	116	8	14	1	108
1973	7,814,710	114	6	9	4	107
1974	7,411,456	112	2	7	2	105
1975	7,393,002	106	2	8	0	99
1976	7,612,508	110	12	6	0	103
1977	9,078,707	116	12	11	5	106
Renaissance						
1978	9,324,044	121	14	9	0	110
1979	10,677,591	122	3	4	0	111
1980	12,261,014	125	9	7	0	116
1981	13,524,996	124	5	4	0	116
1982	14,787,504	134	9	0	0	125
1983	15,604,550	137	6	3	1	130
1984	14,836,883	138	1	6	0	131
1985	15,655,886	138	0	2	0	130
1986	16,262,148	138	3	0	0	135

Appendix A: Minor League Attendance and Number of Teams

Era/Year	Attendance[1]	No. of Teams	Gained[2]	Lost[3]	New[4]	Counties with Teams[5]
1987	17,662,497	144	9	0	0	135
1988	19,225,741	148	4	0	0	135
1989	20,828,049	150	2	0	0	135
1990	22,519,017	150	0	0	0	135

[1] Values for attendance and teams includes communities in Canada and Mexico.
[2] Includes teams that relocated to the county, expansion teams, and teams returning to the county (e.g., after the league disbanded and no team was in existence the previous year). Does not include teams outside of the United States. Note that the number of teams gained minus the number of teams lost does not equal the change in the number of teams from one year to the next due to difficulties in coding some of the franchise shifts and insufficient data.
[3] Includes teams that moved out of the county or disbanded (during or after the season). Does not include teams outside of the United States.
[4] Includes counties in which a team moved or disbanded but was replaced by a new team in the county the next season. The new team may have been in the same league as the previous team, in a new league, or in a different town in the same county.
[5] The number of counties in the data set that had a team for that year. This is less than the actual number of minor league teams for the year because it does not account for counties that had more than one team (nor does it include teams outside of the United States).

Source: Rebecca Susan Kraus, "Sport and Community: The Case of Minor League Baseball, 1950s-1990s" (Doctoral dissertation, The Catholic University of America, 1998) pp. 90-91.

Appendix B

Development of the Data Set

The following is a summary of the Minor League Baseball quality-of-life study I conducted in 1998, and which is referred to throughout this book. Many of the conclusions and much of the data presented in the previous pages are derived from this study. The technical aspects and major findings are presented in this appendix for readers who are interested in more detailed information than that presented in the text.

The collection and analysis of data used in examining the relationship between sports and community required many steps. My review of the literature of sports and community sociology (Chapter 3), and the evolution of Minor League Baseball (Chapters 2 and 4), aided in my development of hypotheses concerning the relationship between Minor League Baseball and the community. With these hypotheses in mind, the next step was to collect data on the teams and to select a data set that would provide information on the social and economic aspects of the communities.

After making these initial decisions, I linked the data on teams to the data on communities and further refined the combined data set. The hypotheses that fueled this investigation, the data used in the creation of the data set, and the variables collected for the study are presented in the following text.

HYPOTHESES

Although many authors have assumed that sports, including Minor League Baseball, have a positive impact on quality of life (QOL), QOL is a difficult topic to measure. However, by comparing various social and economic indicators, we can attempt to estimate the impact of the minor leagues on the QOL of a community. It is assumed that the higher a community ranks on various social and economic indicators, the more likely it is to foster a spirit of community. Two hypotheses were tested and measured in this study:

> Hypothesis 1: The presence of a minor league team will be positively related to a high quality of life in a community.
> Hypothesis 2: The length of time a minor league team has been in the community will be positively related to a high quality of life in the community.

With these hypotheses in mind, the next step was to select the data set to be used and the variables to be analyzed.

CONSTRUCTION OF THE DATA SET

To my knowledge, there has been no previous longitudinal study of quality of life and the impact of sports on a community. Studies have either compared one period of time to another, or merely examined one point in time. This is probably because yearly data are not available to properly measure effects. For example, although decennial census population data are available, data between censuses do not exist for all variables necessary for such a study.

However, the impact of Minor League Baseball over time can be inferred from the data set used in this study. A pooled data set of social, economic, and baseball variables was assembled in the following manner[1]:

1. Data were collected for every minor league team participating in a league organized by the NAPBL between 1946 and 1994. The county for each team was identified using a software program, MapLinx. Separate databases containing information on minor league teams were created for every year from 1946 to 1990.

2. Social and economic variables were obtained from the volumes of the Census Bureau's *County and City Data Book,* which covered the period 1946 to 1990. Five databases were created to cover the decades 1940-1949, 1950-1959, 1960-1969, 1970-1979, and 1980-1990. Each of these data sets contains 2,795 cases (counties). The data are organized by decade because many of the variables (such as population, labor force, number of families, housing value, etc.) were measured at the beginning of each decade in the Census of Population and Housing. Due to a large amount of missing data, data could not be es-

Appendix B: Development of the Data Set   143

timated for each year between 1946 and 1990. County-level data for all necessary variables were not yet available from the 2000 Census. Therefore, there are no estimates of changes in Minor League Baseball during the decade of the 1990s.

3. "Change" variables were calculated to show the percentage change in the social and economic variables from one decade to the next as follows:

$$((\text{Variable}_{t2} - \text{Variable}_{t1})/(\text{Variable}_{t2} + \text{Variable}_{t1})) \times 100$$

4. Dummy variables were created to represent each era in the history of Minor League Baseball: 1946-1950 (the postwar years of prosperity), 1951-1962 (the years of decline), 1963-1967 (the era of major league subsidization), 1968-1977 (the era of indifference toward the minors), and 1978-1990 (the renaissance of minor league baseball). The dummy variable ERA1 equals 1 for the era 1946-1950, and 0 for the other eras; ERA2 equals 1 for the era 1951-1962, and 0 for the other eras; and so forth.

5. Dummy variables to measure the extent of team presence were calculated. "HASANY" equals 0 if the county did not have a team during an era, and equals 1 if the county had a team at any point during the era (for example, HASANY equals 1 whether the county had a team every year during the era or only one year). "HASALL" equals 0 if the county did not have a team during the era, and equals 1 if the county had a team every year. (Note that when HASALL equals 1 for a particular county, HASANY also equals 1.) The dummy variables for era and team presence were added to the separate decade data sets as follows:

Social/Economic Data Sets	Baseball Eras
1940s	1946-1950
1950s	1951-1962
1960s	1963-1967
1970s	1968-1977
1980s	1978-1990

6. To disentangle the main effects of the baseball presence variables and the era variables, interaction terms were created as follows:

ANYERA2 = HASANY×ERA2
ANYERA3 = HASANY×ERA3
ANYERA4 = HASANY×ERA4
ANYERA5 = HASANY×ERA5
ALLERA2 = HASALL×ERA2
ALLERA3 = HASALL×ERA3
ALLERA3 = HASALL×ERA3
ALLERA4 = HASALL×ERA4
ALLERA5 = HASALL×ERA5

Thus, if ANYERA2 equals 1, both HASANY and ERA2 must equal 1; if ANYERA2 equals 0, either HASANY or ERA 2 may equal 0, or both may equal 0. In this way, the interaction of having a team in a particular era can be compared to Era 1 in regression equations.

7. Dummy variables were created to determine movement of teams in and out of a county within a decade. PURETN equals 1 if a county gained ("picked up") a team at some point in the decade and retained it through the end of the decade. PULOST equals 1 if a county gained a team but no longer had a team (i.e., "lost" the team) by the end of the decade.

8. The five decade data sets were pooled to create one data set with 13,975 cases. The five separate data sets were "stacked" together so that the data were matched variable by variable. Some variables do not have data for every decade and thus were coded as "missing" (see Table B.1 for a list of the variables included in the data set and the years for which they were available).

DATA USED

Data were collected on minor league teams as well as the counties in which they were or are located. The complete data set includes more variables than were used in the analyses. The variables used and the sources of the data are discussed in the following. Changes made to the variables and data set are discussed in a later section.

Minor League Data

The data on minor league teams were collected primarily from *The Encyclopedia of Minor League Baseball*.[2] This source provides in-

Appendix B: Development of the Data Set 145

TABLE B.1. Variables in the Data Set and Availability by Decade

Variable	1940	1950	1960	1970	1980	1990
Population	1940	1950	1960	1970	1980	1990
Minority Population	1940	1950	1960	1970	1980	1990
No. of Families	—	1950	1960	1970	1980	1990
No. of Marriages	—	1950	1960	1970	1980	—
No. of Divorces	—	—	—	1970	1980	—
No. of Births	1944	1950	1964	1970	1980	1988
Percent of Population Under Age Five	—	1950	1960	1970	1980	1990
No. of School-Age Children	—	1950	1960	1970	1980	1990
No. of Housing Units	1940	1950	1960	1970	1980	1990
Median Housing Value	—	1950	1960	1970	1980	1990
Median Gross Rent Price	1940	1950	1960	1970	1980	1990
Labor Force	1940	1950	1960	1970	1980	1990
Percent Unemployed	1940	1950	1960	1970	1980	1990
Median Income	—	1950	1960	1970	1979	1989
Percent of Families Living in Poverty	—	1950	1960	1970	1980	1989
Bank Deposits	1944	1950	1960	1970	1980	1992
No. of Manufacturing Establishments	1939	1950	1963	1972	1982	1987
No. of Retail Establishments	1939	1948	1963	1972	1982	1987
No. of Wholesale Establishments	1939	1948	1963	1972	1982	1987
Local Government Revenue	—	1957	1962	1971	1982	1986
Local Government Direct General Expenditures	—	1957	1962	1971	1982	1986
Educational Attainment	—	1950	1960	1970	1980	1990

TABLE B.1 *(continued)*

Variable	1940	1950	1960	1970	1980	1990
Percent of Local Government Expenditures for Education	—	1957	1962	1971	1982	—
No. of Physicians	—	—	—	1970	1980	1990
No. of Hospitals	—	—	—	1975	1980	1991
No. of Hospital Beds	—	—	—	1975	1980	1991
Crime Rate	—	—	—	1975	1980	1990

formation for each minor league team from 1902 to 1992 on the league, playing level (AAA, AA, A, Rookie, B, C, or D), years in the league, attendance, and number of games won and lost. It also provides information on the major league affiliate of each minor league team for the years 1963 to 1992.

The Baseball America Directory for various years also provided the name of the ownership group, from which could be derived the type of ownership (coded as city, county, or municipality; private business group; or major league affiliate); the availability of radio broadcasts (coded as no games broadcast, all games broadcast, home games broadcast, away games broadcast, some games—both home and away—broadcast, some home games broadcast, or some away games broadcast); and stadium capacity.

From the data collected on minor league teams, variables were created to indicate whether a team had changed its name, moved to another town, changed stadiums, or was under new ownership. Information on team relocations and name changes was supplemented with information from *Professional Baseball Franchises: From the Abbeville Athletics to the Zanesville Indians.* Using MapLinx, distances were calculated to create variables for distance from each minor league town to its major league affiliate and to the nearest major league team.

Dummy variables were created to measure the extent of the presence of Minor League Baseball in each county. Preliminary tests showed that the dummy variables "HASANY" and "HASALL" (previously described) were the best predictors of the effect of Minor League Baseball on the community.

The years 1946 to 1990 were chosen as the basis for the analysis for several reasons. First, data were available for a limited number of years. Many of the social and demographic variables are available in the *County and City Data Book* (CCDB) only for the 1950 Census and after. Some economic variables are not available prior to the 1940 Census. For example, information on the number of families, children, and marriages is available for 1950 and after. Data on the noncivilian labor force, number of housing units, and median gross rent price are included in the CCDB for 1940 and after. In addition, some variables for earlier years were measured in a manner that is inconsistent with later years.

Second, previous studies did not conduct time-series analysis using very long periods. Third, the nature of Minor League Baseball has changed over the years, making time-series analysis difficult. The NAPBL organized the minor leagues somewhat in the early 1950s, and the farm system was not introduced until the 1920s. Thus, the present-day experience of baseball is much different from the days of interleague competition for players, looser affiliation with major league teams, and the reserve clause (which tied a player to a team for life). The amateur draft, free agency, farm teams, player development plans, and the Major League Baseball Players Association (which has some indirect affects on minor leaguers) are relatively recent phenomena.

Fourth, Johnson and Wolff identify 1946 as marking a new era in Minor League Baseball.[3] World War II, the introduction of television, and competition from other forms of entertainment had a permanent effect on Minor League Baseball. Thus, this study is limited to the postwar experiences of the industry.

County Data

To represent communities, data on the counties that host minor league teams were collected from the U.S. Department of Commerce, Bureau of the Census *County and City Data Book* for 1947 through 1995, which cover the 1940 through 1990 Censuses. Lyon identifies the CCDB as the best source of local census data. (However, he warns that the CCDB provides only a small portion of the available data on communities. However, much of the data on communities is not publicly available, or is difficult to find.[4])

County was chosen as the unit of analysis for a number of reasons. First, using counties as a proxy for community provides more cases for the analysis. Many minor league towns, particularly in the earlier years, are so small that they do not appear in the CCDB. In addition, in many years, the number of minor league towns was relatively small. Thus, if data were collected on cities instead of counties, many teams would have had to be left out of the analysis. Alternatively, standard metropolitan statistical areas (SMSAs) are too large and often contain two or more teams. (Further, Berger, Blomquist, and Waldner note that using SMSAs excludes rural areas—many of which host Minor League Baseball teams—from the analysis.[5])

Second, many teams are marketed as county or regional teams and are named for the counties in which they are located, not the cities. For example, the Potomac Cannons, which operate in Woodbridge, Virginia, in Prince William County, draw 46 percent of their fans from all over Prince William County, not just Woodbridge. The Cannons also draw fans from Fairfax County, Washington, DC, and Maryland.[6]

In addition, the Bowie Baysox, which operate in Prince George's County, Maryland, are also widely marketed to other towns in Prince George's County, such as Upper Marlboro, as well as other Maryland counties, such as Anne Arundel and Calvert. This suggests that benefits of hosting a minor league team extend beyond the city limits. Thus, using county data to proximate community is more inclusive than using city or other available data for smaller areas, and more convenient than specifying regional boundaries. (In this example, county is also more appropriate than SMSA, since both Potomac and Bowie are in the same SMSA, along with the Hagerstown Suns and the Frederick Keys.)

Third, data at the county level are readily available from the Census Bureau, which provides a variety of social and economic information for counties. County-level data were available on magnetic tape and CD-ROM for the 1947 through 1995 volumes of the *County and City Data Book*.

Fourth, many economic impact studies conducted for cities considering whether to host professional teams were done using county data.[7] However, the reasons for using county data as opposed to city data are not given by the various authors. Johnson suggests, though, that neighboring communities as well as state government should share in the cost of retaining a team, thus suggesting that the team impacts more than just the city in which it is located.[8]

The county-level variables in this analysis were chosen to represent quality of life from both social and economic perspectives. As with the minor league variables, demographic, economic, and social variables were included in response to the survey of the literature presented in this book. For example, family variables were included to measure the extent of *gemeinschaft* and mechanic solidarity. Information on education and government was included to account for services, as identified by various researchers as being an important indicator of quality of life.[9] Further, data on income and population, as well as economic variables (such as unemployment, sales, etc.), were included in many of the analyses reviewed.

In addition, a survey of the quality-of-life (QOL) literature provided some insight as to which variables should be included in this study. Similar to the conflicting opinions on how to measure QOL, there is very little agreement on the variables that measure it. For example, Rossi states that there are at least three important considerations: (1) the indicators should be "based upon a model of how the area of social life in question 'works' "; (2) a small number of indicators should be chosen so that trends are easy to observe; and (3) "the indicators ought to be related to potential social policy."[10] He suggests that the following measures be used: satisfaction with dwelling unit, satisfaction with access to major markets, satisfaction with sociability opportunities, and satisfaction with locality as gratification. Rossi suggests that data to measure such indicators should cover space and cost of dwelling unit, employment opportunities, transportation, local government, public officials, friendliness of neighborhood, number of friends, pride in residence, solidarity, and willingness to move.[11]

Berger, Blomquist, and Waldner and Blomquist, Berger, and Hoehn are more concerned with finding an objective way to weight their QOL indicators than in justifying the choice of amenities. (They do, however, indicate that other amenities, such as number of sports teams, were too highly correlated with city size, and were thus omitted.) They chose indicators such as precipitation, humidity, heating-degree days, cooling-degree days, wind speed, sunshine, coast, violent crime, teacher-pupil ratio, visibility, total suspended particulates, effluent dischargers, landfill waste, superfund sites, treatment, storage, and disposal sites, and residence in central city.[12]

In addition, many researchers have indicated that QOL is a uniquely local experience. Myers, for instance, notes that "most people experience quality of life in a single community."[13] This suggests that measures of migration, which have been omitted from most studies of QOL, may have little, overall, to do with an area's quality of life.

Kasarda and Janowitz argue that "whether a person feels a sense of community is clearly a function of residence," which suggests that certain uncontrollable features of an area, such as climate, may have little effect on QOL. They find social bonds, such as the number of family members and friends, have the greatest effect on community sentiments.[14] Further, Rossi argues that few people move away from or even travel long distances from their place of birth. Even for those who have migrated or traveled, their daily lives are: "acted out within rather narrowly circumscribed areal limits.... These areal characteristics of daily life account for the persistence of local communities as centers of public attention and societal concern."[15] Thus, factors that directly affect the community and its residents should be the most important indicators of QOL. Climatic and environmental indicators may have an indirect effect on QOL through their effects on health or taxes.

Lyon suggests that a high QOL would have to include six "bare necessities": public safety, a strong economy, health care, educational opportunities, a clean environment, and an optimum population size. When these are available, a high QOL becomes more dependent upon individual liberty, categorical equality, communal fraternity, representative/responsive government, community viability, local identification, and resident heterogeneity.[16] However, Lyon admits that such measures are hard to define, measure, and agree upon.

After a review of various attempts to measure QOL, Lyon concludes that there are six basic dimensions that should be included in most attempts to measure QOL. These are: economics, education, health, housing, public safety, and racial and sexual discrimination (measured by unemployment ratios). Lyon suggests that other dimensions such as political activity, ethnic composition, transportation, and environment may also be included.[17]

Given Lyon's discussion concerning the difficulty of obtaining data, and the need for data that are comparable across communities,

I limited my study to county-level data available in the *County and City Data Book*. I identified the six dimensions of QOL to be included in this study: family, economy, housing, education, government, and safety. These dimensions include the following variables:

1. *Family variables*—number of marriages, divorces, families, births, and children (measured as the percentage of the population under the age of five, number of elementary school students, and number of high school students).
2. *Economic variables*—total bank deposits, percentage of families living in poverty, median income, size of the labor force, unemployment rate, and number of manufacturing, wholesale, and retail establishments.
3. *Housing variables*—number of housing units, median housing value, and median rent price.
4. *Education variables*—percentage of the population completing high school or more and percentage of local government expenditures on education.
5. *Government variables*—local government direct general expenditures and local government general revenue.
6. *Health and safety variables*—number of physicians, number of hospitals, number of hospital beds, and the crime rate per 100,000 population.

After running preliminary regression analyses, I determined that not all of these variables were useful in determining the relationship between sports and community. A discussion of the regression models selected is presented next.

Changes to the Data

Approximately 3,185 counties are included in the *County and City Data Books*. Because of shifting boundaries and changes in county designations, the actual number of counties included in the CCDB has changed over the years. These changes and other inconsistencies in the data necessitated the removal of 390 counties. Counties were deleted from the data for a variety of reasons:

1. *Cities/counties that are no longer in existence*. There were some counties that were not included in the 1988 and 1994 CCDBs that

were in previous editions. These were: Ormsby, Nevada; Armstrong, Washabaugh, and Washington, South Dakota; and Elizabeth City, Nansemond, Warwick, and Warwick City, Virginia. Data for these counties/cities were often combined with other counties in the CCDBs, resulting in missing or incomplete data for many of the variables for the years that they were included. Thus, they were not included in the data set for this study.

2. *Counties that were created in the 1980s.* Cibola County, New Mexico, was established in 1981. Formerly it had been part of Valencia County. La Paz County, Arizona, formerly part of Yuma County, was established in 1983.[18] After the creation of these new counties, data for some variables continued to be reported with Valencia and Yuma counties, respectively, resulting in missing data for Cibola and La Paz.[19] There were no baseball teams in any of the four counties at any time between 1946 and 1994. Thus, Cibola and La Paz were excluded from the data set.

3. *Counties constituting Yellowstone National Park.* Data for the counties in Idaho, Wyoming, and Montana, that contain Yellowstone National Park were not measured consistently. For example, in the 1988 CCDB, data for the portions of the park located in Idaho and Wyoming were included with the data for the surrounding counties. The portion of the park in Montana, however, was considered to be an "other unorganized county-type area" and thus data were collected separately from the surrounding counties.[20] All three areas of the park were surveyed separately from their surrounding counties in the 1940 and 1950 Censuses. In addition, for many years, no data were available for most of the variables included in this study for the three areas constituting the park. Given the small population, the incomplete data, and the fact that there was never a Minor League Baseball team in these areas, these were excluded from the data set.

4. *Counties in Alaska.* Much of the data for these counties was incomplete before the 1960 Census. County boundaries underwent extensive revision in 1980, and again in 1990, making it difficult to track changes over time.[21] Given that there never was a minor league team in Alaska, the climate is not conducive to playing Minor League Baseball, and the relative difficulty in traveling to Alaska (compared to other minor league locations), I determined that the social and economic conditions in Alaska were not good predictors of Minor

Appendix B: Development of the Data Set 153

League Baseball outcomes. Thus, all Alaska counties were excluded from the data set.

5. *Counties in Hawaii.* Similar to Alaska, much of the data for Hawaii counties were incomplete before the 1960 Census. In addition, data for more than one Hawaii county were often combined. Although a minor league team, the Hawaii Islanders, did play in Honolulu from 1961 to 1987, the high travel costs associated with the team's distance from the other teams in the league has been cited as the reason for the team relocating to Colorado Springs, Colorado, in 1988.[22] It was thus decided that the social and economic conditions in Hawaii were not good predictors of Minor League Baseball outcomes and Hawaii counties were also excluded from the data set.

6. *Counties with a population of less than 4,000.* During the time covered by this study, the county with the smallest population that had had a Minor League Baseball team was Brewster, Texas, in 1960, with a population of 6,434 persons. It was thus decided that counties with a smaller population would not be sufficient predictors of the existence and impact of Minor League Baseball. In addition, the values of some variables for small population counties were suppressed; because of this, small population counties had many variables with missing data. Therefore, counties with a population of less than 4,000 were removed from the data set (for every year). Four thousand was chosen as the cut-off point, instead of 6,000, because some counties that had teams in later years had populations of less than 6,000 during years when they did not host a team. One hundred eighty-two counties with a population of less than 4,000 in 1940 and 1950, thirty-one in 1960, thirty-one in 1970, fifteen in 1980, and twenty-two in 1990 were excluded from the data set. In total, 281 counties were excluded from the data set based on the size criterion.

7. *Independent cities in Virginia.* Data for the independent cities in Virginia were not measured consistently. In some years, data for an independent city were combined with data for the surrounding county. In some cases, data for one city were combined with different counties, depending on the variable measured. (For example, in the 1994 CCDB some variables for Galax City were included with Grayson County, and others were included with Carroll County.) In other cases, some variables were measured separately for the city and county, and the values for other variables were combined for the city and county yet reported only for the county. This resulted in missing

data for many of the variables for the independent cities. Thirty-eight independent cities in Virginia were deleted from the data set because of missing data. Sixteen of these cities had hosted a minor league team during the period of this study: Bristol, Covington, Danville, Emporia, Franklin, Galax, Hopewell, Lynchburg, Martinsville, Newport News, Norton, Petersburg, Radford, Richmond, Roanoke, and Salem. For the purposes of this study, these teams were classified as being in the counties of Washington, Alleghany, Pittsylvania, Greensville, Southampton, Carroll, Prince George, Campbell, Henry, Hampton (city), Wise, Dinwiddie, Pulaski, Henrico, Roanoke, and Roanoke, respectively. (Because of sufficient data and the fact that they hosted minor league teams during the period under study, the cities of Alexandria, Hampton, Norfolk, Portsmouth, and Suffolk remain in the data set as entities separate from their surrounding counties.)

8. *Other independent cities.* The independent cities of St. Louis, Missouri; Baltimore, Maryland; and Carson City, Nevada, are included in the CCDBs as separate "counties." Carson City was deleted from the data set due to missing data in the earlier censuses. St. Louis and Baltimore have sufficient data and were not removed from the data set.

Other changes were made to the data to accommodate missing data:

1. *Columbus City, Georgia.* For the 1940 through 1970 Censuses, some variables for Columbus City, Georgia (more in the 1940s and 1950s than in the later years), were measured separately from the surrounding county, Muskogee County, Georgia. However, during those years, many variables were measured by combining city and county data. In later censuses, city data were combined with county data for every variable. Thus, the data for Columbus City were combined with the data for Muskogee County for every year in the data set.

2. *Ste. Genevieve, Missouri.* The five-digit county code for Ste. Genevieve, Missouri, was changed between the 1970 and 1980 Censuses from 29193 to 29186. Thus, in my data set, Ste. Genevieve was recoded as 29186 for all years.

3. *Norfolk, Virginia.* In the 1940, 1950, 1960, and 1970 Censuses, Norfolk, Virginia, was classified as a county and an independent city, and had the county codes of 51129 and 51710. In the 1980 and 1990 Censuses, only 51710 was included. Since most of the data in 51710 were missing in earlier years, the data for 51710 was deleted and

51129 was reclassified as 51710 in the data set to be consistent with the later years.

4. *Boroughs of New York City.* For certain variables, the data for the five boroughs of New York City (Bronx, Kings, New York, Queens, and Richmond) were combined and reported for only one of the five boroughs (Kings or New York, depending on the variable), and the other four boroughs reported missing data. To avoid problems with missing data, the values for the approximately twenty affected variables were estimated. Variables presented as rates or percentages were copied for the four boroughs with missing data. Variables presented as whole numbers were divided by five and the one value was repeated for all five boroughs.

Summary

The selection, collection, coding, and cleaning of the data for this study required a number of steps. Minor League Baseball towns had to be linked to the counties in which they reside, and decisions had to be made regarding the exclusion of cases from the data set. Variables included were selected based upon the hypotheses of this study and a review of the literature on quality of life and sports sociology. Such decisions were made in light of the history and nature of Minor League Baseball.

Once the data set was created, I conducted some preliminary analyses to determine the most appropriate statistical methods to use in estimating the relationship between minor league teams and quality of life. A closer examination of the QOL literature and sociological theories enabled me to select the variables and issues I wanted to focus on in this study. The methods and models used in these analyses are discussed next.

STATISTICAL METHODS AND MODELS

A brief discussion of previous models used in sports sociology, community sociology, and the QOL literature is presented to explain my selection of regression models with which I estimate the relationship between certain social, economic, time, and baseball-presence variables and the dependent variables. The final sections of this Appendix discuss the models I chose to estimate and the variables associated with QOL that I focus on in this study.

Method Selection

The measurement of QOL, or quality of place, is a thorny issue. Many attempts have been made at the measurement of such a concept, and many critiques of the various measurement systems have followed.[23] Although the focus of this study is the relationship between Minor League Baseball and QOL, I concluded from my review of the various QOL models that the estimation of a single value of QOL is not feasible for a longitudinal study of almost 3,000 counties. Thus, although the literature was useful in selecting the variables analyzed, I determined that the construction of a QOL index would not be a valuable exercise for this study.

I also reviewed works in which the authors had attempted to analyze the impact of sports on the economy. Most of these analyses have relied on multiplier effects,[24] because communities are concerned with the monetary impact of hosting a team and, therefore, use multiplier effects to estimate the dollar amount of the impact of baseball. Thus, the multiplier effect of gate and parking receipts, taxes, sales of new businesses, etc., are calculated to determine the benefit to the community.[25]

However, analysts do not always agree upon which multiplier to use, and interpretations of the results differ. Further, Euchner argues that analyses that estimate multiplier effects overstate economic outcomes. Such studies neglect to consider that in the absence of a sports team, spending that otherwise would have been generated by the team may be spent elsewhere in the city on other entertainment, thus generating the same revenue as a sports team would. Such studies also do not take into account other development or improvement projects that were forgone to finance a stadium.[26]

In addition, estimation of multiplier effects cannot fully explain the impact of Minor League Baseball on other social phenomena, such as the number of families and children, educational attainment, or the crime rate. Thus, I selected regression analysis for this study so that I could estimate the relationship between Minor League Baseball and the community. Regression analysis allows social scientists to predict the mean value of a dependent variable from a series of independent variables. In this manner, the relationship among the variables can be estimated.[27] Although regression models cannot describe causal direction, theoretical arguments can be made to explain the relationship between the variables.[28]

I determined that regression analysis of a series of dependent variables, which can be used in QOL models, was sufficient in estimating the relationship between Minor League Baseball and the QOL of a community. The dependent variables for the regressions were selected from a review of the sociology of sports, community sociology, and QOL literature, and were selected based on their availability in the *County and City Data Book*.

Six dimensions of QOL were selected as areas to be investigated in this study: the economy, family, education, housing, government, and public safety. At first, I chose seven variables to measure these dimensions of QOL: unemployment, retail establishments, wholesale establishments, families, children, educational attainment, and crime. I developed regression models based on theoretical arguments related to the dependent variable. However, regression analysis suggested that only two variables, educational attainment and the crime rate, appear to be related to Minor League Baseball variables.

Regression Models

Using the data set, I compared communities in their extent of baseball presence, and across the periods in minor league history. Thus, to examine the impact of Minor League Baseball on the counties that host teams, I estimated a number of regression models using indicators of length of team presence and era in which the team operated in a particular county. I analyzed the data using a variety of methods before determining the best model with which to explain the relationship between Minor League Baseball and the community.

Since the dependent variables (social and economic variables selected as measures of QOL) are available in intervals of ten years (measured primarily at the beginning of each decade), I first attempted to measure the effects of Minor League Baseball by measuring the impact of baseball on the change over time for each variable. Thus, change variables were calculated as the percentage rate of change from one decade to the next. These were used as the dependent variables in a series of linear-regression models containing baseball presence variables and population size as the independent variables. I used population as a control variable to account for the differing population sizes among the counties for variables that are not measured as percentages (such as the number of wholesale establishments).

A preliminary set of regression models was run with the five data sets that had been created for each decade: 1940s, 1950s, 1960s, 1970s, and 1980s. The results of these regressions showed a pattern of the effects of baseball presence by decade. This led to a review of the history of the industry, which revealed business patterns that could explain the differing effects of the baseball variables across the decades. To analyze this further, dummy variables were created to represent the five eras in the history of the Minor League Baseball industry (1946-1950, 1951-1962, 1963-1967, 1968-1977, 1978-1990).

Next, the data sets were combined to conduct a pooled time-series analysis to allow for the analysis of a greater number of cases over a period of time.[29] The total number of cases in the pooled data set was 13,975, although some variables had missing data for some decades.[30] Because I created a system of seven models with the unemployment rate, retail establishments, wholesale establishments, families, school-age children, educational attainment, and the crime rate as the dependent variables, my models were considered to be a recursive system.[31] In a recursive system, each of the endogenous variables is determined sequentially. (Endogenous variables are determined within the system; exogenous variables are determined outside the system, i.e., their causes are not explained in the model.[32]) All exogenous variables are determined prior to the dependent variables.[33] Thus, the exogenous variables in an equation will be uncorrelated with the disturbance in the equation.[34] Note that no two variables may be related in such a manner that each is affected by and depends on the other.[35] In other words, one-way causation is acceptable, but a reciprocal relationship will result in biased and inconsistent estimates.[36]

I conducted regression analyses with this system of equations using two-stage least-squares regression. Two-stage least-squares regression analysis is used to estimate structural parameters when equations are overidentified.[37] In this way, the correlations among the independent variables are accounted for, and the biased estimates that would be made with ordinary least-squares regression are eliminated.[38]

Unfortunately, most of the regression models in this system indicated that there is no relationship between Minor League Baseball and community-level social/economic variables. I eventually chose to concentrate on only two of the variables: educational attainment and crime rate. Since these two variables do not predict one another (i.e., are not directly related), my equations were no longer part of a recursive system. Further, after estimating a variety of models, I determined that the most robust models were those that were estimated using separate data sets for each decade, instead of the pooled data set.

Educational Attainment

Education is assumed to be a positive individual quality. Higher education could mean higher community involvement, greater involvement in and awareness of community politics, greater demand for services, better job opportunities, etc. The extent of education achieved is the simplest and best indicator of education within a community. This can be measured with variables such as median school years completed, percent of persons completing high school, and the percent of persons completing college or more (all of which are used, as available, for this study). However, extent of education achieved has been omitted in many QOL studies.

Savageau and Boyer employ such indicators as enrollment in two-year colleges, enrollment in public and private four-year colleges and universities, and access to a metropolitan area.[39] These indicators, however, seem to say very little about how educated a community is. In fact, the presence of four-year colleges and universities may indicate the types of cultural activities available, but tells very little about the amount of education in an area, since many college students may not be from the county in which the college is located. Further, this measure is biased toward metropolitan areas that have more schools.

Berger, Blomquist, and Waldner use only the teacher-pupil ratio.[40] Although this may be an indication of quality of education, it does not seem to measure overall quality of life. Similarly, studies reviewed by Lyon use indicators that do not measure overall educational achievement.[41] The studies in Lyon's review used indicators such as the number of seniors taking college board exams (which does not measure educational achievement), average expenditures per pupil, mean class size, and mean educational level of teachers (most of which measure only quality of education).

Few education variables are included in the CCDB. The percentage of the population completing high school or higher education is available for 1950, 1960, 1970, 1980, and 1990. The percentage completing college or more was available only for 1970, 1980, and 1990, and thus was not included in the data set. Thus, the percentage of the population completing high school or more education is used in this study.

The Model. It has been argued that the more educated the population, the higher the productivity.[42] If Minor League Baseball provides jobs and reduces unemployment, it may also be contributing to the productivity of an area. In addition, if it is located in areas with strong economies, there may be a large proportion of higher-educated persons with higher incomes and more discretionary funds to spend on entertainment such as Minor League Baseball. Further, education, as with Minor League Baseball, has been identified as an economic-development tool.[43] Thus, educational attainment, measured by the percentage of the population completing high school or more, is used as a dependent variable in the following model:

$$EDUC = a + b_1 MEDINC + b_2 BOPOP + b_3 HASANY + b_4 HASYRS + b_5 PURETN + b_6 PULOST + e$$

where:

MEDINC = median income
BOPOP = percentage of the population that is black or other races
HASANY = county hosted a team at any point during the decade
HASYRS = number of years the county hosted a team
PURETN = dummy variable that equals 1 if the county hosted a team during the decade and kept it through the end of the decade
PULOST = dummy variable that equals 1 if the county hosted a team during the decade but lost it by the end of the decade

Educational attainment is affected by a variety of things. However, not all groups have the same probability of completing high school or continuing on to college. Minorities and those with lower incomes historically have achieved lower levels of education than whites. Education is also related to the economic resources one has, which is measured here by the median income.[44]

The Results. The coefficients in Table B.2 show the relationship between the independent variables and educational attainment in the 1950s, 1960s, 1970s, and 1980s. Minor League Baseball is related to educational attainment only in the 1950s. The results suggest that the length of time a team is present in a county is important to its impact on the community. For example, the number of years a team is present in the county (HASYRS) is positively related to educational attainment. Thus, counties with a team for a greater number of years during the 1950s, experienced higher educational attainment. However, hosting a team at any point during the decade (HASANY) is negatively related to educational attainment. Similarly, counties that gained a team during the 1950s, but no longer had a team by the end of the decade (PULOST), experienced lower educational attainment.

However, this pattern was not repeated in the following decades. There appears to be no relationship between Minor League Baseball and educational attainment in the 1960s and 1970s. In the 1980s, the

TABLE B.2. Regression Coefficients, Educational Attainment

Independent Variables	Model 1 1950s	Model 2 1960s	Model 3 1970s	Model 4 1980s
MEDINC	0.01 ***	0.01***	0.00 ***	0.00 ***
BOPOP	0.03 ***	0.02 *	−0.03 ***	−0.04 ***
HASANY	−1.87 ***	1.32	0.33	0.87
HASYRS	0.55 ***	−0.05	0.12	0.27
PULOST	3.19 ***	0.52	0.65	−3.69 *
PURETN	−1.48	−0.06	2.38	1.11
Adjusted R^2	.80	.80	.80	.78
N	2,600	2,795	2,794	2,795

* = $P \leq .05$, *** = $P \leq .001$

only effect of Minor League Baseball was a negative relationship between gaining a team and subsequently losing it (PULOST), and educational attainment.

These results are consistent with the changes in the minor league industry since the 1950s. The 1950s began with a period of prosperity for Minor League Baseball and ended in a long decline in attendance and number of teams. Because communities could not support the number of teams that had been created during the postwar boom, Minor League Baseball declined during the 1950s. Thus, it follows that those communities that were prosperous enough to retain their teams throughout this period (as evidenced by hosting a team for a greater number of years), were also the communities that experienced higher educational attainment and, perhaps, a higher quality of life. Communities that lost a team, or that hosted a team for only part of the decade, were communities that were also suffering from fluctuating social and economic circumstances.

However, in the 1960s and 1970s, Minor League Baseball struggled. The number of teams reached a low point, and the teams themselves were not financially sound. Attendance declined and the minor league industry depended on assistance from Major League Baseball for survival. Thus, it follows that Minor League Baseball would have no impact on the community during this time, as suggested by insignificant regression results.

The 1980s was a period of rebuilding for the minor leagues. During this time, communities began to view Minor League Baseball as an economic-development tool. Thus, it follows that there would be some relationship between Minor League Baseball and the social and economic conditions in the community. The regression results show a negative relationship between gaining a team but losing it and educational attainment. Thus, it is consistent that those communities that attracted a team but could not support it also experienced declining educational attainment and QOL. Such communities, perhaps, were not able to sustain social and economic development during the 1980s.

Crime

It has been argued that Minor League Baseball has a positive impact on the QOL in a community. The one dimension of QOL that researchers have agreed on is public safety. Savageau and Boyer included both the violent crime rate and the property crime rate in their analysis. Berger, Blomquist, and Waldner, and those conducting follow-up studies, included the violent crime rate. Lyon found burglaries, larceny, and auto thefts were used by various researchers in other QOL studies.[45]

The Model. The serious crime rate is used in this study, since it is the one measure of public safety that is included in each *County and City Data Book* after 1970, having been measured in 1975, 1980, and 1990. Thus, a regression model with the crime rate was estimated, as follows:

$$\text{CRIME} = a + b_1\text{MEDINC} + b_2\text{POP} + b_3\text{BOPOP} + b_4\text{HASANY} + b_5\text{HASYRS} + b_6\text{PURETN} + b_7\text{PULOST} + e$$

where:

MEDINC = median income
POP = population
BOPOP = percentage of the population that is black or other races
HASANY = county hosted a team at any point during the decade
HASYRS = number of years the county hosted a team
PURETN = dummy variable that equals 1 if the county hosted a team during the decade and kept it through the end of the decade
PULOST = dummy variable that equals 1 if the county hosted a team during the decade but lost it by the end of the decade

According to Merton, when individuals are unable to achieve their goals (such as acquiring money and goods) through socially approved means, they resort to other methods, such as deviance. Members of minority groups and those facing economic hardships are often the groups shut out from socially approved means to achieve goals.[46] In addition, labor market conditions and prices (measured by the population and median income) may cause economic problems that lead to crime.[47] Those who commit crimes are disproportionately from a lower socioeconomic class and minority groups,[48] thus the inclusion of the minority population. Although, the numbers are controversial, the *Uniform Crime Report* suggests that African Americans account for 45 percent of violent crime arrests and 32 percent of property crime arrests.[49] Of course, it may be that racial profiling and other biases in the criminal justice system have skewed the data. Nonetheless, these are the best data available to estimate the extent of crime on a countywide basis.

The Results. Regression results for the crime rate appear in Table B.3. Data on crime rates are available in the *County and City Data Book* only for the 1970s and 1980s. Thus, only two models were estimated.

These results suggest a positive relationship between Minor League Baseball and the crime rate. Thus, counties that host a team experience higher crime rates. Although on the surface it may appear that Minor League Baseball may "cause" higher crime rates, the relationship is probably more complex. For example, if Minor League Baseball is successful as an economic-development tool, the county will experience a growth in the number of businesses in the area and, perhaps, population. As the regression results indicate, population is positively related to the crime rate. Thus, the more people there are, the greater the opportunity for crimes to occur. Similarly, with more businesses present there is a greater opportunity for shoplifting, armed robbery, and other such crimes.

TABLE B.3. Regression Coefficients, Crime Rate

Independent Variables	Model 1 1970s	Model 2 1980s
MEDINC	0.49 ***	0.19 ***
POP	0.00 ***	0.00 ***
BOPOP	17.53 ***	28.39 ***
HASANY	1141.09 ***	1237.43 *
HASYRS	101.98 **	98.08
PULOST	40.51	−1014.27
PURETN	−594.02	136.85
Adjusted R²	.53	.42
N	2,608	2,736

* = $P \leq .05$, ** = $P \leq .01$, *** = $P \leq .001$

An increased crime rate also can be the result of improved reporting. Larger communities, typically those able to support Minor League Baseball, have larger police forces, better crime tracking systems, and more community watch programs. Thus, with better tracking capabilities, more crimes can be reported. Therefore, there may be other factors that account for the positive relationship between sports and crime.

Notes

Chapter 1

1. Lloyd Johnson and Miles Wolff, eds., *The Encyclopedia of Minor League Baseball,* Second Edition (Durham, NC: Baseball America, Inc., 1997), p. 479; Rebecca Susan Kraus, "Sport and the Community: The Case of Minor League Baseball, 1950s-1990s," (Doctoral dissertation, The Catholic University of America, 1998), pp. 77-78.
2. Neil J. Sullivan, *The Minors: The Struggles and the Triumph of Baseball's Poor Relation from 1876 to the Present* (New York: St. Martin's Press, 1990), p. 256.
3. New York Times Service, "Profitable Days Down on the Farm for Pro Baseball," *St. Louis Post-Dispatch,* 1989, p 3F.
4. See Arthur T. Johnson, *Minor League Baseball and Local Economic Development* (Chicago, IL: University of Illinois Press, 1993), pp. 11-19.
5. Johnson and Wolff, *The Encyclopedia of Minor League Baseball,* p. 11.
6. Ibid.
7. Minor League Baseball, "Frequently Asked Questions," accessed at <www.milb.com/help/faq/>.
8. Judith Blahnik and Phillip S. Schulz, *Mud Hens and Mavericks* (New York: Viking Studio Books, 1995), p. 6.
9. Bruce Adelson, Rod Beaton, Bill Koenig, and Lisa Winston, *The Minor League Baseball Book* (New York: Macmillan, 1995), p. 5.
10. David Lamb, *Stolen Season: A Journey Through America and Baseball's Minor Leagues* (New York: Random House, 1991), p. x.
11. Mike Blake, *The Minor Leagues: A Celebration of the Little Show* (New York: Wynwood Press, 1991), p. 15.
12. Bruce Chadwick, *Baseball's Hometown Teams: The Story of the Minor Leagues* (New York: Abbeville Press, 1994), p. 14.
13. Sullivan, *The Minors,* p. vii.
14. Blahnik and Schulz, *Mud Hens and Mavericks,* p. 1.
15. Kraus, "Sport and the Community," p. 152.

Chapter 2

1. See National Association of Professional Baseball Leagues, "Minor League Baseball—From the Beginning," accessed at <http://www.milb.com/history/100years>. See also Neil J. Sullivan, *The Minors: The Struggles and the Triumph of Baseball's Poor Relation From 1876 to the Present* (New York: St. Martin's Press, 1990), Chaps. 1-3.

2. Lloyd Johnson and Miles Wolff, eds., *The Encyclopedia of Minor League Baseball*, Second Edition (Durham, NC: Baseball America, Inc., 1997), p. 133.

3. Ibid., p. 411.

4. Ibid.

5. Arthur T. Johnson, *Minor League Baseball and Local Economic Development* (Chicago, IL: University of Illinois Press, 1993), pp. 10, 20-21.

6. Jay Acton and Nick Bakalar, *Green Diamonds: The Pleasures and Profits of Investing in Minor League Baseball* (New York: Zebra Books, 1993), pp. 40-41.

7. Johnson and Wolff, *The Encyclopedia of Minor League Baseball*, p. 411; James Edward Miller, *The Baseball Business: Pursuing Pennants and Profits in Baltimore* (Chapel Hill, NC: The University of North Carolina Press, 1990), p. 104.

8. Compiled from *Baseball America 2002 Directory* (Durham, NC: Baseball America, Inc., 2002), pp. 135-142.

9. Bill O'Neal, *The International League: A Baseball History, 1994-1991* (Austin, TX: Eakin Press, 1992), p. 1.

10. International League, "An Outline History of the International League," accessed at <http://www.ilbaseball.com/aboutext.html>.

11. O'Neal, *The International League*, pp. 3-4.

12. International League, "An Outline History of the International League," accessed at <http://www.ilbaseball.com/aboutext.html>.

13. O'Neal, *The International League*, p. 54; Johnson and Wolff, *The Encyclopedia of Minor League Baseball*, p. 25. Prior to 1963, Class AA was an intermediate level of the minors, below Class A, but above Classes B, C, D, and E; Johnson and Wolff, *The Encyclopedia of Minor League Baseball*, p. 11.

14. O'Neal, *The International League*, pp. 68-69.

15. Ibid., p. 69; International League, "An Outline History of the International League"; Johnson and Wolff, *The Encyclopedia of Minor League Baseball*, p. 213.

16. Johnson and Wolff, *The Encyclopedia of Minor League Baseball*, pp. 213-214. See also O'Neal, *The International League*, pp. 69-70. The Southern Association, the Blue Ridge League, and the Virginia League suspended operations in June that year, and the American Association, the Pacific Coast League, the Western League, the Texas League, and the Eastern League ceased play in July. The Pacific Coast International League disbanded in May.

17. Johnson and Wolff, *The Encyclopedia of Minor League Baseball*, p. 25.

18. O'Neal, *The International League*, p. 133.

19. Ibid., pp. 133-153.

20. Ibid., pp. 169-170.

21. O'Neal, *The International League*, pp. 205-206.

22. Johnson and Wolff, *The Encyclopedia of Minor League Baseball*, p. 505.

23. Ibid., p. 587; *Baseball America 1998 Directory* (Durham, NC: Baseball America, Inc., 1998), pp. 128, 137.

24. Bruce Chadwick, *Baseball's Hometown Teams: The Story of the Minor Leagues* (New York: Abbeville Press, 1994), p. 90.

25. Johnson and Wolff, *The Encyclopedia of Minor League Baseball*, p. 11. See also Sullivan, *The Minors*, p. 222.

26. Bill O'Neal, *The Pacific Coast League: 1903-1988* (Austin, TX: Eakin Press, 1990), pp. 89-91; Sullivan, *The Minors*, pp. 216-219.

27. Ibid., pp. 57-61.

28. Ibid., p. 78.
29. Ibid., pp. 112-114.
30. Chadwick, *Baseball's Hometown Teams*, p. 90.
31. Ibid., pp. 92-93.
32. See Johnson and Wolff, *The Encyclopedia of Minor League Baseball*, pp. 33-34.
33. Ibid., pp. 16, 89-90.
34. Ibid., pp. 27, 435, 441.
35. *Baseball America 2002 Directory* Nineteenth Edition (Durham, NC: Baseball America, Inc., 2002), p. 287.
36. John Thorn and Bob Carroll, eds., *The Whole Baseball Catalogue* (New York: Fireside, 1990), p. 240.
37. Eastern League, "History," accessed at <http://www.easternleague.com/history.htm>.
38. Johnson and Wolff, *The Encyclopedia of Minor League Baseball*, pp. 36-37.
39. Southern League of Professional Baseball, "A Brief History of the Southern League," accessed at <http://www.southernleague.com/history.htm>.
40. See Johnson and Wolff, *The Encyclopedia of Minor League Baseball*, p. 36.
41. Ibid.; Bill O'Neal, *The Southern League: Baseball in Dixie, 1885-1994* (Austin, TX: Eakin Press, 1994), pp. 21-22.
42. Mike Blake, *The Minor Leagues: A Celebration of the Little Show* (New York: Wynwood Press, 1991), pp. 165-166. See also Johnson and Wolff, *The Encyclopedia of Minor League Baseball*, p. 36.
43. Johnson and Wolff, *The Encyclopedia of Minor League Baseball*, p. 36.
44. Southern League of Professional Baseball, "A Brief History of the Southern League."
45. Ibid.
46. Johnson and Wolff, *The Encyclopedia of Minor League Baseball*, p. 38.
47. Blake, *The Minor Leagues*, p. 154; Johnson and Wolff, *The Encyclopedia of Minor League Baseball*, pp. 38, 113-114.
48. Johnson and Wolff, *The Encyclopedia of Minor League Baseball*, p. xx.
49. Blake, *The Minor Leagues*, p. 156; Southern League of Professional Baseball, "A Brief History of the Southern League."
50. Thorn and Carroll, *The Whole Baseball Catalogue*, pp. 245-246.
51. Johnson and Wolff, *The Encyclopedia of Minor League Baseball*, p. xx; California League, "Cal League History," accessed at <http://www.californialeague.com/history.html>.
52. Bruce Adams and Margaret Engel, *Ballpark Vacations* (New York: Fodor's Travel Publications, Inc., 1997), pp. 1-4; Bruce Adelson, Rod Beaton, Bill Koenig, and Lisa Winston, *The Minor League Baseball Book* (New York: Macmillan Travel, 1995), p. 116; Thorn and Carroll, *The Whole Baseball Catalogue*, p. 247.
53. Carolina League, "Carolina League's History A Rich One," accessed at <http://www.carolinaleague.com/league/history>.
54. Jim L. Sumner, *Separating the Men from the Boys: The First Half-Century of the Carolina League* (Winston-Salem, NC: John F. Blair, Publisher, 1994), pp. 3-5, 13-14.
55. See Johnson and Wolff, *The Encyclopedia of Minor League Baseball*, pp. 79-80, 83-84. See also Sumner, *Separating the Men from the Boys*, pp. 40-42.

56. Sumner, *Separating the Men from the Boys*, p. 41.

57. Thorn and Carroll, *The Whole Baseball Catalogue*, p. 248; *Baseball America 2002 Directory*, pp. 111-113, 181-186.

58. Florida State League, "History," accessed at <http://www.fslbaseball.com/frmwelcome.htm>. See also Johnson and Wolff, *The Encyclopedia of Minor League Baseball*, p. x.

59. Ibid.

60. Compiled from *Baseball America 2002 Directory*, pp. 194-201.

61. Johnson and Wolff, *The Encyclopedia of Minor League Baseball*, pp. 36, 38, 42. See also South Atlantic League, "Welcome to the Official Web Site of the League of Choice," accessed at <http://www.southatlanticleague.com>.

62. Compiled from Johnson and Wolff, *The Encyclopedia of Minor League Baseball*, pp. 71-73.

63. The Midwest League, "History," accessed at <http://www.midwestleague.com/mwlhistory.html>; See also Johnson and Wolff, *The Encyclopedia of Minor League Baseball*, pp. x, xxx.

64. The Midwest League, "History."

65. Adams and Engel, *Ballpark Vacations*, pp. 102-104, 141-147.

66. Compiled from *Baseball America 2002 Directory*, pp. 202-208.

67. See Johnson and Wolff, *The Encyclopedia of Minor League Baseball*, pp. xxx.

68. Northwest League, "League History," accessed at <http://www.northwestleague.com/about1.html>.

69. Thorn and Carroll, *The Whole Baseball Catalogue*, p. 260.

70. Compiled from *Baseball America 2002 Directory*, pp. 170, 176, 181, 187, 194, 214-218.

71. See Johnson and Wolff, *The Encyclopedia of Minor League Baseball*, p. x.

72. Ibid., p. 70-71, 77, 86, 88.

73. The Pioneer League, "A Brief history of the Pioneer Baseball League," accessed at <http://www.pioneerleague.com/History/history.htm>.

74. See Johnson and Wolff, *The Encyclopedia of Minor League Baseball*, p. x.

75. Steve Perlstein, *Rebel Baseball: The Summer the Game Was Returned to the Fans* (New York: Henry Hold and Company, 1994), p. 5.

76. Johnson and Wolff, *The Encyclopedia of Minor League Baseball*, pp. 135, 156, 161-162, 166.

77. Ibid., p. 185.

78. Ibid., pp. 35, 375, 387, 393.

79. Ibid., p. 609.

80. Ibid.

81. Ibid.

82. All-American Association, "League," accessed at <http://www.allamericanassociation.com>.

83. Northern League, "Historical Overview, The Northern League: Proud Tradition," by David Kemp, accessed at <http://www.northernleague.com/history.html> (emphasis in original).

84. Northern League, "Historical Overview."

85. Northern League, "Historical Overview." See also Johnson and Wolff, *The Encyclopedia of Minor League Baseball*, p. 32.

86. Northern League, "Historical Overview."
87. Northern League, "History of the Northeast League," accessed at <http://www.northernleague.com/northeastlg.html>.
88. Frontier League, "Frontier League Online: League History," accessed at <http://www.frontierleague.com/history.htm>.
89. *Baseball America 1996 Directory* (Durham, NC: Baseball America, Inc., 1996), pp. 217-218; *Baseball America 1997 Directory* (Durham, NC: Baseball America, Inc., 1997), pp. 222-223.
90. *Baseball America 1999 Directory* (Durham, NC: Baseball America, Inc., 1999), pp. 255, 257-260.
91. Frontier League, "Frontier League Online: Teams," accessed at <http://www.frontierleague.com/teams.htm>.
92. Central League, "History," accessed at <http://www.centralleaguebaseball.com/history.html>; Central League, "Wolff Named Central League Commissioner," news release, March 1, 2002; Mark Derewicz, "Fort Worth, Tyler Find Greener Indy Pastures," *Baseball America Online,* Jan. 7, 2002, accessed at <http://www.baseballamerica.com/today/leagues/independent/indy0107.html>.
93. Derewicz, "Fort Worth, Tyler Find Greener Indy Pastures"; Mike Christensen, "Jackson to Get Former Tyler, Texas, Ballclub," *The Clarion-Ledger,* Jan. 31, 2002, accessed at <http://www.clarionledger.com>.
94. Western Baseball League, "A Brief History of the Western Baseball League," accessed at <http://www.westernbaseball.com/league_history.html>.
95. Ibid.
96. Atlantic League of Professional Baseball Clubs, Inc., "League Information," accessed at <http://www.atlanticleague.com/league.html>.

Chapter 3

1. There have been numerous social science research studies that focus on Minor League Baseball: William G. Colclough, Lawrence A. Daellenbach, and Keith R. Sherony, "Estimating the Economic Impact of a Minor League Baseball Stadium," *Managerial and Decision Economics,* vol. 15 (1994), pp. 497-502; Arthur T. Johnson, "Professional Baseball at the Minor League Level: Considerations for Cities Large and Small," *State and Local Government Review,* vol. 22, no. 2 (1990), pp. 90-96; Arthur T. Johnson, "Local Government, Minor League Baseball, and Economic Development Strategies," *Economic Development Quarterly,* vol. 5, no. 4 (1991), pp. 313-324; Kenneth C. Land, Walter R. Davis, and Judith R. Blau, "Organizing the Boys of Summer: The Evolution of U.S. Minor League Baseball, 1883-1990," *American Journal of Sociology,* vol. 100, no. 3 (1994), pp. 781-813; Mark S. Rosentraub and David Swindell, "'Just Say No?' The Economic and Political Realities of a Small City's Investment in Minor League Baseball," *Economic Development Quarterly,* vol. 5, no. 2 (1991), pp. 152-167.
2. Janet Lever, *Soccer Madness* (Chicago: The University of Chicago Press, 1983); Bruce Kucklick, *To Everything a Season: Shibe Park and Urban Philadelphia, 1909-1976* (Princeton, NJ: Princeton University Press, 1991); Steven Riess, *City Games: The Evolution of American Urban Society and the Rise of Sports* (Chicago: University of Illinois Press, 1989); Neil J. Sullivan, *The Dodgers Move West* (New York: Oxford University Press, 1987).

3. Charles C. Euchner, *Playing the Field: Why Sports Teams Move and Cities Fight to Keep Them* (Baltimore: Johns Hopkins University Press, 1993); Rosentraub and Swindell, "Just Say No?", pp. 152-167; David Whitson and Donald Macintosh, "Becoming a World-Class City: Hallmark Events and Sports Franchises in the Growth Strategies of Western Canadian Cities," *Sociology of Sport Journal,* vol. 10, no. 3, pp. 221-240.

4. Robert A. Baade and Richard F. Dye, "Sports Stadiums and Area Development: A Critical Review," *Economic Development Quarterly,* vol. 2, no. 3 (1988), p. 46; Robert A. Baade and Richard F. Dye, "An Analysis of the Economic Rationale for Public Subsidization of Sports Stadiums," *The Annals of Regional Science,* vol. 22, no. 2 (1988), p. 274; Johnson, "Local Government, Minor League Baseball, and Economic Development Strategies," pp. 313-324; Benjamin A. Okner, "Subsidies of Stadiums and Arenas," in Roger N. Noll, ed., *Government and the Sports Business* (Washington: The Brookings Institution, 1974), p. 327.

5. Roger N. Noll, "Attendance and Price Setting," in Roger N. Noll, ed., *Government and the Sports Business* (Washington: The Brookings Institution, 1974), p. 121; Gerald W. Scully, *The Business of Major League Baseball* (Chicago: The University of Chicago Press, 1989), p. 112.

6. Sullivan, *The Dodgers Move West,* p. 194.

7. John P. Marcum and Theodore N. Greenstein, "Factors Affecting Attendance of Major League Baseball: II. A Within-Season Analysis," *Sociology of Sport Journal,* vol. 2 (1985), pp. 314-322.

8. Robert A. Baade and Laura J. Tiehen, "An Analysis of Major League Baseball Attendance, 1969-1987," *Journal of Sport and Social Issues,* vol. 14, no. 1 (1990), pp. 14-32.

9. Ibid., p. 22.

10. Ibid., p. 17.

11. Barry Schwartz and Stephen F. Barsky, "The Home Advantage," *Social Forces,* vol. 55, no. 3 (1977), p. 642.

12. Ibid., p. 651.

13. Ibid., p. 657.

14. Mark S. Mizruchi, "Local Sports Teams and Celebration of Community," *The Sociological Quarterly,* vol. 26, no. 4 (1985), p. 508.

15. Ibid., p. 509.

16. Lever, *Soccer Madness,* p. 13.

17. Ibid., p. 145.

18. Garry J. Smith, "The Noble Sports Fan," *Journal of Sport and Social Issues,* vol. 12, no. 1 (1988), p. 59.

19. Nick Trujillo and Bob Krizek, "Emotionality in the Stands and in the Field: Expressing Self Through Baseball," *Journal of Sport and Social Issues,* November 1994, p. 306.

20. Riess, *City Games,* p. 236.

21. Sullivan, *The Dodgers Move West,* p. 194.

22. Ibid.

23. Kuklick, *To Everything a Season,* p. 53.

24. Ibid., p. 190.

25. Ibid., p. 191.

26. Ibid., p. 6.

27. Ibid., p. 190.

28. Rob Ruck, *Sandlot Seasons: Sport in Black Pittsburgh* (Urbana, IL: The University of Illinois Press, 1993), p. 3.

29. Ibid.

30. James Bankes, *The Pittsburgh Crawfords* (Dubuque, IA: C. Brown Publishers, 1991), pp. 102-105.

31. Alan G. Ingham, Jeremy W. Howell, and Todd Schilperoot, "Professional Sports and Community: A Review and Exegesis," in Art Johnson and Jim Frey, eds., *Government and Sport: The Public Policy Issues* (Totowa, NJ: Rowan and Allanheid, 1986), p. 431.

32. Ibid., p. 441.

33. Ibid., p. 461.

34. Gregory P. Stone, "Sport As a Community Representation," in Gunter R.F. Luschen and George H. Sage, eds., *Handbook of Social Science of Sport* (Champaign, IL: Stipes Publishing Company, 1981), p. 224.

35. Ibid., p. 243.

36. David Montgomery, "With Minor Leagues Blooming, Bowie Can't Wait to 'Play Ball!'" *The Washington Post,* August 1, 1993, p. B1; Eugene L. Meyer, "Bowie's Roads of Discovery," *The Washington Post,* April 21, 1999, p. M16; Jackie Spinner, "A Life of Luxury in Bowie," *The Washington Post,* May 15, 1999, p. H1; Joel Furfari, "Bases Loaded: As Bowie Enters 10th Season, Bowie Savors Team's Impact on City's Economy, Leisure," *The Bowie Star,* April 11, 2002, p. A1.

37. Scott Graham, "Aberdeen Stadium Already Spurs Growth," *Baltimore Business Journal,* June 21-27, 2002, p. 5.

38. Okner, "Subsidies of Stadiums and Arenas," p. 327.

39. Ibid.

40. Ibid., p. 346.

41. Frank L. Hefner, "Using Economic Models to Measure the Impact of Sports on Local Economies," *Journal of Sport and Social Issues,* vol. 14, no. 1 (1990), p. 2.

42. Baade and Dye, "Sports Stadiums and Area Development: A Critical Review," p. 46.

43. Baade and Dye, "An Analysis of the Economic Rationale for Public Subsidization of Sports Stadiums," p. 274.

44. Ibid., p. 273.

45. Johnson, "Local Government, Minor League Baseball, and Economic Development Strategies," p. 315.

46. Ibid., p. 322.

47. Arthur T. Johnson, "The Uneasy Partnership of Cities and Professional Sport: Public Policy Considerations," in Nancy Theberge and Peter Donnelly, eds., *Sport and the Sociological Imagination* (Fort Worth, TX: Texas Christian University Press, 1984), p. 216.

48. Ibid., pp. 216-217.

49. Ibid., p. 218.

50. Ibid., p. 224.

51. Johnson, "Professional Baseball at the Minor League Level," p. 96.

52. John P. Pelissero, Beth M. Henschen, and Edward I. Sidlow, "Urban Regimes, Sports Stadiums, and the Politics of Economic Development," *Policy Studies Review,* vol. 10, no. 2/3 (1991), p. 125.

53. Ibid.

54. Arthur T. Johnson, "The Sports Franchise Relocation Issue and Public Policy Response," in Art Johnson and Jim Frey, eds., *Government and Sport: The Public Policy Issues* (Totowa, NJ: Rowan and Allanheid, 1986), pp. 219-247.

55. Ibid., p. 236.

56. Colclough, Daellenbach, and Sherony, "Estimating the Economic Impact of a Minor League Baseball Stadium," p. 501.

57. Euchner, *Playing the Field,* p. 20.

58. Ibid., p. 168.

59. David Whitson and Donald Macintosh, "Becoming a World-Class City: Hallmark Events and Sport Franchises in the Growth Strategies of Western Canadian Cities," *Sociology of Sport Journal*, vol. 10, no. 3 (1993), pp. 221-240.

60. Rosentraub and Swindell, "Just Say No?," p. 166.

61. Ibid.

62. Baade and Dye, "Sports Stadiums and Area Development," pp. 272-274; Johnson, "Local Government, Minor League Baseball, and Economic Development Strategies," pp. 321-323; Baade and Dye, "An Analysis of the Economic Rationale for Public Subsidization of Sports Stadiums," p. 46; Johnson, "Local Government, Minor League Baseball, and Economic Development Strategies," pp. 321-323; Colclough, Daellenbach, and Sherony, "Estimating the Economic Impact of a Minor League Baseball Stadium," p. 501.

63. Robert M. MacIver, *Society: Its Structure and Changes* (New York: Ray Long and Richard R. Smith, Inc., 1931), quoted in Dennis E. Poplin, *Communities: A Survey of Theories and Methods of Research* (New York: The Macmillan Company, 1972), p. 16.

64. Poplin, *Communities,* pp. 14-15.

65. Roland L. Warren, *The Community in America* (Chicago: Rand McNally College Publishing Company, 1972), p. 6.

66. Ibid., Chapter 3.

67. Poplin, *Communities,* pp. 16-17.

68. Roland L. Warren, ed., *New Perspectives on the American Community* (Chicago: Rand McNally College Publishing, 1977), p. 260; Warren, *The Community in America,* pp. 161-166.

69. Eastern League, "Political Parties Battle in 41st Annual Congressional Game at Prince George's Stadium," news release, June 17, 2002; Tynisa E. Trapps, "Republicans Tattoo Democrats," *The Prince George's Sentinel Newspaper,* June 27, 2002, accessed at <http://www.thesentinel.com/pgfolder/020627baseball.htm>.

70. Robert A. Nisbet, *The Sociological Tradition* (New York: Basic Books, Inc., Publishers, 1966), p. 47.

71. Warren, *New Perspectives,* p. 6.

72. Poplin, *Communities,* p. 7.

73. Robert A. Nisbet, "Moral Values and Community," *International Review of Community Development,* vol. 5 (1960), p. 7-85; reprinted in Warren, *New Perspectives*, p. 100.

74. Coleman McCarthy, "Minor League Game is Major Source of Joy," *The Washington Post,* Aug. 15, 1990, p. B6.

75. David Lamb, "The Major Pleasures of the Minor Leagues," *USA Weekend,* June 5-7, 1992, pp. 4-6.

76. Bruce Chadwick, *Baseball's Hometown Teams: The Story of the Minor Leagues* (New York: Abbeville Press Publishers, 1994), p. 144.
77. Mark Newman, "That's Life on the Farm," *Sporting News,* April 24, 1995, p. 35.
78. Bruce Adelson, "Take Me Out to the Ball Game—And Make It a Minor League," *The Washington Post,* March 1, 1992, p. E1.
79. Lamb, "The Major Pleasures," p. 4.
80. Joseph R. Gusfield, *The Community: A Critical Response* (New York: Harper Colophon, 1975), p. 24.
81. Poplin, *Communities,* p. 65.
82. Warren, *New Perspectives,* p. 4.
83. Robert Ezra Park, "Human Ecology," *American Journal of Sociology,* vol. XLII, no. 1 (1936), pp. 1-15; reprinted in Warren, *New Perspectives,* p. 45.
84. Park, "Human Ecology," p. 47.
85. John D. Kasarda, "Urbanization, Community, and the Metropolitan Problem," David Street and Associates, eds., *Handbook of Contemporary Urban Life* (Washington: Jossey-Bass Publishers, 1978), p. 29.
86. Ernest W. Burgess, "The Growth of the City: An Introduction to a Research Project," Robert E. Park, Ernest W. Burgess, and R.D. McKenzie, eds., *The City* (Chicago: University of Chicago Press, 1925), p. 50; Larry Lyon, *The Community in Urban Society* (Philadelphia: Temple University Press, 1987), pp. 35-37.
87. Lyon, *The Community in Urban Society,* p. 35.
88. Kasarda, "Urbanization, Community, and the Metropolitan Problem," p. 28.
89. Riess, *City Games.*
90. Amos H. Hawley, "Ecology and Human Ecology," *Social Forces,* vol. 22 (1944), p. 403.
91. Amos. H. Hawley, *Human Ecology: A Theory of Community Structure* (Chicago: The University of Chicago Press, 1950), p. 180.
92. Ibid., p. 209.
93. Ibid.
94. Lever, *Soccer Madness.*
95. Kuklick, *To Everything a Season,* p. 190.
96. See, for example, David McLellan, ed., *Karl Marx: Selected Writings* (New York: Oxford University Press, 1990); Hans Gerth and C. Wright Mills, *From Max Weber* (New York: Oxford University Press, 1958).
97. Anthony Giddens, ed., *Emile Durkheim: Selected Writings* (New York: Cambridge University Press, 1972).
98. Emíle Durkheim, *The Division of Labor in Society,* translated by George Simpson (New York: The Free Press, 1933).
99. Ibid., p. 70.
100. Ibid., pp. 28-29.
101. Ferdinand Tonnies, *Gemeinschaft und Gesellschaft,* translated by Charles P. Loomis (East Lansing, MI: The Michigan State University Press, 1957).
102. Warren, *The Community in America,* p. 2.
103. Tonnies, *Gemeinschaft and Gesellschaft,* p. 33.
104. Ibid., p. 42.
105. Poplin, *Communities,* pp. 115-116.
106. Ibid., p. 83, 267.

107. Ibid., p. 65.
108. Murray Ross, "Football Red and Baseball Green," in Peter I. Rose, eds., *The Study of Society* (New York: Random House, 1977), p. 114.
109. Wilbert Marcellus Leonard, II, *A Sociological Perspective of Sport*, third edition (New York: Macmillan Publishing Company, 1988), p. 72.
110. Ira Berkow, "Basketball the New National Pastime? Don't Rule Out Baseball," *The Baltimore Sun*, June 30, 1993, p. 1D.
111. Seymour B. Sarason, "Commentary: The Emergence of a Conceptual Center," *Journal of Community Psychology*, vol. 14 (1986), pp. 405-407.
112. Joseph R. Gusfield, *The Community: A Critical Response* (New York: Harper Colophon, 1975), p. xvi.
113. David W. McMillan and David M. Chavis, "Sense of Community: A Definition and Theory," *Journal of Community Psychology*, vol. 14 (1986), p. 9.
114. Warren, *The Community in America*, p. 5.
115. Ibid., p. 17.
116. John D. Kasarda and Morris Janowitz, "Community Attachment in Mass Society," *American Sociological Review*, vol. 39 (1974), pp. 328-339.
117. Randy Roberts and James Olson, *Winning is the Only Thing: Sports in America Since 1945* (Baltimore, MD: The Johns Hopkins University Press, 1989), p. 214.
118. David Lamb, *Stolen Season: A Journey Through America and Baseball's Minor Leagues* (New York: Random House, 1991).

Chapter 4

1. National Association of Professional Baseball Leagues, "Minor League Baseball to Open 100th Season at Memphis," Press release, Dec. 9, 2000.
2. Steven A. Riess, *City Games: The Evolution of American Urban Society and the Rise of Sports* (Chicago: University of Illinois Press, 1989), pp. 231-245.
3. Randy Roberts and James Olson, *Winning Is the Only Thing: Sports in America Since 1945* (Baltimore, MD: The Johns Hopkins University Press, 1989), p. 214.
4. Ibid., p. 216.
5. Johnson and Wolff divide minor league history from World War II to the 1990s into four eras: the Golden Years (1946-1951), the Decline (1952-1962), the Subsistence Years (1963-1977), the Revival (1978-1991), and the Boom (1992-1996). Lloyd Johnson and Miles Wolff, eds., *The Encyclopedia of Minor League Baseball*, Second Edition (Durham, NC: Baseball America, Inc., 1997), p. 105.
6. Ibid., p. 107.
7. Neil J. Sullivan, *The Minors: The Struggles and Triumph of Baseball's Poor Relation* (New York: St. Martin's Press, 1990), pp. 42-46.
8. Johnson and Wolff, *The Encyclopedia of Minor League Baseball*, 1997, pp. 193, 219, 263.
9. Sullivan, *The Minors*, pp. 96-98.
10. Johnson and Wolff, *The Encyclopedia of Minor League Baseball*, 1997, pp. 321, 354.
11. Lloyd Johnson and Miles Wolff, eds., *The Encyclopedia of Minor League Baseball*, First Edition (Durham, NC: Baseball America, Inc., 1993), p. 219.

12. Ibid.
13. Ibid., p. 263; Sullivan, *The Minors*, pp. 235-251.
14. Johnson and Wolff, *The Encyclopedia of Minor League Baseball*, 1993, p. 263.
15. Ibid.
16. Ibid., p. 309.
17. Sullivan, *The Minors*, p. 256.
18. Jay Acton and Nick Bakalar, *Green Diamonds: The Pleasures and Profits of Investing in Minor League Baseball* (New York: Kensington Publishing Corporation, 1993), p. 24.
19. New York Times News Service, "Profitable Days Down on the Farm for Pro Baseball," *St. Louis Post-Dispatch*, 1989, p. 3F.
20. David Lamb, "A Minor Happening: Farm Team in Durham, N.C., Cultivates Success," *Los Angeles Times*, August 1989, p. 3.
21. Arthur T. Johnson, *Minor League Baseball and Local Economic Development* (Chicago: University of Illinois Press, 1993), pp. 78-95.
22. Johnson and Wolff, *The Encyclopedia of Minor League Baseball*, 1993, p. 309.
23. Wilbert Marcellus Leonard II, *A Sociological Perspective of Sport*, Third Edition (New York: Macmillan Publishing Company, 1988), p. 335.
24. Johnson and Wolff, *The Encyclopedia of Minor League Baseball*, 1993, p. 309.
25. Acton and Bakalar, *Green Diamonds*, p. 52.
26. Ibid., p. 145; Johnson, *Minor League Baseball and Local Economic Development*, p. 212.
27. Acton and Bakalar, *Green Diamonds*, pp. 13-14.
28. Ray Waddell, "'94 Season One of the Best Ever for Minor League Baseball," *Amusement Business*, vol. 106, no. 43 (1994), p. 16.
29. Ray Waddell, "Buffalo Bisons Top Draw in AAA Baseball," *Amusement Business*, vol. 104, no. 41 (1992), p. 14.
30. Johnson, *Minor League Baseball and Local Economic Development*, pp. 115-119; Ray Wadell, "Baseball's AA Attendance on Par with '91's Turnout," *Amusement Business*, vol. 105, no. 40 (1993), p. 16; Jack Cavanaugh, "Major Boom for Minor Leagues: Nationwide Attendance Hits Highest Level in 37 Years," *Chicago Tribune*, Sept. 24, 1989, p. 8.
31. Linda Deckard, "Young Lining Up Investors and Financing to Purchase Mets' AAA Tidewater Tides," *Amusement Business*, vol. 104, no. 36 (1992), p. 18.
32. David Lamb, *Stolen Season: A Journey Through America and Baseball's Minor Leagues* (New York: Random House, 1991).
33. Ibid., p. x.
34. *Baseball America 2001 Almanac* (Durham, NC: Baseball America, Inc., 2001), p. 263.
35. Johnson, *Minor League Baseball and Local Economic Development*, pp. 21-22.
36. Johnson and Wolff, *The Encyclopedia of Minor League Baseball*, 1997, p. 609.
37. Ibid.
38. Ibid.
39. Acton and Bakalar, *Green Diamonds*, pp. 89-92.

40. Mike Blake, *The Minor Leagues: A Celebration of the Little Show* (New York: Wynwood Press, 1991), quoted in Tim Warren, "Going to the Minors," *Baltimore Sun,* July 25, 1992, p. 1D.

41. Acton and Bakalar, *Green Diamonds,* pp. 94-96.

42. David Lamb, "The Major Pleasures of the Minor Leagues," *USA Weekend,* June 5-7, 1992, p. 6.

43. Bill Koenig, "He's the P.T. Barnum of the Minor Leagues," *Baseball Weekly,* Sept. 9-15, 1992, p. 24.

44. Richard Panek, *Waterloo Diamonds: A Midwestern Town and Its Minor League Team* (New York: St. Martin's Press, 1995), p. 54.

45. Quoted in John Thorn and Bob Carroll, eds., *The Whole Baseball Catalogue* (New York: Fireside, 1990), p. 236.

46. Ibid.

47. Johnson and Wolff, *The Encyclopedia of Minor League Baseball,* 1997, p. 74.

48. Bill O'Neal, *The International League: A Baseball History, 1994-1991* (Austin, TX: Eakin Press, 1992), pp. 236-243.

49. Johnson and Wolff, *The Encyclopedia of Minor League Baseball,* 1997, p. 207.

50. Ibid., pp. 227-387. Also see, William W. Mowbray, *The Eastern Shore Baseball League* (Centreville, MD: Tidewater Publishers, 1989).

51. Jim L. Sumner, *Separating the Men from the Boys: The First Half-Century of the Carolina League* (Winston-Salem, NC: John F. Blair, Publisher, 1994), p. 159.

52. *Baseball America 1996 Directory* (Durham, NC: Baseball America, Inc., 1996), p. 166.

53. *Baseball America 1997 Directory* (Durham, NC: Baseball America, Inc., 1997), pp. 124-125.

54. Miles Wolff, "New Nicknames Get Out of Control," *Baseball America,* vol. 14, no. 24, p. 6.

55. *Baseball America 1996 Directory* (Durham, NC: Baseball America, Inc., 1996); *Baseball America 1997 Directory* (Durham, NC: Baseball America, Inc., 1997).

56. Will Lingo, "Minors' Worst Fears Prove to Be Unfounded," *Baseball America,* June 9-22, 1997, p. 12.

57. *Baseball America 2001 Almanac,* pp. 264-266.

58. Ibid.

59. Ibid., p. 266.

60. *Baseball America 2002 Directory* (Durham, NC: Baseball America, Inc., 2002), p. 203.

61. Frontier League, "League History," accessed at <http://www.frontierleague.com/history.htm>; *Baseball America Directory* (Durham, NC: Baseball America, Inc., 1993-2001); Johnson and Wolff, *The Encyclopedia of Minor League Baseball.*

62. Frontier League, "League History" *Baseball America Directory;* Johnson and Wolff, *The Encyclopedia of Minor League Baseball,* 1997.

63. Compiled from *Baseball America 1998 Directory* (Durham, NC: Baseball America, Inc., 1998); *Baseball America 1999 Directory* (Durham, NC: Baseball America, Inc., 1999).

64. Compiled from *Baseball America 1999 Directory* (Durham, NC: Baseball America, Inc., 1999); *Baseball America 2000 Directory* (Durham, NC: Baseball America, Inc., 2000); *Baseball America 2001 Directory* (Durham, NC: Baseball America, Inc., 2001); *Baseball America 2002 Directory* (Durham, NC: Baseball America, Inc., 2002).

65. John Rofé, "Naming Deals Plug Holes in Financing," *Street & Smith's Sports Business Journal,* July 26-August 1, 1999, p. 30; *Baseball America 1996 Directory* (Durham, NC: Baseball America, Inc., 1996), pp. 158-159; *Baseball America 2000 Directory* (Durham, NC: Baseball America, Inc., 2000), pp. 148-149.

66. Rofé, "Naming Deals Plug Holes in Financing," p. 30; *Baseball America 1995 Directory* (Durham, NC: Baseball America, Inc., 1995), p. 98; *Baseball America 1996 Directory* (Durham, NC: Baseball America, Inc., 1996), p. 104; *Baseball America 1997 Directory* (Durham, NC: Baseball America, Inc., 1997), p. 108; *Baseball America 1998 Directory* (Durham, NC: Baseball America, Inc., 1998), p. 129; *Baseball America 1999 Directory* (Durham, NC: Baseball America, Inc., 1999), p. 136; *Baseball America 2000 Directory* (Durham, NC: Baseball America, Inc., 2000), p. 136.

67. Lamb, "The Major Pleasures of the Minor Leagues," p. 4.

Chapter 5

1. See Lloyd Johnson and Miles Wolff, eds., *The Encyclopedia of Minor League Baseball,* Second Edition (Durham, NC: Baseball America, Inc., 1997), p. 74.

2. Bill O'Neal, *The International League: A Baseball History, 1994-1991* (Austin, TX: Eakin Press, 1992), pp. 236-245.

3. Ibid.

4. Ibid.

5. See Johnson and Wolff, *The Encyclopedia of Minor League Baseball,* p. 207.

6. Johnson and Wolff, *The Encyclopedia of Minor League Baseball,* pp. 200-271.

7. Ibid., p. 22.

8. William W. Mowbray, *The Eastern Shore Baseball League* (Centreville, MD: Tidewater Publishers, 1989).

9. See Johnson and Wolff, *The Encyclopedia of Minor League Baseball,* pp. 53, 62.

10. Ibid.

11. Ibid.

12. Bruce Adams and Margaret Engel, *Ballpark Vacations: Great Family Trips to Minor League and Classic Major League Baseball Parks Across America* (New York: Fodor's Travel Publications, Inc., 1997), p. 90.

13. Paul Hendrickson, "At Play in a Fading Light: In Hagerstown, a Golden Image of Baseball Is Going, Going . . ." *The Washington Post,* August 26, 1997, p. C1.

14. City of Hagerstown, "Historic Preservation in Hagerstown: Background," accessed at <http://www.hagerstownmd.org/html/historic_preservation1.html>. See also State of Maryland, Maryland Manual Online, community information, accessed at <http://www.mdarchives.state.md.us>; Sue Anne Pressley, "Hagerstown: Hardship and Hope; Residents Defend Struggling City from Scorn of Outsiders," *The Washington Post,* March 25, 1985, p. D1.

15. Carl W. Disque, Preservation Design District Commission, "Introduction," p. 11 in Susan Levitas, ed., *Railroad Ties: Industry and Culture in Hagerstown, Maryland* (Crownsville, MD: The Maryland Historical Trust, 1994).

16. Ibid.

17. City of Hagerstown, "Historic Preservation in Hagerstown."

18. Pressley, "Hagerstown: Hardship and Hope."

19. See Johnson and Wolff, *The Encyclopedia of Minor League Baseball,* pp. 200-267.

20. Johnson and Wolff, *The Encyclopedia of Minor League Baseball,* p. 221. See also Hagerstown Suns, "History of Professional Baseball in Hagerstown, Maryland," compiled by David F. Chrisman, Bob Miller, Mike Oraves, and Dave Collins.

21. See Johnson and Wolff, *The Encyclopedia of Minor League Baseball,* p. 269.

22. Adams and Engel, *Ballpark Vacations,* p. 90; Bruce Adelson, Rod Beaton, Bill Koenig, and Lisa Winston, *The Minor League Baseball Book* (New York: Macmillan, 1995), p. 174; Hendrickson, "At Play in a Fading Light." For an in-depth discussion of integration in the southern minor leagues, see Bruce Adelson, *Brushing Back Jim Crow: The Integration of Minor-League Baseball in the American South* (Charlottesville, VA: University Press of Virginia, 1999).

23. Hendrickson, "At Play in a Fading Light." See also Adams and Engel, *Ballpark Vacations,* p. 90.

24. See Johnson and Wolff, *The Encyclopedia of Minor League Baseball,* p. 34.

25. Rick Gano, "Suns Have Their Day in the Sun," *The Hagerstown Morning Herald,* April 9, 1981, p. C1; Rick Gano, "It's Opening Day: Pro Baseball Returns as Suns Host Pilots," *The Hagerstown Morning Herald,* April 10, 1981, p. C1.

26. Rick Gano, "A Team of Strangers Pulls Together," *The Hagerstown Morning Herald,* April 11, 1981, p. B5; Darrell Kepler, "No Apology Necessary," *The Hagerstown Morning Herald,* April 11, 1981, p. B5; Marie Lanser, "6-2: Sums Open with a Win," *The Hagerstown Morning Herald,* April 11, 1981, p. A1.

27. Hagerstown Suns, "History of Professional Baseball in Hagerstown, Maryland."

28. See Johnson and Wolff, *The Encyclopedia of Minor League Baseball,* pp. 53, 58, 389-390.

29. Ibid.; *Baseball America 2000 Directory* (Durham, NC: Baseball America, Inc., 2000).

30. U.S. Census Bureau, *County and City Data Book: 1994,* Twelfth Edition, Table C, pp. 746-753.

31. See Hendrickson, "At Play in a Fading Light;" Scott Butki, "County Oks Stadium Spending," *The Hagerstown Herald-Mail,* May 9, 2000; Bruce Hamilton, "Group Offers New Stadium Plan," *The Hagerstown Herald-Mail,* Oct. 26, 1999; Dan Kulin, "Stadium Group to Propose Funding," *The Hagerstown Herald-Mail,* April 20, 2000.

32. Hagerstown Suns, "History of Professional Baseball in Hagerstown, Maryland."

33. *Baseball America 2001 Directory* (Durham, NC: Baseball America, 2001), p. 194. Attendance in the South Atlantic League ranged mostly between 264,924 (Delmarva Shorebirds) and 91,437 (Charleston Alley Cats). That year, the Cape Fear Crocs attendance was only 32,641. The team moved to a new stadium in Lakewood, NJ, for the 2001 season.

34. Eugene L. Meyer, "Bowie's Roads of Discovery," *The Washington Post,* April 21, 1999, p. M16.

35. City of Bowie, "Welcome to the City of Bowie on the Web," accessed at <http://www.cityofbowie.org/Welcome.htm>.

36. City of Bowie, "City of Bowie [history]," accessed at <http://www.cityofbowie.org/aboutmain.htm>; Meyer, "Bowie's Roads of Discovery."

37. City of Bowie, "City of Bowie [history]."

38. City of Bowie, "Welcome to the City of Bowie on the Web."

39. City of Bowie, "City of Bowie [history]."

40. International Council of Shopping Centers, "Their Town: Residents of Bowie Get a New Lifestyle Center—and a Downtown," accessed at <http://www.icsc.org/srch/sct/current/sct0401/page1c.html>.

41. City of Bowie, "Welcome to the City of Bowie on the Web." See also Kristin Collins, "Bowie Anticipates Challenges of the New Century," *The Bowie Star,* Dec. 31, 1999, accessed at <http://www.gazette.net>.

42. Maryland Department of Business and Economic Development, "Population," accessed at <http://www.dbed.state.md.us/datacenter/demographics/population.asp>.

43. Jeremy Breningstall, "County Now Maryland's Second-most Populous," *Gazette Newspapers,* March 22, 2001, accessed at <http://www.gazette.net>.

44. City of Bowie, "City of Bowie [history]."

Chapter 6

1. Roland L. Warren, *The Community in America* (Chicago: Rand McNally College Publishing Company, 1972), p. 6; Dennis M. Poplin, *Communities: A Survey of Theories and Methods of Research* (New York: The Macmillan Company, 1972), pp. 16-17.

2. Robert A. Nisbet, *The Quest for Community: A Study in the Ethics and Order of Freedom* (San Francisco: Institute for Contemporary Studies Press, 1990), pp. xxi-xxxii.

3. Roland L. Warren, *New Perspectives on the American Community* (Chicago: Rand McNally College Publishing Company, 1977), p. 6.

4. Nick Trujillo and Bob Krizek, "Emotionality in the Stands and in the Field: Expression Self Through Baseball," *Journal of Sport and Social Issues,* vol. 18 (1994), pp. 303-325.

5. Amos H. Hawley, *Human Ecology: A Theory of Community Structure* (New York: Ronald Press Company, 1950), p. 209.

6. Garry J. Smith, "The Noble Sports Fan," *Journal of Sport and Social Issues,* vol. 12, no. 1 (1988), pp. 54-65; Janet Lever, *Soccer Madness* (Chicago: The University of Chicago Press, 1983).

7. John Bale, *Sports Geography* (New York: E. and F. Spon, 1989); Trujillo and Krizek, "Emotionality in the Stands and in the Field," pp. 303-325.

8. See Robert A. Baade and Richard F. Dye, "Sports Stadiums and Area Development: A Critical Review," *Economic Development Quarterly,* vol. 2, no. 3 (1988), pp. 265-275; Mark S. Rosentraub and David Swindell, "'Just Say No?' The Economic and Political Realities of a Small City's Investment in Minor League Baseball," *Economic Development Quarterly,* vol. 5, no. 2 (1991), pp. 152-167.

9. Rebecca Susan Kraus, "Sport and the Community: The Case of Minor League Baseball, 1950s-1990s" (Doctoral dissertation, The Catholic University of America, 1998).

10. See David Savageau and Richard Boyer, *Places Rated Almanac* (New York: Macmillan, 1993), pp. 401-410.

11. Arthur T. Johnson, "Professional Baseball at the Minor League Level: Considerations for Cities Large and Small," *State and Local Government Review,* vol. 22 (1990), p. 95.

Epilogue

1. See Ken Gurnick, "MLB, Players Association Donate $10 Million to Relief Fund: Teams, Individual Players Also Making Contributions to Help Victims," Sept. 19, 2001, accessed at <http://www.mlb.com>; Mike Bauman, "Bonds Grappling with Emotions," September 20, accessed at <http://www.mlb.com>; Baltimore Orioles, "Orioles to Honor Victims of Terrorist Attack on Friday," press release, September 20, 2001, accessed at <http://baltimore.orioles.mlb.com>.

2. Major League Baseball, "MLB Cancels All Wednesday Games," press release, September 12, 2001, accessed at <http://www.mlb.com>.

3. Bakersfield Blaze, press release, September 12, 2001, accessed at <http://www.bakersfieldblaze.com/index2.htm>.

4. Information summarized from Rebecca Susan Kraus, "Baseball Responds to Terrorism," unpublished manuscript, September 2001.

Appendix B

1. The variables included in the data set were chosen based on the literature reviews of sports, community, and organization theories that were presented in Chapters 2 and 3. In addition, a review of the current literature on quality of life aided in the selection of variables with which to measure the impact of Minor League Baseball on the community.

2. This study was limited to baseball for several reasons. The primary reason is its long history as part of the national pastime. In addition, data are not readily available in a similar format as that used for Minor League Baseball (NFL, NBA, and NCAA yearbooks and references are not available for all years included in this study). Further, due to the difficulty in assigning teams to counties, the data set was limited to Minor League Baseball only. Besides, I only like baseball.

3. Lloyd Johnson and Miles Wolff, eds., *The Encyclopedia of Minor League Baseball,* First Edition (Durham, NC: Baseball America Inc., 1993), p. 219.

4. Larry Lyon, *The Community in Urban Society* (Philadelphia: Temple University Press, 1987), pp. 150, 151, 158.

5. Mark C. Berger, Glenn C. Blomquist, and Werner Waldner, "A Revealed-Preference Ranking of Quality of Life for Metropolitan Areas," *Social Science Quarterly,* vol. 68 (1987), pp. 760-778.

6. Prince William Cannons Advertising Brochure, 1993. (The Potomac Cannons were previously known as the Prince William Cannons.)

7. See William G. Colcough, Lawrence A. Daellenbach, and Keith R. Sherony, "Estimating the Economic Impact of a Minor League Baseball Stadium," *Managerial and Decision Economics,* vol. 15 (1994), pp. 497-502.

8. Arthur T. Johnson, "The Sports Franchise Relocation Issue and Public Policy Response," in Art Johnson and Jim Frey, eds., *Government and Sport: The Public Policy Issues* (Totowa, NJ: Rowan and Allanheid, 1986), pp. 219-247.

9. Charles C. Euchner, *Playing the Field: Why Sports Teams Move and Cities Fight to Keep Them* (Baltimore, MD: Johns Hopkins University Press, 1993), p. 20; Morris Janowitz and David Street, "Changing Social Order of the Metropolitan Area," in David Street and Associates, eds., *Handbook of Contemporary Urban Life* (Washington: Jossey-Bass Publishers, 1978), pp. 96-98.

10. Peter H. Rossi, "Community Social Indicators," in Angus Campbell and Philip E. Converse, eds., *The Human Meaning of Social Change* (New York: Russell Sage Foundation, 1972), p. 124.

11. Ibid., p. 125.

12. Berger, Blomquist, and Waldner, "A Revealed-Preference Ranking . . . ," p. 768; Glenn C. Blomquist, Mark C. Berger, and John P. Hoehn, "New Estimates of Quality of Life in Urban Areas," *The American Economic Review,* vol. 78 (1988), pp. 89-107.

13. Dowell Myers, "Community-Relevant Measurement of Quality of Life: A Focus on Local Trends," *Urban Affairs Quarterly,* vol. 23, no. 1 (1987), p. 109.

14. John D. Kasarda and Morris Janowitz, "Community Attachment in Mass Society," *American Sociological Review,* vol. 39 (1974), pp. 334-335.

15. Rossi, "Community Social Indicators," p. 87.

16. Larry Lyon, *The Community in Urban Society* (Philadelphia, Temple University Press, 1987), pp. 243-245.

17. Ibid., p. 158.

18. U.S. Bureau of the Census, *County and City Data Book, 1988: Files on CD-ROM Technical Documentation,* prepared by Data User Services Division, Bureau of the Census (Washington: Bureau of the Census, 1989), p. 7-1.

19. U.S. Bureau of the Census, *County and City Data Book, 1994: Files on CD-ROM* [machine-readable data file], prepared by Data User Services Division, Bureau of the Census (Washington: Bureau of the Census, 1994), footnotes.

20. U.S. Bureau of the Census, *County and City Data Book, 1988: Files on CD-ROM Technical Documentation,* p. 7-5.

21. Ibid., p. 7-1.

22. Arthur T. Johnson, *Minor League Baseball and Economic Development* (Chicago: University of Illinois Press, 1993), p. 235.

23. See Dowell Myers, "Building Knowledge About Quality of Life," *Journal of the American Planning Association,* vol. 54 (1988), p. 354; Mark Edward Stover and Charles L. Leven, "Methodological Issues in the Determination of the Quality of Life in Urban Areas," *Urban Studies,* vol. 29, no. 5 (1992), p. 744; John D. Landis and David S. Sawicki, "A Planner's Guide to the *Places Rated Almanac,*" *Journal of the American Planning Association,* vol. 54 (1988), p. 341.

24. Frank L. Hefner, "Using Economic Models to Measure the Impact of Sports on Local Economies," *Journal of Sport and Social Issues,* vol. 14, no. 1 (1990), pp. 1-13; Colclough, Daellenbach, and Sherony, "Estimating the Economic Impact . . . ," pp. 497-502.

25. Telephone conversation with Cindy Richmond, deputy director of economic development, Loudon County, Virginia, May 7, 1997.

26. Euchner, *Playing the Field*, pp. 68-73.

27. Hubert M. Blalock Jr., *Social Statistics*, Revised Second Edition (New York: McGraw-Hill, Inc., 1979), p. 452.

28. Ibid., p. 468.

29. Lois W. Sayrs, *Pooled Time Series Analysis* (New York: Sage Publications, 1989), p. 7.

30. For the purposes of this study, a case is defined as a "county decade"—each county (there are 2,795 counties included in the data set) appears in the data set five times as a separate case with data for each decade. For example, Washington County, Maryland, has data points for the 1940s, 1950s, 1960s, 1970s, and 1980s; data for each of these years for Washington County (and all counties) are reported as five cases. The era dummy variables indicate which era is represented by the data.

31. A recursive system allows us to consider each equation in the system separately from the others so that ordinary least-squares regression analysis may be used. Using this method, the variables are arranged hierarchically, based on "causal priorities." In this way, "it becomes possible to neglect variables that are clearly dependent on a given subset of variables." H.M. Blalock Jr., editor, *Causal Models in the Social Sciences* (Chicago, IL: Aldine-Atherton, Inc., 1971), pp. 1-2.

32. Robert S. Pindyck and Daniel L. Rubinfeld, *Econometric Models and Economic Forecasts* (New York: McGraw-Hill, Inc., 1991), pp. 288-289, 298; Otis Dudley Duncan, *Introduction to Structural Equation Models* (Boston, MA: Academic Press, Inc., 1975), pp. 25-26.

33. Duncan, *Introduction to Structural Equation Models*, p. 26.

34. Ibid., p. 28. In such a system, independent variables in one equation may be dependent variables in others, as long as such equations are causally prior to the equation in which they are independent variables. In this way, dependent variables are assumed to be uncorrelated to the independent variables. However, the "correlation between any pair of variables can be written in terms of the paths leading from common antecedent variables." Otis Dudley Duncan, "Path Analysis: Sociological Examples," in H.M. Blalock Jr., ed., *Causal Models in the Social Sciences* (New York: Aldine-Atherton, 1971), p. 120.

35. Duncan, *Introduction to Structural Equation Models*, p. 25.

36. Harry H. Kelejian and Wallace E. Oates, *Introduction to Econometrics: Principles and Applications* (New York: Harper and Row, Publishers, 1981), p. 240.

37. Pindyck and Rubinfeld, *Economic Models and Economic Forecasts*, pp. 298-301.

38. Marija J. Norusis, *SPSS for Windows Professional Statistics Release 6.0* (Chicago, IL: SPSS Inc., 1993), p. 233.

39. David Savageau and Richard Boyer, *Places Rated Almanac* (New York: Macmillan, 1993), pp. 135-140.

40. Berger, Blomquist, and Waldner, "A Revealed-Preference Ranking . . . ," pp. 760-778.

41. Lyon, *The Community in Urban Society*, pp. 145-159.

42. Gerald A. Carlino, "Do Education and Training Lead to Faster Growth in Cities?" *Business Review* (Federal Reserve Bank of Philadelphia), vol. 90, no. 2, January/February (1995), pp. 15-22.

43. Joan Fitzgerald, "Labor Force, Education, and Work," in Richard D. Bingham and Robert Mier, eds., *Theories of Local Economic Development* (Newbury Park, CA: Sage Publications, Inc., 1993), pp. 125-146.

44. Peter M. Blau and Otis Dudley Duncan, *The American Occupational Structure* (New York: John Wiley and Sons, 1967); Richard A. Easterlin, *Population, Labor Force, and Long Swings in Economic Growth* (New York: National Bureau of Economic Research, 1968).

45. Savageau and Boyer, *Places Rated Almanac,* pp. 212-216; Berger, Blomquist, and Waldner, "A Revealed-Preference Ranking of Quality...," pp. 760-778; Lyon, *The Community in Urban Society,* pp. 145-159.

46. Robert K. Merton, "Social Structure and Anomie," *American Sociological Review,* vol. 3, pp. 672-682.

47. Larry J. Siegel, *Criminology,* Fifth Edition (New York: West Publishing Company, 1995), pp. 60-72.

48. Ian Robertson, *Sociology,* Third Edition (New York: Worth Publishers, Inc., 1987), p. 204.

49. Siegel, *Criminology,* p. 70.

Index

Page numbers followed by the letter "f" indicate figures; those followed by the letter "t" indicate tables.

A. *See* Class A; *individual leagues and teams*
AA. *See* Class AA; *individual leagues and teams*
AAA. *See* Class AAA; *individual leagues and teams*
Aberdeen IronBirds
    franchise relocation and affiliation changes, 104, 105t, 108t
    owned by Ripken Professional Baseball, LLC, 67, 104
    New York-Penn League, 37t, 117t
Academia, 58
Acereros del Norte, 20t
Adelanto, CA, 28t
Adelson, Bruce, 8
Adirondack Lumberjacks, 49t
Advanced Rookie Leagues. *See also individual leagues and teams;* Rookie Leagues
Affiliation changes, 100, 101-111
African-American
    importance of sport to communities, 65
    population of Prince George's County, MD, 124, 124t
    population of Washington County, MD, 122t
Akron Aeros, 21, 22t, 50, 100, 107
Alabama, location of All-American Association teams, 48. *See also individual cities and teams*
Alameda Encinals, 44
Albany, NY
    Albany-Colonie Diamond Dogs, 49t
    International League, 15
    Northern League, 49t

Albany Polecats, 15, 33t, 100
Alberta, Canada. *See also individual cities and teams*
    Pacific Coast League, 18
    Pioneer League, 41
Albuquerque, NM, 9, 101, 112
Alexandria Aces, 50, 52t
Algodoneros de Unión Laguna, 20t
All-American Association, 45t, 47-48, 50
Allentown, PA
    Allentown Ambassadors, 49t
    International League, 14
    Northern League, 49t
Alliance Classic, 15
All-Star Game, 15, 125
Altoona Curve, 22t
Amarillo Dillas, 52t
American Association
    class A, 6
    class AA, 6
    class AAA, 6, 14-15
    independent league, 45t
American League, 17, 89, 114
American League Park, 114
American Legion, 39
American Red Cross, 134
Anaheim, CA, Pacific Coast League, 17. *See also* Anaheim Angels
Anaheim Angels
    California League, 25
    class A affiliates, 11, 28t, 35t
    class AA affiliates, 26t
    class AAA affiliates, 19t
    rookie league affiliates, 42t
Appalachian (APPY) League. *See also individual teams*
    advanced rookie league, 5, 5f, 39, 40t

187

Appalachian (APPY) League *(continued)*
   description 39
   history, 39
   stadiums, 39
Applebee's Park, 31
Appleton, WI, 35t
Arizona. *See also individual cities and teams*
   Arizona League, 5f, 43
   Arizona-Mexico League, 18
   Arizona-Texas League, 18
   location of Western League teams, 52
Arizona Diamondbacks
   class A affiliates, 28t, 35t, 38t, 104
   class AA affiliates, 26t
   class AAA affiliate, 17, 19t
   relationship with Mexican League, 20
   rookie league affiliates, 42t
Arkansas, location of Texas League teams, 23. *See also individual cities and teams*
Arkansas Travelers, 26t
Arlington Stadium, 63
Asheville Tourists, 1, 2, 33t
Ashland, KY, 50, 107, 109t
Atlanta, GA. *See also* Atlanta Braves
   International League, 15
   Milwaukee Braves move, 21
Atlanta Braves, 13
   class A affiliates, 30t, 33t
   class AA affiliate, 24t
   class AAA affiliate, 16t
   rookie league affiliates, 40t
Atlantic City Surf, 53, 54t
Atlantic Coast League, 45t
Atlantic League, 6f, 45t, 53, 54t
Attendance
   Bowie Baysox, 121f, 125
   during the 1970s, 3
   during the 1990s, 27
   effects on, 60, 88-95, 129
   estimate for community support, 61
   Hagerstown Suns, 121f, 122
   studies of, 59
Auburn, NY
   affiliation changes, 108t
   Auburn Astros, 104, 105t
   Auburn Doubledays, 36, 37t, 104, 105t

Augusta, NJ, 37t
Augusta GreenJackets, 33t
Austin, TX, 25, 95
AutoZone Park, 95, 111

Baade, Robert A., 68-69
Baker, Frank "Home Run," 115
Bakersfield, CA
   Bakersfield Blaze, 28t, 100, 101, 102t
   Bakersfield Dodgers, 100, 102t
   name changes and franchise relocation, 102t, 103t, 104
Baltimore, MD. *See also* Baltimore Orioles
   Baltimore and Potomac Railroad, 123
   International League, 14, 15
   location of baseball teams, past and present, 99, 117t
   stadiums, teams, and ballparks, 114
Baltimore Orioles
   Bowie Baysox affiliate, 2, 21, 100, 120, 123
   class A affiliates, 30t, 33t, 37t, 100, 115
   class AA affiliates, 21, 22t
   class AAA affiliate, 13, 16t
   fans, 62
   farm system, 4-5
   Hagerstown Suns affiliate, 100, 115, 120
   International League teams, 14, 15, 99, 114
   rookie league affiliate, 40t
   Prosperity Era, 90
   World Series, 57
Barsky, Stephen F., 60-61
Baseball America, 48, 101
Batavia, NY
   Batavia Clippers, 105tt, 104
   Batavia Muckdogs, 37t, 105t, 104
   New York-Penn League teams, 37t, 104, 108t
Battle Creek, MI
   Battle Creek Golden Kazoos, 100
   Michigan Battle Cats, 35t
   Midwest League, 35t
Beaton, Rod, 8

Beaumont, TX, 50
Belair. *See* Bowie, MD
Belleville, IL, 31, 34
Beloit Snappers, 35t
Bend, OR, 51
Berkshire Black Bears, 49t
Big South League, 45t
Billings Mustangs, 42t
Binghamton Mets, 21, 22t
Birmingham Barons, 24t
Blahnik, Judith, 7, 9
Blake, Mike, 8
Blue Ridge League, 115, 117t, 118
Blue Ridge Mountains, 39
Bluefield Orioles, 5, 40t
Boca del Río, Veracruz, Mexico, 20t
Boise Hawks, 38t
Boston Red Sox
    class A affiliates, 32t, 33t, 37t
    class AA affiliate, 22t
    class AAA affiliate, 16t
Bowie, MD. *See also* Bowie Baysox; Prince George's County, MD
    Belair Estate and Stable, 123
    Bowie Town Center, 123
    comparison to Hagerstown, 113, 130-131
    Eastern League team, 22t, 116, 117t
    economic development, 123-125
    franchise relocation, 100
    history and description of, 122-125
    Huntington, 123
    Levitt, 123
    minor league town, 2, 10, 122-123
    new baseball team in town, 95
    new stadium, 130
    population characteristics, 120, 123-125, 124t
    retail, 123-124
Bowie, Ogden, 123
Bowie Baysox
    attendance, 121f, 125
    Baltimore Orioles affiliate, 5, 21, 22t
    Bowie, MD, 122, 123
    Eastern League, 21, 22t
    games played at Memorial Stadium, 114, 123
    naming trends, 101
    role in economic development, 67, 123-125

Bowman Field, 36
Brazil, 62-63
Brevard County Manatees, 32t
Brewster, TX, 3
Bridgeport Bluefish, 53, 54t
Bridgewater, NJ, 54t
Bristol, VA
    Bristol Red Sox, 93
    Bristol White Sox, 40t
British Columbia, Canada, location of Northwest League teams, 36. *See also individual cities and teams*
Brockton Rox, 49t
Broncos de Reynosa, 20t
Brooklyn Cyclones
    franchise relocation and affiliation changes, 101, 104, 105t, 108t
    New York-Penn League, 37t
    relief fund for victims of terrorist attacks, 134
Brooklyn Dodgers, 63-64
Buffalo, NY
Buffalo Bisons, 16t, 111
    international league teams, 15, 111
Bull Durham, 2, 27, 57
Bureau of Economic Analysis, 70
Burgess, Ernest W., 77
Burlington Bees, 35t
Burlington Indians, 39, 40t
Butte, MN, 101
Buzas, Joe, 93

Cafeteros de Córdoba, 20t
Calfee Park, 39
Calgary, Alberta, Canada
    Calgary Cannons, 19t
    location of Pioneer League teams, 41
    Pacific Coast League, 19
California. *See also individual cities and teams*
    location of California League teams, 27
    location of independent league teams, 47
California League
    class A, 5f, 25
    class C, 25

California League *(continued)*
　description, 25, 27, 28t
　franchise relocation, 101, 102t, 103t, 104
　history, 27, 44
　independent league, 44, 45t
　name changes in, 101, 102t, 103t, 104
Cambridge, MD
　Cambridge Canners, 99
　Cambridge Cardinals, 99
　Cambridge Dodgers, 99, 115
　Eastern Shore League teams, 99, 115, 117t
Camden Riversharks, 54t
Campeche Pirates, 20, 20t
Canada. *See also individual cities, states, and teams*
　franchise relocation, 111
　hallmark events and communal sentiment, 71
　home to minor league teams, 4, 36, 47, 53
　Western Canada League, 41
Canal Park, 100
Cancún, Quintana Roo, Mexico, 20t
Canton, OH
　Canton Coyotes, 51t, 107, 109t
　Canton Crocodiles, 107, 109t
　Canton-Akron Indians, 100
　Frontier League, 50, 109t
　Thurman Munson Memorial Stadium, 62
Cape Fear Crocs, 101
Capital City Bombers, 33t
Capitales de Quebec, 49t
Carolina League
　Baltimore Orioles affiliate, 5
　class A advanced, 5f, 27, 29, 30t
　class C, 27
　description, 27, 29
　franchise relocation, 100, 115, 120, 130
　history, 27, 29, 92
　teams in Maryland, 117t
Carolina Mudcats, 24t, 100, 134
Carroll, Bob, 39
Casper Rockies, 41, 42t, 101
Cedar Rapids Kernels, 35t
Centennial Field, 36

Central Association, 34
Central Interstate League, 34
Central Islip, NY, 54t
Central League
　description and history, 50, 52t
　independent league, 6f, 45t
Centralia, IL, 34
Centreville, MD
　Centreville Colts, 99
　Centreville Orioles, 99
　Centreville Red Sox, 99
　Eastern Shore League, 115, 117t
Chadwick, Bruce, 9, 17
Chamber of Commerce, 75
Chambersburg, PA
　Blue Ridge League, 118
　Chambersburg Marooners, 119t
　Chambersburg Maroons, 119t
　Chambersburg Young Yanks, 119t
Championship Series, 134
Charleston, SC
　Charleston RiverDogs, 33t
　South Atlantic League, 33t
　Southern League, 21
Charleston, WV
　Charleston Alley Cats, 33t
　Charleston Wheelers, 98
　International League, 15
　South Atlantic League, 31, 33t
　Watt Powell Park, 31
Charlotte, NC, 23, 100, 120
Charlotte Knights, 16t, 32t
Charm City. *See* Baltimore, MD
Chattanooga Lookouts, 23, 24t
Chavis, David M., 82, 84
Chicago, IL. *See also* Chicago Cubs; Chicago White Sox
　economic development study, 70
　Leland Hotel and creation of NAPBL, 11
Chicago Cubs
　class A affiliates, 35t, 38t
　class AA affiliate, 24t
　class AAA affiliate, 19t
Chicago White Sox
　class A affiliates, 30t, 33t
　class AA affiliate, 24t
　class AAA affiliate, 16t
　rookie league affiliate, 40t
Chico Heat, 52, 53t

Chihuahua, Mexico, 18
Chillicothe Paints, 50, 51t, 109t
Cincinnati Reds
    class A affiliates, 35t, 38t
    class AA affiliate, 24t
    class AAA affiliate, 16t
    rookie league affiliate, 42t
    spring training stadium, 29
Class A. *See also individual leagues and teams*
    league classifications and restructuring, 6, 7t, 13
    leagues and teams, 5f, 27-38
    salaries, 7
    short-season leagues and teams, 5f, 34-38
    value of teams, 94
Class A1, 6
Class AA. *See also individual leagues and teams*
    league classifications and restructuring, 6, 7t, 13, 114
    leagues and teams, 5f, 21-25
    salaries, 7
Class AAA. *See also individual leagues and teams*
    AAA Alliance, 15
    AAA All-Star Game, 15
    league classifications and restructuring, 6, 7t, 13, 114
    leagues and teams, 5f, 13-20
    salaries, 7
    value of teams, 94
Class B, 6, 13
Class C, 6, 13
Class D, 6, 13
Class E, 6
Class Four-A, 17
Clear Lake, IA, 31, 34
Clearwater Phillies, 29, 32t
Cleveland, OH, location of United States League team, 44. *See also* Cleveland Indians
Cleveland Indians
    class A affiliates, 30t, 33t, 37t
    class AA affiliate, 21, 22t
    class AAA affiliate, 13, 16t
    rookie league affiliate, 40t
Clinton LumberKings, 34, 35t, 39
Clubhouse, 96
Coahuila, Mexico, 20
Coastal Plain League, 29
Cohen Stadium, 112
Colclough, William G., 70
Collinsville, IL, 50, 51t, 107
Colonial League, 44, 45t
Colorado Rockies
    class A affiliates, 30t, 33t, 38t
    class AA affiliate, 24t
    class AAA affiliate, 19t
    rookie league affiliate, 42t
Colorado Springs Sky Sox, 19t
Columbia, SC, 33t
Columbus Clippers, 15, 16t
Columbus RedStixx, 31, 33t
Comiskey Park, 63
Commissioner of Baseball, 12, 133
Community
    anomie (loss of community), 79
    attachment, 60, 64
    concept/definition of, 72-81, 82-83, 127
    development of, 2
    identity, 59, 69
    pride, 59, 85, 128
    psychology of, 82
    relationship between communities and sports teams, 59
    representation, 66
    sense of, 128
    sociology of, 73-81
    solidarity, 66, 83, 88
    spirit, 113, 128
    studies of, 66, 82
    support, 61
Comstock Park, MI, 35t
Concentric zones, 77
Congress, 70
Congressional Baseball Game for Charity, 75
Connecticut, location of Eastern League teams, 21. *See also individual cities and teams*
Cook County Cheetahs, 51t, 107, 109t
Cooperstown, NY, 34, 116
Córdoba, Veracruz, Mexico, 20t
Corporate sponsorship, 111
Corpus Christi, TX, 50

Crestwood, IL, 50, 51t, 107
Crisfield, MD
　Crisfield Crabbers, 99
　Eastern Shore League, 115, 117t
Cuba, 15
Cumberland, MD
　Blue Ridge League, 99, 117t, 118
　Cumberland Colts, 115, 119t
　Cumberland Rooters, 99, 114, 115
　Cumberland Valley, 116
Customers, 96, 97-98

Daellenbach, Lawrence A., 70
Dallas, TX, 25
Damaschke Field, 36
Danville Braves, 40t
Davenport, IA, 35t, 112
Dayton Dragons, 35t
Daytona Cubs, 29, 32t
Decline, era of, 88, 90-92, 129, 130, 137t
Delmarva Shorebirds, 5, 33t, 100, 116
Dems Donkeys, 75
Des Moines, IA, 19t
Detroit Tigers
　class A affiliates, 32t, 35t, 37t, 104
　class AA affiliate, 22t
　class AAA affiliate, 16t
Developmental leagues, 43
Diablos Rojos del México, 20t
Dixie Association, 23, 25
Dominican Summer League, 43
Doubleday, Abner, 36
Drummondville, Quebec, Canada, 44
Dubois County Dragons, 51t, 107, 108t
Dubuque, IA, 34
Duluth-Superior Dukes, 48, 49t
Dunedin Blue Jays, 29, 32t
Dunn, Jack, 99, 114
Dunn Tire Park, 111
Durham, NC
　Durham Bulls, 16t, 27, 48, 94, 134
　Durham Bulls Athletic Park, 59, 134
　historical baseball town, 95
Durkheim, Emile, 60, 66, 82
Dye, Richard F., 68-69
Dyersville, IA, 31

Early Years of Minor League Baseball, 88-90
Eastern Carolina League, 27
Eastern League. *See also* Class AA; *individual leagues and teams*
　Akron Aeros, 22t, 50, 107
　Baltimore, MD, 99
　Baltimore Orioles' affiliate, 2
　Bowie Baysox, 21, 22t
　class A, 6
　class AA, 5f, 6, 21, 22t, 117t
　description, 21, 22t
　Eastern Circuit, 14
　Hagerstown Suns, 115, 120, 130
　history, 21
　predecessor of International League, 14
Eastern Shore League, 99, 115, 117t
Easton, MD
　Eastern Shore League, 115, 117t
　Easton Browns, 99
　Easton Cubs, 99
　Easton Farmers, 99, 115
　Easton Yankees, 99, 115
Economic benefits of minor league baseball, 128, 131
Economic development, 59, 66-72, 94, 129
Economic impact of sports, 59, 63, 66-72, 85
Ed Smith Stadium, 29
Edinburg Roadrunners, 50, 52t
Edison International Field, 11
Edmonton Trappers, 18, 19t
El Paso Diablos, 25, 26t
Elizabethton Twins, 39, 40t
Elizabethtown, MD. *See* Hagerstown, MD
Elmira Pioneers, 49t, 104, 105t, 108t
Engel, Bruce L., 51
Erie, PA
　Erie Sailors, 107, 109t
　Erie SeaWolves, 22t, 105t
　franchise relocation and affiliation changes, 104, 105t, 108t, 109t
Euchner, Charles C., 71
Eugene Emeralds, 36, 38t
Evansville, IN
　Evansville Otters, 51t, 108t
　Frontier League, 50, 51t, 107, 108t
　Southern League, 23

Everett AquaSox, 38t
Expansion teams, 70, 101

Fall leagues, 5
Fan(s)
   attachment, 59, 64, 97
   community, 79, 84-85, 128
   loyalty, 60
Fargo-Moorhead RedHawks, 49t
Farm system/team, 4, 89, 120
Farnham, Quebec, Canada, 44
Federal League, 44, 45t, 89, 114
Federalsburg, MD
   Eastern Shore League, 115, 117t
   Federalsburg A's, 99
   Federalsburg Athletics, 99
   Federalsburg Feds, 99
Field of Dreams, 31
Fifth Third Field, 13
Florida. *See individual cities, leagues, and teams*
Florida Marlins
   class A affiliates, 32t, 35t, 37t
   class AA affiliate, 21, 22t
   class AAA affiliate, 19t
Florida State League (FSL)
   class A Advanced, 5f, 29, 31, 32t
   description, 29, 31
   history, 29
   teams abolished in 2002, 101
Fodor's, 1, 116
Football, 81, 90
Fort Mill, SC, 16t
Fort Myers Miracle, 29, 32t
Fort Wayne Wizards, 35t
Fort Worth, TX
   Central League, 50, 52t
   Fort Worth Cats, 52t
   Texas League, 25
Foxx, Jimmy, 115
Franchise relocation
   case studies of, 71, 84
   economic development strategy, 67
   examples of, 98-111
   Major League Baseball, 17
Frederick, MD
   Blue Ridge League teams, 117t, 118
   Carolina League, 30t
   Frederick Hustlers, 115, 119t

Frederick, MD *(continued)*
   Frederick Keys, 5, 30t, 100, 112, 116
   Frederick Warriors, 119t
   location of minor league teams, 1, 117t, 120
   population of Frederick County, 120
   stadium construction, 93, 130
Fresno, CA
   California League, 44
   Fresno Grizzlies, 19t
   Pacific Coast League, 19t
Frick, Ford, 12
Frontier Field, 134
Frontier League
   description and history, 50, 51t
   franchise relocation and name changes, 107, 108t
   independent league, 6f, 43, 45t
Frostburg, MD, 99, 115, 117t
Functions of minor league baseball, 128
Furillo, Carl, 115

Galveston, TX, 25
Gary Southshore RailCats, 49t
Gastonia, NC, 98
Gateway Grizzlies, 51t, 107, 109t
Gemeinschaft, 80-82, 84, 127-128
Geneva, IL, 35t
Georgia. *See also individual cities and teams*
   Georgia-Florida League, 92
   location of All-American Association teams, 48
Gesellschaft, 80-82, 84
Gettysburg, PA
   Gettysburg Patriots, 119t
   Gettysburg Ponies, 119t
   location of Blue Ridge League teams, 118
Glens Falls, NY, 49t
Golden Park, 31
Golden State League, 45t
Granby, Quebec, Canada, 44
Grand Old Party Elephants, 75
Grapefruit League, 29
Grays Harbor, WA, 51, 52
Great Central League, 45t

Great Depression, 17, 89, 91
Great Falls Dodgers, 42t
Greensboro Bats, 33t
Greenstein, Theodore N., 60
Greenville Braves, 23, 24t
Guerreros de Oaxaca, 20t
Gulf Coast League, 5, 5f
Gusfield, Joseph R., 76

Hager, Jonathan, 116
Hagerstown, MD. *See also* Hagerstown Suns
    Blue Ridge League teams, 115, 117t, 118, 119t
    comparison to Bowie, 113, 130-131
    franchise relocation, 100
    Hagerstown Blues, 115, 118, 119t
    Hagerstown Braves, 115, 118
    Hagerstown Champs, 118, 119t
    Hagerstown Hubs, 115, 118, 119t
    Hagerstown Municipal Stadium, 31, 116, 121
    Hagerstown Owls, 118
    Hagerstown Packets, 120
    Hagerstown Suns, 33t
    Hagerstown Terriers, 115, 118, 119t
    history and description of, 116-122
    population characteristics, 120
Hagerstown Suns
    attendance, 122
    franchise relocation, 100, 115, 120, 123
    return to Hagerstown, 120
    South Atlantic League team, 33t, 130
Hamilton, Ontario, Canada, 15, 36
Hannibal, MI, 34
Hanover, MD
    Eastern Shore League, 117t, 118
    Hanover Hornets, 119t
    Hanover Raiders, 119t
Hardware City Rock Cats, 100
Harford County, MD, 67
Harlingen, TX, 52t
Harrisburg Senators, 14, 22t
Harry Grove Stadium, 116
Hawaii Islanders, 18
Hawley, Amos H., 78
Heartland League, 45t, 50

Hefner, Frank, 68
Helena, MN, 101
Henschen, Beth M., 70
Hickory Crawdads, 33t
High Desert Mavericks, 28t, 102t, 103t, 104
Hollywood Stars, 18
Holman Stadium, 29
Home court advantage, 61
Homestead Grays, 65
Hooker Field, 39
Hoover, AL, 23, 24t
Houston, TX, 25. *See also* Houston Astros
Houston Astros, 107
    class A affiliates, 33t, 35t, 37t, 107
    class AA affiliate, 26t
    class AAA affiliate, 19t
    rookie league affiliate, 40t
Howell, Jeremy M., 65-66
Hub City. *See* Hagerstown, MD
Hudson Valley Renegades, 37t, 105t
Human ecology, 73, 77-79, 84
Hunnicutt Field, 39
Hunter Wright Stadium, 39
Huntingburg, IN, 50, 51t, 107
Huntington, MD. *See* Bowie, MD
Huntsville Stars, 23, 24t

Idaho. *See also individual cities and teams*
    location of Northwest League teams, 36
    location of Pioneer League teams, 41
    Utah-Idaho League, 41
Idaho Falls Padres, 42t
Illinois, 34, 48, 107. *See also individual cities and teams*
Independent Leagues. *See also individual leagues and teams*
    definition of, 5, 7t
    growth of, 55
    leagues, 6f, 13, 43-55, 45t-46t
    number of leagues in 2002, 87
    relationship to Major League Baseball, 5, 43, 55
    relationship to Minor League Baseball, 43, 55

Indiana, location of Midwest League teams, 34. *See also individual cities and teams*
Indianapolis Indians, 15, 16t
Indifference, era of, 88, 92-93, 129, 130, 138t
Industrial Revolution, 82
Ingham, Alan M., 65-66
Intangible benefits of sport, 59, 62-66, 71
Inter-Mountain League, 41
International League. See also individual teams
   AAA All-star Game, 15
   AAA Alliance, 15
   Baltimore Orioles affiliate, 5
   class AA, 13, 117t
   class AAA, 5f, 13, 117t
   current teams, 16t
   description, 13-15
   history, 13-15
   interleague play, 15
   New International League, 14
Interstate League, 115, 117t, 118
Iowa. *See also individual cities and teams*
   Iowa Cubs, 19t
   location of International League teams, 15
   location of Midwest League teams, 34
   location of Northern League teams, 48

Jackson, TN, 23, 24t
Jackson Senators, 52t
Jacksonville, MS, 50
Jacksonville Suns, 15, 21, 23, 24t
Jamestown Jammers, 37t, 105t, 108t
Jersey City, NJ, 15, 99, 114
Joe O'Brien Field, 39
Johnson, Arthur T., 69
Johnson, Lloyd, 47, 96
Johnson City Cardinals, 40t
Johnstown, PA
   franchise relocation and name changes, 107, 109t
   Johnstown Johnnies, 50, 51t, 109t
   Johnstown Steal, 109t
Joliet JackHammers, 49t
Jupiter Hammerheads, 29, 32t

Kalamazoo, MI
   Kalamazoo Kings, 50, 51t, 107, 109t
   Kalamazoo Kodiaks, 107, 109t
Kane County Cougars, 35t
Kannapolis Intimidators, 33t
Kansas City, MI, major league expansion, 90. *See also* Kansas City Royals
Kansas City Royals
   class A affiliates, 30t, 35t, 38t
   class AA affiliate, 26t
   class AAA affiliate, 19t
Keizer, OR, 38t
Kennewick, WA, 38t
Kent, OH, 62
Kentucky Rifles, 107, 108t
Key, Francis Scott, 116
Kinas, Patrick, 134-135
Kingsport Mets, 39, 40t
Kinston Indians, 30t
Kissimmee, FL, 23, 24t, 101
Kodak, TN, 23, 24t
Koenig, Bill, 8
Kokomo, IN, 34
Korean War, 90
Kraus, Rebecca Susan, 9
Krizek, Bob, 63
Kuklick, Bruce, 64

La Crosse County, WI, 70
La Liga Mexicana de Béisbol. *See* Mexican League
Lafayette, IN, 34
Lake Elsinore Storm, 27, 28t, 102t, 103t
Lakeland Tigers, 29, 32t, 39
Lakewood BlueClaws, 33t, 101
Lamb, David, 8, 76, 93, 112
Lancaster, OH, 50
Lancaster JetHawks, 28t, 101, 102t, 103t
Lancaster Scouts, 107, 108t
Lansing Lugnuts, 35t, 101, 111
Las Vegas 51s, 19t
Legitimization, era of, 88, 94-95, 130
Leones de Yucatán, 20t
Lever, Janet, 62-63, 79, 84
Lewiston, ID, 36, 41
Lexington Legends, 31, 33t, 101

Lincoln Saltdogs, 49t
Lincolnton, NC, 90
Little Falls, NJ, 49t
Little League Baseball, 34, 36, 111
Little Rock, AR, 15, 25, 26t
Little World Series, 114
Logos, 62, 100-101
Lonaconing, MD, 99, 115, 117t
London Werewolves, 50, 107, 109t
Long Beach Breakers, 51, 53t
Long Island Ducks, 53, 54t
Longosteros de Cancún, 20t
Lord Baltimores, 114
Los Angeles, CA. *See also* Los Angeles Dodgers
   California League, 44
   Los Angeles Angels, 18
   major league expansion and relocation, 3, 90
   Pacific Coast League, 17
Los Angeles Dodgers
   affiliation changes, 101
   Brooklyn Dodgers move, 63
   California League, 25, 29, 101
   class A affiliates, 32t, 33t
   class AA affiliate, 24t
   class AAA affiliate, 19t
   rookie league affiliate, 42t
   spring training site, 29
Louisiana. *See also individual cities and teams*
   location of All-American Association teams, 48
   location of Central League teams, 50
   Texas-Louisiana League, 50
Louisville Bats, 13, 15, 16t
Louisville Slugger Field, 13
Lowell Spinners, 37t, 104, 105t, 108t
Luther Williams Field, 31
Lynchburg, VA
   Carolina League, 30t
   Lynchburg Hillcats, 30t
   Southern League, 23

Macintosh, Donald, 71, 72
MacIver, Robert M., 73
Macon Braves, 31, 33t
Madison Hatters, 100

Mahoning Valley Scrappers, 37t, 104, 105t, 108t
Maine, location of Eastern League teams, 21. *See also individual cities and teams*
Major League Baseball
   assignment of players to minor league teams, 4
   disaster relief fund, 133
   disenchantment with, 58, 76
   expansion and relocation, 17, 90, 94
   Major League Baseball Properties, 96
   ownership of minor league teams, 3
   Professional Baseball Agreement, 47, 96-97
   relationship to independent leagues, 5, 43
   relationship to Mexican League, 18, 25
   relationship to Minor League Baseball, 2-6, 12, 54, 57, 87-90
   response to terrorism, 133
   stadiums, 2
   strike, 76
Major League Baseball Players Association, 133
Manitoba, Canada. *See also individual cities and teams*
   Northern League, 48
   Pioneer League, 48
Marcum, John P., 60
Marion, IL, 34
Martinsburg, WV
   Blue Ridge League, 118
   Martinsburg Blue Sox, 119t
   Martinsburg Champs, 119t
   Martinsburg Mountaineers, 119t
Martinsville Astros, 39, 40t
Marx, Karl, 79
Maryland. *See also individual cities and teams*
   location of Eastern League teams, 21, 117t
   Maryland Base Ball Club, 114
   Maryland Department of Business and Economic Development, 124

Maryland *(continued)*
   minor league teams located in, 98-100, 114-116, 117t
   Pennsylvania-Ohio-Maryland League, 99, 114, 117t
Marysville, CA, 52, 53t
Mason-Dixon line, 116
Mattoon, IL, 34
Mays, Willie, 120
McAllen, TX, 50
McCarthy, Coleman, 76
McCoy Field, 13
McCurdy Field, 116
McMillan, David W., 82, 84
Medicine Hat Blue Jays, 41, 42t
Melbourne, FL, 29, 32t
Memphis Redbirds, 15, 19t, 95, 111
Mérida, Yucatán, Mexico, 20t
Metairie, LA, 19t
Mexican League
   class AAA, 5f, 18, 20, 20t
   description, 18, 20
   history, 18
   Pan-American Association, 25
   relationship to Major League Baseball, 18, 20
   relationship to Minor League Baseball, 18, 25
Mexico. *See also individual cities, leagues, and teams*
   baseball leagues, 18
   home to minor league baseball, 4, 18, 53
   Mexican Center League, 18
   Mexican Northern League, 18
   Mexican Southeast League, 18
México, D.F., 18, 20, 20t
Michigan. *See also individual cities and teams*
   location of Midwest League teams, 34
   Michigan Battle Cats, 35t, 100-101
Mid-America League, 45t
Middle Atlantic League, 115, 117t, 118
Midland RockHounds, 25, 26t
Midwest League
   class A, 5f, 35t
   history and description of, 31, 34

Milwaukee, WI. *See also* Milwaukee Brewers
   major league expansion and relocation, 90
   Milwaukee Braves, 8, 21
   Seattle Pilots move, 36
Milwaukee Brewers
   class A affiliates, 28t, 35t
   class AA affiliate, 24t
   class AAA affiliate, 16t
   rookie league affiliate, 42t
Minnesota, location of Northern League teams, 48, 49t. *See also individual cities and teams*
Minnesota Twins
   class A affiliates, 32t, 35t
   class AA affiliate, 22t
   class AAA affiliate, 19t
   rookie league affiliate, 40t
Minor League Baseball. *See also* Farm system; Independent leagues
   attendance, 3-4, 121f, 122, 125
   business aspects, 2, 4, 95-98, 111
   contests, giveaways, and promotions, 4
   divisions and classifications of, 4-5, 6, 54
   economic development tool, 2, 66-67
   family atmosphere, 131
   franchise relocation and name changes, 98-111
   functions of, 128
   history, 3-4, 11-13, 129
   impact on community, 54, 58
   logos, 62, 100-101
   marketing and commercialization, 1, 58
   popularity and recognition of, 1, 27, 57
   relationship between community and team, 2, 7, 9
   relationship to independent leagues, 7t, 43, 44
   relationship to Major League Baseball, 2-6, 12, 54, 57, 87-90
   restructuring of leagues, 6
   salaries, 6-7, 8, 89, 112

Minor League Baseball *(continued)*
   stabilization, 12-13
   towns and cities, 6-7, 11, 47
Mississippi. *See also individual cities and teams*
   location of Central League teams, 50
   location of independent league teams, 47
   location of Texas League teams, 23
   Mississippi River, 112
   Mississippi-Ohio Valley League, 34
Missoula Osprey, 42t
Missouri, location of Central League teams, 50. *See also individual cities and teams*
Mizruchi, Mark S., 61
Mobile, AL
   Mobile BayBears, 24t
   Southern League, 23, 24t
   Texas-Louisiana League, 50
Modesto A's, 27, 28t, 102t, 103t
Monclova, Coahuila, Mexico, 20t
Montana. *See also individual cities and teams*
   location of Pioneer League teams, 41
   Montana League, 41
Monterrey, Nuevo León, Mexico, 18, 20t
Montgomery, AL, 23
Montgomery County, MD, 124
Montreal, Quebec, Canada. *See also* Montreal Expos
   Eastern League, 99, 114
   International League, 15
Montreal Expos
   class A affiliates, 32t, 35t, 37t
   class AA affiliate, 22t
   class AAA affiliate, 16t
Monumentals, 114
Morganna the Kissing Bandit, 4, 98
Mount Vernon, IL, 34
Mudville Nine, 104
Murphysboro, IL, 34
Murray, Eddie, 57
Myrtle Beach, SC, 29, 30t, 100
   Carolina League, 29, 30t
   Myrtle Beach Hurricanes, 100
   Myrtle Beach Pelicans, 30t
   South Atlantic League, 120

Naming rights. *See* Team names
Nashua Pride, 53, 54t
Nashville, TN
   International League, 15
   Nashville Sounds, 18, 19t
   promotions and contests, 98
   stadium scoreboard, 112
National Agreement, 89
National anthem, 9, 62
National Association of Professional Baseball Leagues (NAPBL). *See* Minor League Baseball
National Baseball Hall of Fame and Museum, 34
National Basketball Association, 81
National League, 17, 25, 89
Nebraska, location of Northern League teams, 48. *See also individual cities and teams*
Negro Leagues, 65
New Britain Rock Cats, 22t, 100
New Hampshire, location of independent league teams, 47. *See also individual cities and teams*
New Haven Ravens, 22t
New Jersey. *See also individual cities and teams*
   location of Eastern League teams, 21
   New Jersey Cardinals, 37t, 105t
   New Jersey Jackals, 49t, 108t
   Northern League, 48
   South Atlantic League, 101
New Mexico, location of Texas League teams, 23. *See also* individual cities and teams
New Orleans, LA
   American Association, 15
   International League, 15
   New Orleans Zephyrs, 19t
   Pacific Coast League, 19t
   Texas League, 25
New York. *See also individual cities and teams*
   location of Eastern League teams, 21
   location of Northern League teams, 48

New York *(continued)*
    location of United States League
        teams, 44
    New York Fire Department, 134
    New York State League, 14
    Pennsylvania-Ontario-New York
        (PONY) League, 36
New York Mets
    class A affiliates, 32t, 33t, 37t
    class AA affiliate, 21, 22t
    class AAA affiliate, 13, 16t
    rookie league affiliates, 40t
New York Yankees
    class A affiliates, 32t, 33t, 37t, 58
    class AA affiliate, 22t
    class AAA affiliate, 13, 16t
New York-Penn League, 101, 104,
        117t, 134
    Aberdeen, MD, 117t
    Baltimore Orioles affiliates, 5
    current teams, 34, 36, 37t
    name changes and franchise
        relocation, 101, 104,
        105t-106t
    New York-Pennsylvania League, 21
    Short season class A, 5f
Newark, NJ
    International League, 14, 15
    Newark Bears, 54t
    Newark Bison, 107, 109t
    Newark Buffalos, 107, 109t
Niles, OH, 37t, 104
Nisbet, Robert A., 75
Noah Night, 98
Nogales, Sonora, Mexico, 18
Norfok Tides, 13, 16t, 95, 100
North AmeriCare Park, 111
North Atlantic League, 45t, 47
North Carolina. *See also individual
        cities and teams*
    location of Appalachian League
        teams, 29
    location of Carolina League teams,
        27
    location of South Atlantic League
        teams, 101
    North Carolina State League, 27
North Central League, 45t
North Dakota, location of Northern
        League teams, 48. *See also
        individual cities and teams*

Northeast League, 47
Northern League
    alignment with Central League, 50
    absorption of Northeast League, 47
    commissioner, Miles Wolff, 50
    demise of original Northern League,
        92
    history and description of, 47, 48,
        49t
    independent league, 6f, 45t
    revival of independent baseball, 43,
        47
Northwest League
    class A league, 5f, 36, 38t
    franchise relocation, 101
    history and description of, 36
Northwestern League, 34, 89
Norwich Navigators, 22t
Nuevo Laredo, 18, 20t
Nuevo León, Mexico, 20

Oakland Athletics (A's)
    class A affiliates, 25, 28t, 38t, 104
    class AA affiliate, 26t
    class AAA affiliate, 19t
Oakland Invaders, 44
Oaxaca, Mexico, 20, 20t
O'Fallon, MO, 50, 51t, 107
Ogden Raptors, 42t
Ogle, Samuel, 123
Ohio. *See also individual cities and
        teams*
    location of Eastern League teams,
        21
    location of Midwest League teams,
        34
    Mississippi-Ohio Valley League, 34
    Pennsylvania-Ohio-Maryland
        League, 99, 114, 117t
Ohio Valley Redcoats, 107, 108t
Oklahoma, location of International
        League teams, 15. *See also
        individual cities and teams*
Oklahoma RedHawks, 19t
Okner, Benjamin A., 67
Oldsmobile Park, 111
Olmecas de Tabasco, 20t
Olson, James, 83, 88
Omaha Royals, 15, 19t

O'Neal, Bill, 14, 17
Oneonta, NY
   Oneonta Tigers, 34, 37t, 105t, 108t
   Oneonta Yankees, 105t, 108t
Ontario, Canada. *See also individual cities and teams*
   independent leagues, 47
   Ontario League, 14
   New York-Penn League, 36
   Pennsylvania-Ontario-New York (PONY) League, 36
Oregon, location of Northwest League teams, 36. *See also individual cities and teams*
Oriole Park, 114
Orioles. *See* Baltimore Orioles
Orlando Rays, 24t
Ottawa Lynx, 15, 16t
Owners, 84, 94
Oxley, Mike, 75
Oxnard, CA, 51, 52
Ozark, MO, 52t

Pacific Coast International League, 36
Pacific Coast League (PCL)
   absorption of American Association teams, 15
   class A, 6
   class AA, 6, 13
   class AAA, 5f, 6, 13, 19t, 45t
   franchise relocation, 101
   history and description of, 15-18
Pacific Northwest League, 36, 41
Pacific Suns, 52
Paducah, KY, 34
Palm Springs Suns, 51, 52
Pan-American Association, 25
Park, Robert E., 77
Parkersburg, WV, 50, 107
Pasco, WA, 101
Patriotism, 134
Pawtucket Red Sox, 9, 14, 15, 16t
Pelissero, John P., 70
Pennsylvania. *See also individual cities and teams*
   location of Blue Ridge League teams, 115

Pennsylvania *(continued)*
   location of Eastern League teams, 21
   location of Northern League East teams, 48
   Pennsylvania-Ohio-Maryland League, 99, 114, 117t
   Pennsylvania-Ontario-New York (PONY) League, 36
   Western Pennsylvania League, 117t
Pennsylvania Road Warriors, 54t
Peoria Chiefs, 35t
Perdue Stadium, 31
Pericos de Puebla, 20t
Perlstein, Steve, 43
PGE Park, 15
Philadelphia, PA. *See also* Philadelphia Phillies
   Eastern League, 14
   Philadelphia Athletics, 64
   Shibe Park, 64
Philadelphia Athletics, 64
Philadelphia Phillies
   class A affiliates, 32t, 33t, 37t
   class AA affiliate, 21, 22t
   class AAA affiliate, 16t
Piedmont, WV
   Piedmont League, 115, 118
   Piedmont/Westernport Drybugs, 115, 119t
   Western Pennsylvania league team, 99
Piedmont League, 115, 117t, 120
Pikeville, KY, 50
Pilot Field, 93, 111
Pioneer League
   advanced rookie league, 5f, 41, 42t
   franchise relocation 101
   history and description of, 41
Piratas de Campeche, 20t
Pittsburgh, PA. *See also* Pittsburgh Pirates
   African-American community, 65
   Homestead Grays, 65
   Pittsburgh Crawfords, 65
Pittsburgh Pirates
   class A affiliates, 30t, 33t, 37t, 104, 120
   class AA affiliate, 22t
   class AAA affiliate, 19t

Pittsfield, MA
  New York-Penn League teams, 49t, 105t, 108t
  Pittsfield Astros, 105t, 107, 108t
  Pittsfield Mets, 104, 105t, 108t
Player Development Contract (PDC), 13, 96
Player Development Plan, 12, 92
Playoffs. *See* Championship series
Pocomoke City, MD
  Eastern Shore League, 115, 117t
  Pocomoke City Chicks, 100, 115
  Pocomoke City Red Sox, 100
  Pocomoke City Salamanders, 100
Poplin, Dennis E., 77
Port Charlotte, FL, 29, 32t
Port St. Lucie, FL, 29, 32t
Portland, OR
  Pacific Coast League, 15, 19t, 101
  PGE Park, 15
  Pioneer League, 41
  Portland Beavers, 15, 19t
Portland Sea Dogs, 21, 22t
Portsmouth, OH, 50
Portsmouth Explorers, 107, 108t
Potomac Cannons, 30t, 58
Potomac League, 99, 115, 117t
Prairie League, 45t, 47
Presley, Elvis, 97
Prince George's County, MD. *See also* Bowie, MD
  Hagerstown Suns move to, 123
  population, 124, 124t
  Prince George's Stadium, 2, 67, 75, 122
Prince William Cannons, 58
Princeton Devil Rays, 39, 40t
Professional Baseball Agreement (PBA)
  established, 12
  impact on teams, 96
  specifications, 47, 96-97, 101
Professional Baseball Fund, 12
Promotions, 96
Prosperity, Era of, 88, 90, 129, 130, 137t
Provincial League, 44, 45t
Provo Angels, 41, 42t, 101
Public subsidies for stadiums, 67, 84
Puebla, Mexico, 20, 20t

Puerto Rico, 5, 15
Pulaski Rangers, 39, 40t

Quad City River Bandits, 35t
Quality of life (QOL)
  building blocks of, 71
  impact of Minor League Baseball on, 112, 113, 128, 141
  impact of sports on, 131
  measurement of, 141, 155-165
  studies of, 149-151
Quebec, Canada. *See also individual cities and teams*
  Capitales de Quebec, 49t
  Northern League, 48, 49t
  Provincial League, 44
Queens Kings, 21, 101, 104, 105t, 108t
Quintana Roo, Mexico, 20

Rancho Cucamonga Quakes, 11, 28t, 102t, 103t
Reading, PA
  International League, 14, 22t
  location of United States League team, 44
  Reading Phillies, 4, 21, 22t, 93
Renaissance, era of, 88, 93-94, 129, 130, 138t
Reno, NV, 51
Reserve clause, 89
Reynosa, Tamaulipas, Mexico, 20t
Rhode Island, home of McCoy Field, 13-14. *See also individual cities and teams*
Richmond, VA
  franchise relocation, 99, 114
  International League, 14, 15, 16t
  Richmond Braves, 16t, 59
Richmond Roosters, 50, 51t, 107, 108t
Rickey, Branch, 89
Riess, Steven, 63, 78
Rio Grande Valley White Wings, 52t
Ripken Jr., Cal
  Aberdeen IronBirds, 67, 104
  Baltimore Orioles player, 57
  Ripken Professional Baseball, LLC, 104
Ripken Stadium, 67

River City Rascals, 51t, 107, 109t
Riverside Pilots, 101, 102t, 103t
Roberts, Randy, 83, 88
Rochester Red Wings, 5, 13, 16t, 134
Rockford RiverHawks, 51t, 109t, 111
Rocky Mount Pines, 100
Rohnert Park, CA, 53t
Rojos del Aguila de Veracruz, 20t
Rookie Leagues
    Appalachian League, 5t, 39, 40t, 43
    Arizona League, 43
    Baltimore Orioles rookie league affiliate, 5
    classification of Minor League Baseball, 7t
    Gulf Coast League, 43
    other rookie and lower leagues, 41, 43
    Pioneer League, 41, 42t, 43
Rosentraub, Mark S., 72
Round Rock Express, 25, 26t, 95
Ruck, Rob, 65
Ruth, Babe, 34, 114, 116

Sabo, Martin Olav, 75
Sacramento, CA
    Sacramento River Cats, 19t, 95
    Sacramento Senators, 44
    Western League, 52
Salaries, 6-7, 8, 89, 112
Salem, OR, 1, 36
Salem Avalanche, 30t
Salem-Keizer Volcanoes, 38t
Salinas Peppers, 51, 52
Salisbury, MD
    Eastern Shore League, 115, 116, 117t
    Salisbury Cardinals, 100
    Salisbury Indians, 100
    Salisbury Senators, 100
    South Atlantic League, 31, 33t
Salt Lake City, UT
    Pacific Coast League, 15, 19t
    Salt Lake City Bees, 18
    Salt Lake Stingers, 19t
Saltillo, Coahuila, Mexico, 20t
San Angelo Colts, 52t
San Antonio, TX
    San Antonio Missions, 26t
    Texas League, 25, 26t
    Texas-Louisiana League, 50

San Bernardino, CA
    California League, 28t, 102t, 103t
    San Bernardino Spirit, 101, 102t
    San Bernardino Stampede, 28t, 101, 102t
San Diego, CA. *See also* San Diego Padres
    Pacific Coast League, 17
    San Diego Chicken, 98
San Diego Padres
    class A affiliates, 28t, 35t, 38t
    class AA affiliate, 24t
    class AAA affiliate, 19t
    relationship with Mexican League, 20
    rookie league affiliate, 42t
San Francisco, CA. *See also* San Francisco Giants
    California League, 44
    major league stadium, 2
    major league expansion and relocation, 90
    Pacific Coast League, 17
    San Francisco Orphans, 44
San Francisco Giants
    class A affiliates, 25, 28t, 33t, 38t, 104
    class AA affiliate, 26t
    class AAA affiliate, 19t
San Jose, CA
    California League, 28t
    San Jose Giants, 28t, 102t, 103t
    San Jose Prune Pickers, 44
San Juan, Puerto Rico, 15
Santa Cruz Sand Crabs, 44
Saraperos de Saltillo, 20t
Sarason, Seymour B., 82
Sarasota, FL
    Florida State League, 29, 32t
    Gulf Coast League, 5
    Sarasota Orioles, 5
    Sarasota Red Sox, 29, 32t
Saskatchewan, Canada, 41
Savannah, GA
    Savannah Sand Gnats, 33t
    South Atlantic League, 33t
    Southern League, 21
Schaumburg Flyers, 49t
Schilperoot, Todd, 65-66

Schulz, Phillip S., 7, 9
Schwartz, Barry, 60-61
Scottsdale, AZ, 52
Scranton/Wilkes-Barre Red Barons, 16t
Scully, Gerald W., 60
Seattle, WA. *See also* Seattle Mariners
 minor league teams, 2, 3, 36
 Pacific Coast League, 17
 Seattle Pilots, 36
 Seattle Rainiers, 18
Seattle Mariners
 class A affiliates, 25, 28t, 35t, 38t
 class AA affiliates, 26t
 class AAA affiliates, 19t
Selig, Bud, 133
Semipro teams, 90
Shenandoah Valley, 39
Sherbrooke, Quebec, Canada, 44
Sherony, Keith R., 70
Shibe Park, 64
Short Season Class A, 5f, 34-38
Shreveport Swamp Dragons, 25, 26t
Sidlow, Edward I., 70
Sioux City Explorers, 49t
Sioux Falls Canaries, 48, 49t
SkyDome, 62
Smith, Garry J., 63
Soccer, 62-63
Social construction, 73, 76-77
Socialization, 128
Sociological theory/theorists, 66, 73-81, 82-85, 127
Solano Steelheads, 53t
Somerset, PA, 99, 115
Somerset Patriots, 53, 54t
Sonoma County Crushers, 51, 53t
South Atlantic League (SALLY)
 Baltimore Orioles affiliate, 5
 class A, 5f, 31, 33t, 117t
 franchise relocation and expansion, 100, 101, 116, 120
 Hagerstown, Maryland, 122, 130
 history and description of, 31
 predecessor of Southern League, 23, 31
 successor of Western Carolina League, 31
South Bend Silver Hawks, 35t

South Dakota. *See also individual cities and teams*
 location of independent league teams, 47
 location of Northern League teams, 48
South Georgia Waves, 33t
Southern League. *See also individual cities and teams*
 class AA, 5f, 21, 23
 description, 21, 23, 24t
 history, 21, 23
 member of Dixie Association, 23
 Southern Association, 23
 Southern League of Professional Baseball Clubs, 23
 successor of South Atlantic League, 23, 31
 teams, 23, 24t
Spokane Indians, 36, 38t
Sport(s)
 administration, 94
 economic impact of, 59, 63, 66-72, 85
 franchises, 63, 65-66
 history, 58
 impact on community identity, 50, 63, 72
 investment in, 71
 intangible benefits of, 59, 62-66, 67, 71
 popularity of, 83
 sociology of, 58, 61, 128, 131
 source of solidarity, 66
 symbolic of city, 65
 teams and their communities, 59, 72
Sporting News, 23, 76
Spring training, 20, 29
Springfield, IL
 franchise relocation, 50, 107, 109t, 111
 Frontier League, 50, 109t
 Springfield Capitals, 107, 109t
 Springfield Cardinals, 107
Springfield/Ozark Mountain Ducks, 52t
St. Catharines, Ontario, Canada
 St. Catharines Blue Jays, 36, 104, 105t, 108t
 St. Catharines Stompers, 105t
St. Hyacinthe, Quebec, Canada, 44

St. Jean, Quebec, Canada, 44
St. Louis, MO. *See also* St. Louis
    Cardinals
  major league city, 18
  St. Louis Browns, 99, 114
St. Louis Cardinals
  development of farm system, 89, 90
  minor league affiliates, 19t, 22t, 30t,
    35t, 37t, 40t
St. Lucie Mets, 32t
St. Paul Saints, 42, 48, 49t
St. Petersburg, FL, 101
Stadiums. *See also individual stadiums*
  atmosphere of, 64, 127, 131
  classic ball parks, 13-14
  construction of, 93, 95
  economic development, 64, 71
  expenditures for, 59
  International League stadiums, 2
  major league stadium, 2, 58
  Mexican League stadiums, 20
  minor league stadiums, 2, 59, 76,
    130
  need for, 64
  public ownership of, 67
  subsidies, 67, 68
  seating capacity, 39
  specifications for, 96
Staten Island Yankees, 37t, 104, 105t,
    108t
Stockton, CA
  California League, 27, 28t
  Mudville Nine, 102t, 103t, 104
  Stockton Ports, 28t, 102t, 103t, 104
  Stockton Tigers, 44
Stone, Gregory, 66
Strike, 76
Subsidization, era of, 88, 92, 138t
Sullivan, Neil J., 9, 64
Sultanes de Monterrey, 20t
Summer Leagues, 43
Sumner, Jim, 29
Surrey, British Columbia, 51
Swindell, David, 72
Syracuse SkyChiefs, 15, 16t
Systems theory, 73-75, 127

Tabasco Cattlemen, 20, 20t
Tacoma Rainiers, 15, 19t

Tamaulipas, Mexico, 20
Tampa Bay Devil Rays
  class A affiliates, 28t, 33t, 37t
  class AA affiliate, 24t
  class AAA affiliate, 16t
  rookie league affiliate, 40t
Tampa Yankees, 29, 32t
Tar Heel League, 27, 31
Team names
  naming rights, 111
  naming trends, 101
Tecolotes de Los Dos Laredos, 20t
Television, 88
Tennessee. *See also individual cities
    and teams*
  location of All-American
    Association teams, 48
  location of Appalachian League
    teams, 39
  Tennessee Smokies, 24t
Terrapin Park, 114
Terre Haute, IN, 31
Terreón, Coahuila, Mexico, 20t
Terrorism, 133
Texas, location of Central League
    teams, 50. *See also individual
    cities, leagues, and teams*
Texas League. *See also individual
    cities and teams*
  attendance record, 95
  class AA, 5f, 25, 26t
  history and description of, 23, 24
  member of Dixie Association, 23,
    25
  member of Pan-American
    Association, 25
Texas Rangers
  class A affiliates, 32t, 33t
  class AA affiliate, 24t
  class AAA affiliate, 19t
  rookie league affiliate, 40t
Texas-Louisiana League, 6f, 45t, 50
Textile leagues, 90
"Third" Minor League, 17
Thorn, John, 39
Three-I League, 34
Thunder Bay, Ontario, 48
Thurman Munson Memorial Stadium,
    50, 62, 100, 107

Tidewater Tides, 100
Tiehen, Laura J., 60
Tigres del México, 20t
Tijuana, 18
Tobacco State League, 27, 29
Toledo Mud Hens, 9, 13, 16t
Tonnies, Ferdinand, 80-81, 82
Toronto, Ontario, Canada. *See also* Toronto Blue Jays
    International League, 15
    SkyDome, 62
Toronto Blue Jays
    class A affiliates, 32t, 33t, 37t, 100, 120
    class AA affiliate, 24t
    class AAA affiliate, 16t
    rookie league affiliate, 42t
    SkyDome, 62
Tourism, 1, 71
Traditionalism and attachment, 73, 75-76
Trenton, NJ
    Eastern League, 22t
    International League, 14
    Trenton Giants, 120
    Trenton Thunder, 22t
Tri-City, WA, 36, 51
Tri-City Dust Devils, 38t, 101
Tri-City ValleyCats, 37t, 104, 105t, 108t
Tri-State League, 45t
Tri-State Tomahawks, 109t. *See also* Ashland, KY
Troy, NY, 37t
Trujillo, Nick, 63
Tucson, AZ
    Pacific Coast League, 16-17, 19t
    Tucson Electric Park, 15, 134
    Tucson Sidewinders, 17, 19t, 134
Tulsa Drillers, 25, 26t
Twin Ports League, 6
Two-I League, 34
Tyler, Texas, 50

Union Association, 41
United States, 47, 53, 83, 111
United States League, 44, 45t

Utah. *See also individual cities and teams*
    location of Pioneer League teams, 41
    Utah-Idaho League, 41
Utica, NY
    franchise relocation and affiliation changes, 104, 105t, 108t
    Utica Blue Sox, 105t
    Utica Blue Marlins, 105t

Vacaville, CA, 52, 53t
Valley Vipers, 52
Vancouver, British Columbia, Canada
    Northwest League, 38t
    Pacific Coast League, 18
    Pioneer League, 41
    Vancouver Canadians, 38t
    Vancouver Mounties, 18
Venezuela
    fall and winter leagues, 5
    Venezuelan Summer League, 43
Vermont Expos, 36, 37t, 105t, 108t
Vero Beach Dodgers, 29, 31, 32t
Villahermosa, Tabasco, Mexico, 20t
Vincennes, Indiana, 34
Virginia. *See also individual cities and teams*
    location of Appalachian League teams, 39
    location of Carolina League teams, 27
Visalia, CA
    minor league affiliations, 101, 104
    stadium, 39
    Visalia Oaks, 27, 28t, 102t, 103t, 104

Waco, TX, 25
Wappingers Falls, NY, 37t
Warren, Roland, 74, 82
Washington, location of Northwest League teams, 36. *See also individual cities and teams*
Washington, DC, 2, 44, 116, 134
Washington, PA, 51t, 111
Washington County, MD, 116

Washington Wild Things, 51t, 109t, 111
Watertown, NY, 104, 105t, 108t
Watt Powell Park, 31
Wayne County, WV, 50, 107
Waynesboro, PA
   location of Blue Ridge League teams, 118
   Waynesboro Red Birds, 119t
   Waynesboro Villagers, 119t
Weber, Max, 66, 79
Wenatchee, WA, 36
West Frankfort, IL, 34
West Haven, CT, 22t
West Michigan Whitecaps, 35t
West Sacramento, CA, 19t
West Tenn Diamond Jaxx, 24t
West Virginia. *See also individual cities and teams*
   location of Appalachian League teams, 39
   location of Blue Ridge League teams, 115
   West Virginia Coal Sox, 109t
Western Baseball League, 6f, 51-52, 53t
Western Canada League, 41
Western Carolina(s) League, 27, 31, 92
Western International League, 36
Western League
   description and history, 51-52, 53f
   independent league, 5f, 45t, 47
Western Pennsylvania League, 99, 114, 117t
Western Tri-State League, 41
Westernport, MD, 115, 117t, 118
Whitson, David, 71, 72
Wichita Wranglers, 25, 26t
Wilkes-Barre Barons, 21
Williams, Bernie, 58
Williamsport, PA
   home of Little League Baseball, 34, 36
   location of Bowman Field, 35

Williamsport, PA *(continued)*
   Williamsport Billies, 21
   Williamsport Crosscutters, 34, 37t, 104, 105t, 108t
   Williamsport Cubs, 104, 105t
Wilmington, NC, 101
Wilmington Blue Rocks, 14, 29, 30t, 95
Winnipeg Goldeyes, 48, 49t
Winooski, VT, 37t
Winston, Lisa, 8
Winston-Salem Warthogs, 30t
Winter leagues, 5
Wisconsin. *See also individual cities and teams*
   location of Midwest League teams, 34
   Wisconsin Timber Rattlers, 35t
Wolff, Miles, 47, 50, 96
Woodbridge, VA, 30t
Works Projects Administration, 91
World Series, 57, 89
World War I, 14, 89
World War II
   cancellation of playoffs due to, 133
   impact on leagues, 14, 27, 29, 41
   patriotism and Minor League Baseball, 135
   post-war prosperity and Minor League Baseball, 88

Yakima Bears, 36, 38t
"YMCA," 97
Yuma Bullfrogs, 52, 53t
Yuma-Sutter Gold Sox, 53t

Zanesville, OH, 50, 107, 109t
Zebulon, NC, 23, 24t
Zimmer, Don, 115

SPECIAL 25%-OFF DISCOUNT!
Order a copy of this book with this form or online at:
http://www.haworthpressinc.com/store/product.asp?sku=4720

MINOR LEAGUE BASEBALL
Community Building Through Hometown Sports

_____ in hardbound at $37.46 (regularly $49.95) (ISBN: 0-7890-1755-5)

_____ in softbound at $14.96 (regularly $19.95) (ISBN: 0-7890-1756-3)

Or order online and use Code HEC25 in the shopping cart.

COST OF BOOKS_____

OUTSIDE US/CANADA/
MEXICO: ADD 20%_____

POSTAGE & HANDLING_____
(US: $5.00 for first book & $2.00
for each additional book)
Outside US: $6.00 for first book
& $2.00 for each additional book)

SUBTOTAL_____

IN CANADA: ADD 7% GST_____

STATE TAX_____
(NY, OH & MN residents, please
add appropriate local sales tax)

FINAL TOTAL_____
(If paying in Canadian funds,
convert using the current
exchange rate, UNESCO
coupons welcome)

☐ **BILL ME LATER:** ($5 service charge will be added)
(Bill-me option is good on US/Canada/Mexico orders only;
not good to jobbers, wholesalers, or subscription agencies.)

☐ Check here if billing address is different from
shipping address and attach purchase order and
billing address information.

Signature_____

☐ **PAYMENT ENCLOSED:** $_____

☐ **PLEASE CHARGE TO MY CREDIT CARD.**

☐ Visa ☐ MasterCard ☐ AmEx ☐ Discover
☐ Diner's Club ☐ Eurocard ☐ JCB

Account #_____

Exp. Date_____

Signature_____

Prices in US dollars and subject to change without notice.

NAME_____
INSTITUTION_____
ADDRESS_____
CITY_____
STATE/ZIP_____
COUNTRY_____ COUNTY (NY residents only)_____
TEL_____ FAX_____
E-MAIL_____

May we use your e-mail address for confirmations and other types of information? ☐ Yes ☐ No
We appreciate receiving your e-mail address and fax number. Haworth would like to e-mail or fax special discount offers to you, as a preferred customer. **We will never share, rent, or exchange your e-mail address or fax number.** We regard such actions as an invasion of your privacy.

Order From Your Local Bookstore or Directly From
The Haworth Press, Inc.
10 Alice Street, Binghamton, New York 13904-1580 • USA
TELEPHONE: 1-800-HAWORTH (1-800-429-6784) / Outside US/Canada: (607) 722-5857
FAX: 1-800-895-0582 / Outside US/Canada: (607) 722-6362
E-mail to: getinfo@haworthpressinc.com
PLEASE PHOTOCOPY THIS FORM FOR YOUR PERSONAL USE.
http://www.HaworthPress.com